Business/Science/Technology
Division

© THE BAKER & TAYLOR CO.

The Hidden Addiction
And How to Get Free

Other books by Alan E. Nourse, M.D.

Intern by Dr. X
The Practice
The *Ladies' Home Journal* Family Medical Guide
The Fourth Horseman

The Hidden Addiction

And How to Get Free

Janice Keller Phelps, M.D.

Alan E. Nourse, M.D.

LITTLE, BROWN AND COMPANY   Boston   Toronto

FIRST EDITION

Library of Congress Cataloging in Publication Data

Phelps, Janice Keller, 1932–
    The hidden addiction: and how to get free.

    Includes index.
    1. Substance abuse—Treatment.   I. Nourse, Alan Edward.
II. Title
RC564.P49   1985   616.86   85–6820
ISBN 0-316-70470-9 (HC)
ISBN 0-316-70471-7 (PB)

BP

Designed by Patricia Girvin Dunbar

Published simultaneously in Canada
by Little, Brown & Company (Canada) Limited

PRINTED IN THE UNITED STATES OF AMERICA

To my parents, Eunice and Harold Keller, whose unconditional love has always been my foundation; to my friend Jack Smith, journalist and sportswriter, who urged me to write this book and guided my first steps; and to all recovering alcoholics and addicts who are now free to be all they can be.

Janice Keller Phelps, M.D.

Contents

Introduction

DO YOU control your own life?

Think hard for a moment before you answer. If you are one of the many millions who

- have gone through the torture of trying to give up smoking cig-arettes, without success
- fluctuate between binge eating and radical diets
- need a "sugar fix" between meals
- find alcohol becoming an increasingly important part of daily life
- secretly dread the possibility that a drug prescription won't be renewed
- can't get started in the morning without that first cup of coffee

then you may have to realize that some chemical substance has more control over your daily life than you do — in short, that you are an addict.

I'm writing for all such people, and for those who care about them and live with them.

This book is a tool. It is designed to help you discover and break free from your addictions, and regain control of your life.

Perhaps no other illness touches as many people as addiction does. I am convinced that at least four of every ten people are born with a potential for addiction to dozens of common substances, most of them perfectly legal and condoned by society.* The odds are overwhelmingly great that you or someone you love is already a victim of addiction, and that because of it life is less satisfying than it ought to be.

This doesn't have to be so. Addiction can be treated and controlled. I know. I've helped hundreds of my patients overcome it; and in 1980 I was helped with my own alcoholism and found in sobriety how jealously possessive my addiction was.

I began to look seriously at addiction sixteen years ago, as medical director of a children's correctional institution. I saw cases of what is commonly thought of as "real addiction" — hard drug habits. But for every kid hooked on an illegal street drug, I saw dozens more who were in trouble because they weren't able to handle substances usually considered far less dangerous, such as sugar. They made me think back to the children I had seen in my pediatric practice, children whose behavior was often erratic, frustrating, and unpredictable.

That experience gave me my first insight into addiction. I saw more when, in 1977, I became medical director of the Center for Addiction Services in Seattle, Washington. I treated addicts, but *they* taught *me* the basics of addiction. They helped me realize the awful, crippling way that drugs and chemicals, and sometimes even food, can take over a life and restrict its growth. And I began to see, for the first time, the curious and intriguing similarities and relationships among what doctors have always assumed were a variety of different addictions.

I'm challenging that assumption, and many others as well. After several years as a staff physician at an alcohol treatment hospital, and as one of the few physicians in the country with a private practice specializing in addiction therapy, I have treated more than 5,000 addicts. From that experience, I'm convinced that there is only one basis for addiction, regardless of the substances involved. I'm also convinced that addicts literally are born, not made, and that the sooner addictive or addiction-prone people face that real-

---

*Between 10 and 20 percent of the population is addicted to alcohol, according to the most knowledgeable authorities on alcoholism that I've talked to. I estimate that another 10 to 20 percent is addicted to prescription drugs, street drugs, or hard narcotics, and that an equal number have the potential for addiction even if they are not now actively addicted.

ity, the better their chances of coping with their problem and enriching their lives. More than anything else, I'm concerned about the insidious damage of addiction and its unrecognized, widespread prevalence.

Much of what follows in this book will be a source of controversy and argument. The ideas I'm setting forth are based empirically on observations and conclusions drawn from my own extensive clinical experience dealing with addictive people and treating addiction. Addiction is still largely unexplored territory; we've spent woefully little time, energy, and money trying to understand it. We need effective treatment methods *now* — the controlled double-blind studies will be welcome when the money is available to do them properly. Some doctors may criticize my concept of addiction or my methods of treatment, but I know I have found a system that works. Although this book is directed primarily at the general reader, chapter 14 is addressed specifically to practicing physicians, who know the problems in treating addiction and who want and need better tools and resources to help their patients.

The first step in the process of coping with addiction is accepting the fact that it exists. That's difficult for many of us. An increasing number of recovering people are stepping forward to be recognized, however, and are finding that their careers are not jeopardized, but enhanced. They discover the joys of sobriety and many new avenues toward self-discovery and growth. They want to share these rewards with others.

Addicted individuals may find much to criticize in my book. Denial of addiction can render people totally unaware of how their addiction is affecting every aspect of their lives in a hazardous way. They may become angry or put off by the slightest suggestion that they have a problem. For example, when I was a practicing alcoholic, I kept coming across magazine quizzes headlined "Are You an Alcoholic?" I always managed to keep my "yes" answers under the diagnostic number, even though I had to lie to do it. Some of the questions I discounted as ambiguous or meaningless, and therefore I answered "no." Many of my recovering patients laugh with me over similar experiences. It's clear to us now that our addiction impaired our judgment, thinking, and emotions, but we were the last to know.

I have written this book as a self-help guide in the hope that it will be read and shared by those of you who have concerns about your own addictions or the addictions of your loved ones. May this book be a guide that moves you into the joyous experience of sobriety and drug-free living. I trust that you, too, will find the true freedom and expanding goal achievements that I have found, as well as a world filled with love.

This is not to say that overcoming addiction isn't difficult and trying. It requires hard work, patience, and commitment, but the choice is between a life out of control and a life that is truly your own. And I'd say that is no choice at all.

Janice Keller Phelps, M.D.
Seattle, Washington

Part One

Identifying Addiction

1

Addictiveness and Addiction

A FUNNY THING happened at a medical meeting I attended recently.

The topic of the conference was "Addictive Behavior," and I was one of four or five people scheduled to speak to the fifty doctors in attendance. The organizers of the meeting had decided to change a practice usual at such functions: they would employ some holistic health techniques and substitute fresh fruit, cheese, and fruit juice for coffee that is almost always offered in the morning before the day's program begins.

Neither I nor the conference sponsors were quite prepared for the outrage that greeted the decision. The doctors were furious. Some of the most virulent reactions came from three of the speakers scheduled to deliver addresses. They flatly refused to start the program until they had their morning cup of coffee. They couldn't possibly go on, they insisted. The sponsors had to order up a special urn of coffee on the double, and we all had to sit around and wait until it was made and brought out before we could get on with the meeting. The program finally began an hour and twenty minutes late.

I was supposed to talk about addiction that day, but the scene we had just witnessed said more about it than I could have if I had talked all day.

I'm telling this story now for a couple of reasons. First, it illustrates with blinding clarity just how insidious and pervasive the effects of addiction really can be. I do not believe that the speakers were merely annoyed because a simple and harmless habit pattern had been disrupted unexpectedly. If that had been so, the speakers — like rational, civilized people — would have shrugged and said, "Oh, well, we'll have coffee later; let's get on with the show." Something far deeper was biting at them. They had come to the meeting expecting their regular morning caffeine fix before anything else happened, and when they didn't get it they were furious. They were hooked — addicted to caffeine. As a result, the absence of a common, supposedly harmless chemical substance had caused a group of intelligent professional people to neglect the serious business of the day, waste about seventy man-hours, and behave as irrationally as children having tantrums.

That's the classical way that an addiction controls our lives: it always has to be satisfied first, before we can get on with what we want to do.

Myths about Addiction

Equally important, this rather silly little story may help to dispel some very commonplace myths and misunderstandings about addicts, addiction, and withdrawal. Let's tackle some of the false ideas about addicts and addiction one at a time.

Myth: Addicts are criminals. By any reasonable standards, the doctors who clamored for their morning coffee that day were perfectly upstanding, law-abiding people. But they were addicts, and the fact that they happened to be addicted to a legal substance changes nothing. Most of the substances to which we're addicted are legal and easily available. It's a myth that addicts are criminals. (However, the reverse — that imprisoned criminals are addicts — has a high probability of being true.)

Myth: Only illegal drugs are addicting. Most addictive people get hooked on the drug or chemical of their choice long before they are exposed to heroin or street speed — if they ever are. In fact, two of the most addicting substances I know of — nicotine and diazepam (Valium) — are legal.

Myth: Problems, pressure, or stress can turn somebody into an addict. I have yet to meet one person who doesn't experience problems, pressure, or stress. If people became addicts because of them, then at least 95 percent of the population would be addicts, and that, fortunately, is not the case. Addictive or addiction-prone people are born that way. Pressure and stress have little, if anything, to do with it.

Myth: Addiction is immoral, and addicts have weak characters. Addicts do not choose to be addictive. Addiction is not a moral issue at all, because no amount of inner strength, willpower, or moral purity can change the physical fact of addictiveness.

Myth: Addiction is a psychological problem. Addiction often gets thrown into the catchall of "psychological problem" because orthodox medicine, by treating peripheral symptoms but not the root cause, fails to cope with addiction effectively. When treating the symptoms doesn't work, doctors and their patients come to believe that since the body has been treated without success, the trouble must be in the patient's mind.

During my work in alcohol treatment centers I've encountered many alcoholics who were treated psychiatrically long before they realized their true disorder and discovered that their problems weren't with their minds at all, but with booze. *The primary cause of an addict's problems isn't psychological illness, but addiction.* Addiction may, and indeed often does, bring psychological or emotional problems in its wake, but the basic problem is the addiction itself.

Myth: Withdrawal is violent and dangerous. As a matter of fact, in certain cases it *can* be, and we will deal with this in detail later. Not every withdrawal is gut-wrenching and traumatic, however. The symptoms often are far more subtle — even deceptively so. Withdrawal may manifest itself as mental depression, as headaches or as a mild case of flu, as unfocused anxiety, or simply as general malaise — a feeling that all is not well. Always, however, withdrawal is just unpleasant enough that untreated addicts try to avoid it by going back to the addictive chemical of their choice.

Myth: There are different kinds of addiction. In my years of work with addictions to many different substances, I have found no evidence to support this belief. Many doctors try to make a distinction between "physical" and "psychological" addictions, or claim there's a difference between the ways different drugs addict people, or insist that there are "addictive personalities." I don't buy any of this. From my experience, I am convinced that *there is only one kind of addiction, and that one addiction is the same as every other.* Valium addicts the way Demerol addicts, the way nicotine addicts, the way alcohol addicts, and so on.

I think the mistaken idea of "different kinds of addiction" has led to a great deal of medical mistreatment of addicts. Doctors trying to help an alcoholic stay off booze will prescribe a dosage of Valium. Wrong! There's a good reason why Valium works for alcoholics: it satisfies the alcohol addiction by staving off the withdrawal symptoms. So the patient, though not using alcohol at the moment, now risks becoming a Valium addict.

I got my first clue to how one addictive substance can replace another when I noticed the huge amounts of sugar that heroin addicts consume. They know that if they can't score dope, they can get by — for a while, at least — by consuming large quantities of candy, soda pop, and other sweets.

That's why it's so important to recognize that you're addictive, if you are. Even if you're hooked on a relatively harmless substance, such as caffeine, you have to deal with the fact of your addictiveness, because having become addicted to one substance, you've shown that you're susceptible to dozens of others that are dangerous and destructive.

Myth: Many books have explored the question of what addiction really is. Wrong again! That extremely basic question is seldom addressed in most books and articles on addiction.

Myth: You can deal with addiction by "cutting down." An addict can't lose an addiction simply by imitating the way nonaddictive or nonaddicted people use the same chemical. A nonaddictive person uses a drug out of choice. An addict uses the same drug, in whatever quantity, to prevent withdrawal.

A common corollary to the misconception that an addict can "cut down" is the practice of some alcoholics, for example, to characterize themselves as "social drinkers." Because alcoholics tend to surround themselves with other alcoholics, they find it easy to rationalize that they can't have a drinking problem because, after all, they don't drink any more than their friends do.

Myth: Addiction always wrecks your life. The fact is that most addicts are at least reasonably functioning people. Many are happy and successful in spite of their addiction. But they very likely are not as happy and successful as they might be if they did not have to share their life with a chemical. Most alcoholics — that is, people addicted to alcohol — are not blubbering, falling-down, pathetic characters. Comparatively few are lying in the gutter down in Muscatel Park clutching wine bottles in brown paper bags. Multitudes of alcoholics hold good jobs; many are bright, talented achievers. Few of the people around them would call them alcoholics. You can indeed be firmly addicted to alcohol even though your life isn't a shambles.

Myth: When you're addicted to something, you use it all the time in increasingly larger amounts. The size or frequency of dosage isn't necessarily a reliable indicator of addiction — at least not for every substance. A Valium addiction, for example, can be maintained for many years at a constant dosage. Often an addict will use a substance only as often as necessary to stave off withdrawal symptoms. In the case of some alcoholics, for example, that may simply mean drinking in the evening after work — but *only* after work. Just a little something, they'll say, to help them unwind after a hard day. The truth is, however, that the tension they have to "unwind" from is, in fact, one of the early withdrawal symptoms that begin to appear after twenty hours or so without alcohol.

Myth: Anyone can become addicted to strong drugs, such as morphine or heroin. On the contrary, I believe it would be very difficult to make an addict of a person who was not born addictive. Although there are no statistics, it is universal medical knowledge that thousands of hospitalized patients who receive powerful narcotics, sometimes in large doses, for days on end for the control of pain, never become addicted. I personally treated many such patients during the years I spent as a hospital resident and then as a pediatrician before I ever became involved in addiction therapy. The same principle applies to other addictive substances, too. Many people drink alcohol in moderation more or less regularly, yet never become addicted. There are even people who smoke just two or three cigarettes a week, when they feel like it, without ever becoming addicted.

The Role of Addictiveness

Years of work with addicts of all sorts have convinced me that addiction is a matter of biochemistry and genetics. *Addictiveness —*

the capacity to become an addict to anything — is a built-in physio-logical state, something you are born with. Either you are born ad-dictive or you are born nonaddictive.

Underlying this addictiveness, I am convinced, is a biochemical error of carbohydrate metabolism. If you are an addictive person, your body simply doesn't handle sugars the way other people's bodies do. No one has yet discovered exactly where the basic error lies. It may be in the adrenals, in the pancreas, in the pituitary, or in that vital neurochemical regulatory center in the brain known as the limbic system. Whatever its origin is, people with this underlying metabolic error — addictive people — are capable of becoming ad-dicts.

In later chapters we will discuss the many different forms that ad-diction takes. But first, how can addictiveness be recognized and identified? Are *you* an addictive person? How can you tell? As it happens, there are medical, physical, and behavioral clues. In chap-ter 2 we will use a self-administered test to help you develop your own Individual Addictiveness Profile and make a start in determin-ing whether you are addictive.

2.

A Test for Addictiveness

ARE YOU AN addictive person? As yet there is no single laboratory test that can provide you with a reliable, definitive, yes-or-no answer to that question. Nor is it really possible for most people to look at themselves objectively for possible clues to addictiveness and come up with a meaningful answer, no matter how sincere their motivation. It is part of the nature of addictiveness that even the most obviously addicted person may vigorously deny that any addiction exists.

Many factors are helpful in identifying a person's addictiveness: the way one consumes and metabolizes sugars and refined carbohydrates, the person's family history, the possible presence of a significant amount of depression, personal history relevant to drinking habits or prescription drug use, overt history of use of addictive drugs, and certain aspects of the quality of one's life. This test seeks to uncover clues or risk factors in each of these areas. The test is not designed or intended for anyone to "do well at" — it doesn't matter in the least how "well" or "badly" you do. It is intended solely to help you discover some useful and important information about yourself, namely the risk factors that you may have suggesting addictiveness.

This profile is a self-administered test that will result in a numerical score. The different parts of the test deal with a number of addictiveness risk factors that may be present in your life. The test will *not* tell you whether or not you are an addictive person in absolute terms; indeed, by the nature of the test, the same person taking the same test on several successive days will probably not get precisely the same score twice. What this profile *will* do is suggest — with some validity — whether there is a high, moderate, or low likelihood that you are an addictive person.

Answer each question in each part of the following test with the utmost honesty and objectivity you can manage, and score each question in the right-hand margin according to the instructions with each individual question. Do not worry about interpreting the questions — all aspects of this test will be discussed in detail in other parts of this book. If you feel that any question has absolutely no relationship to your life in any way, score 0 for that question.

THE PHELPS-NOURSE INDIVIDUAL ADDICTIVENESS PROFILE
(a self-administered test)

Part I   Diet

1. How often have you eaten the following foods? (Less than once a week, score 0; once a week, score 1; once a day, score 2; twice a day, score 3; three times a day, score 4; more than three times a day, score 5.)

    sugar, honey, or syrup   _____

    jams or jellies   _____

    chocolate, candy   _____

    ice cream or sherbet   _____

    cake, pie, or cookies   _____

    doughnuts, sweet rolls, or pastries   _____

    other desserts (pudding, canned fruit in syrup, fruited yogurt, ice cream topping, and so on)   _____

    white breads or dinner rolls   _____

    soft drinks (nondiet)   _____

2. Have you ever craved one of the foods on the above list so much that it distracted you? (Once a week or less, score 0; once a day, score 2; more than once a day, score 4.)   _____

3. Has eating a moderate amount of one of the above foods made you lose your appetite for more, or has it made

you want more immediately? (Lose appetite, score 0; want more, score 3.) _____

4. Have you ever overeaten any of the foods listed above to the point of discomfort? (Never, score 0; once a month, score 1; once a week, score 3; once a day, score 5.) _____

5. Have you ever gone on food binges, eating many helpings of *any* kind of food? (Rarely or never, score 0; once a month, score 1; once a week, score 3; once a day, score 5.) _____

6. How much sugar have you used a day? (None to two teaspoons a day, score 0; three to five teaspoons a day, score 2; six or more teaspoons a day, score 4.) _____

7. Have you had trouble controlling your weight? (Never, score 0; occasional trouble, score 1; constant trouble, score 4.) _____

8. Have you had any of the following symptoms regularly — daily or more than three times a week? (No, score 0; yes, score 2 for *each group* of symptoms.)

unexplained or undiagnosed stomachache, backache, or indigestion

unexplained headache _____

trouble sleeping _____

low energy or fatigue _____

trouble getting started, getting things accomplished _____

trouble concentrating or reading _____

angry outbursts for trivial reasons _____

daytime faintness, sleepiness, cold spells, or shakiness _____

discouraged with nothing to look forward to _____

9. If you have had any of the above symptoms, were they noticeably or reliably relieved by eating sweets or starchy foods? (For each symptom that was, score 2 additional points.) _____

10. How long have you been able to stay on a reducing diet that severely restricts or eliminates all sweets or starchy foods, including bread, pasta, potatoes, and so on? (Indefinitely, these foods are not a problem, score 0; only one week, score 2; 1–2 days, score 3; less than a day, score 5.) _____

Total score for Part I   _____

Part II Family History

The questions in this section refer exclusively to blood relatives, both living and dead, in your immediate family. The relatives referred to are your parents, grandparents, brothers, sisters, or your own children. The term does not include aunts, uncles, cousins, steprelatives, marital partners, or in-laws.

1. Have any blood relatives in your immediate family habitually consumed food high in starch and sugar, to excess? (None, score 0; one or two, score 3; most, score 5.)   ___

2. Have any relatives been heavy coffee or tea drinkers — more than three cups per day? (None, score 0; one or more, score 2.)   ___

3. Have any relatives had serious trouble controlling their weight — are they twenty-five pounds overweight or more? (None, score 0; one, score 1; two, score 2; more than two, score 4.)   ___

4. Have any relatives been alcoholics or recovering alcoholics, including relatives who are no longer living? (None, score 0; for each one who qualifies, score 5.)   ___

5. Have there been any relatives who were not acknowledged alcoholics but who were probably alcoholic — who had four or more drinks of alcohol daily, from what you personally know about their drinking habits? (None, score 0; for each one who qualifies, score 5.)   ___

6. Have there been any relatives you think were probably not alcoholic but who have had occasional or periodic episodes of heavy drinking or getting drunk? (None, score 0; for each one who qualifies, score 3.)   ___

7. Have there been any relatives who, in your private opinion, may have been "problem drinkers" or alcoholics, even though you have no specific evidence to support this feeling? (None, score 0; for each one who qualifies, score 2.)   ___

8. Have any relatives been hard narcotic addicts, using either prescribed or street drugs, now or in the past? (None, score 0; for each one who qualifies, score 5.)   ___

9. To your knowledge, have any relatives been regu-

lar — virtually every day — users of tranquilizers, such as meprobamate, Valium, or Xanax? (None, score 0; for each one who qualifies, score 3.)

10. Have any relatives been long-term heavy smokers? (None, score 0; for each one who qualifies, score 2.)

11. Have any relatives been regular — virtually every night — users of sleeping pills, whether prescribed or over-the-counter? (None, score 0; for each one who qualifies, score 3.)

12. Have any relatives been regular users of so-called recreational drugs — marijuana, cocaine, speed, peyote, LSD, and so on? (None, score 0; for each one who qualifies, score 3.)

13. Have any relatives been known to have suffered long or severe spells of depression? (None, score 0; for each one who qualifies, score 3.)

14. If your answer to question 13 is yes, have any of those relatives been treated with antidepressant drugs, been hospitalized for treatment, or received electroshock therapy? (None, score 0; for each relative receiving treatment, score 3.)

15. Have any relatives ever been diagnosed as hyperactive during their childhood? (None, score 0; for each one who qualifies, score 3.)

16. Have any relatives committed suicide or made suicide attempts? (None, score 0; for each one who qualifies, score 5.)

Total score for Part II

Part III Depression

1. Have you usually had trouble getting to sleep or staying asleep at night? (No or infrequently, score 0; some, score 2; frequently, score 3.)

2. Have you cried easily or felt like crying a lot? (No or infrequently, score 0; some, score 2; frequently, score 3.)

3. Have you regularly had to push yourself to get things done? (No or infrequently, score 0; some, score 2; frequently, score 3.)

4. Have you often felt fatigued or excessively drowsy

during the day? (No or infrequently, score 0; some, score 2; frequently, score 3.)   ——

5. Has your sexual response changed for the worse? (No or infrequently, score 0; some, score 2; frequently, score 3.)   ——

6. Have you often felt fearful, tense, or anxious? (No or infrequently, score 0; some, score 2; frequently, score 3.)   ——

7. Have you quickly lost interest or enthusiasm for what you are doing? (No or infrequently, score 0; some, score 2; frequently, score 3.)   ——

8. Have you found yourself looking for escapes? (No or infrequently, score 0; some, score 2; frequently, score 3.)   ——

9. Have you often felt guilty about things that happen? (No or infrequently, score 0; some, score 2; frequently, score 3.)   ——

10. Have you ever considered suicide? (Never, score 0; once or twice, vaguely, score 1; once or twice, seriously, score 3; more often and more detailed than that, score 5.)   ——

11. All of the factors mentioned in questions 1 through 10 are frequently associated with depression. Do you feel that any of these factors have interfered with your life or achievements? (No, score 0; at one time but not now, score 2; repeatedly, score 5.)   ——

12. Have you regularly eaten to relieve depression or because of a gnawing, insatiable hunger? (No or infrequently, score 0; some, score 2; frequently, score 3.)   ——

13. Have you regularly used alcohol to relieve depression? (No or infrequently, score 0; some, score 2; frequently, score 5.)   ——

14. Have you ever taken drugs or medicines, other than prescribed antidepressants, to relieve depression? (No or infrequently, score 0; some, score 2; frequently, score 5.)   ——

15. Have you ever been subject to prolonged or serious episodes of depression? (No, score 0; once only, score 1; two or three times that you can remember, score 3; frequently, score 5.)   ——

16. Have you ever been hospitalized for depression or had electroshock therapy? (No, score 0; yes, score 5.)   ____

17. Have you ever taken antidepressant drugs on prescription for depression? (Some common antidepressant drugs include Elavil, imipramine, Ludiomil, Norpramine, Tofranil, Asendin, and Desyrel.) (No, score 0; yes, for one month or less, once, score 2; yes, for longer than a month or more than once, score 5.)   ____

Total score for Part III   ____

Part IV   Alcohol Use

1. Have you drunk alcohol regularly in the past, or do you now? (Never, score 0; once a month, score 1; once a week, score 2; daily, score 4.)   ____

2. Indicate the average quantity you drank in a day. (Not very much — up to 1½ oz. of hard liquor, one beer, or one glass of wine in a day — score 0; a moderate amount — 2-3½ oz. of hard liquor, two beers, or two glasses of wine in a day — score 2; quite a bit — 4-6 oz. of hard liquor, three to four beers, or three to four glasses of wine in a day — score 4; a heavy amount — 8 or more oz. of hard liquor, five or more beers, or five or more glasses of wine in a day — score 6.)   ____

3. Have you ever suffered one or more of the following events because of overdrinking: Throwing up from drinking too much? Passing out or being unable to remember what you did the night before? Missing work on account of your drinking? (Never any of them, score 0; one or more of them rarely, score 2; one or more of them occasionally, score 4; one or more of them frequently, score 6.)   ____

4. Has drinking made your home life unhappy or interfered with your goals or achievements? (Not at all, score 0; maybe a little, score 2; quite a bit, score 4; very seriously, score 6.)   ____

5. Have you ever felt remorseful, ashamed, or guilty about drinking? (Never, score 0; occasionally, score 1; frequently, score 2.)   ____

6. Have you craved a drink at a regular time each day? (No, score 0; yes, score 2.)   ____

7. Have you drunk to relieve tension or escape pressure or unwind? (No, score 0; yes, score 2.) _____

8. Have you drunk alone? (Never, score 0; very rarely, score 2; occasionally, score 4; frequently, score 6.) _____

9. Have you wanted to drink in the morning? (Never, score 0; very rarely, score 2; occasionally, score 4; frequently, score 6.) _____

10. Have you ever been medically treated, hospitalized, or admitted to an institution because of drinking? (No, score 0; once, score 3; more than once, score 6.) _____

11. Have you ever been cited for DWI (driving while intoxicated)? (No, score 0; yes, score 4 for each time.) _____

12. Have you ever drunk more than you intended to? (Never, score 0; rarely, score 1; occasionally, score 3; often, score 5.) _____

13. Have other people (close friends, your children, employer, doctor, or spouse) ever commented negatively on your drinking or urged you to cut down? (No, score 0; yes, score 3 for one of the above or score 6 for two or more of the above.) _____

14. Have most fun things and good times in your life now or in the past been associated with alcohol? (No, score 0; yes, score 2.) _____

15. Have you declined a drink or left your first drink unfinished? (Sometimes or often, score 0; once or twice, score 2; almost never, score 3.) _____

16. Have you been comfortable associating socially with people who do not drink at all? (Yes, score 0; no, score 2.) _____

Total score for Part IV _____

Part V   Drug Use

1. Have you regularly taken prescription drugs of any of the following types for any reason? (No, score 0; yes, score 5 for each type.)
    sleeping pills _____
    tranquilizers _____
    diet pills _____
    pain pills _____

2. Have you taken any kind of pills (excluding vitamins) on a daily basis to "feel better"? (No, score 0; yes, score 2.)

3. Have you ever sought prescriptions from two or more doctors simultaneously for the same pills? (No, score 0; yes, score 5.)

4. Have you ever been addicted to a narcotic such as opium, morphine, heroin, Demerol, methadone, Dilaudid, or codeine? (No, score 0; yes, score 5.)

5. Have you ever used any of the following drugs: marijuana, speed, downers, acid, or cocaine? (Never, score 0; once, score 1; occasionally, score 2; frequently, score 3; daily, score 4 for each drug used.)

6. Have you ever had medical or institutional treatment for a drug habit? (No, score 0; yes, score 5.)

7. Have you personally known a ready source of marijuana, cocaine, heroin, or other street drugs? (No, score 0; yes, score 2.)

8. How many cigarettes have you smoked daily? (None, score 0; less than a pack a day, score 2; more than a pack a day, score 3.)

9. Have you ever chewed tobacco or smoked a pipe or cigars on a regular basis? (No, score 0; yes, score 3.)

10. Have discussions of drug abuse made you uncomfortable? (No, score 0; yes, score 2.)

11. How much coffee, tea, or cola have you drunk daily? (Less than 16 oz., score 0; more than 16 oz., score 2.)

12. Have you suffered a financial strain, family problems, or work difficulties because of drug use? (No, score 0; yes, score 4 for each one.)

Total score for Part V

Total score for Parts I–V

Interpreting Your Test

A relatively low score indicates that the individual has comparatively few risk factors suggesting that he or she may be addictive. A high score suggests a large number of such clues or risk factors; a

PHELPS/NOURSE INDIVIDUAL
ADDICTIVENESS PROFILE

SCORE SHEET

Part I	*Part II*	*Part III*	*Part IV*	*Part V*
1. a._____	1._____	1._____	1._____	1. a._____
b._____	2._____	2._____	2._____	b._____
c._____	3._____	3._____	3._____	c._____
d._____	4._____	4._____	4._____	d._____
e._____	5._____	5._____	5._____	2._____
f._____	6._____	6._____	6._____	3._____
g._____	7._____	7._____	7._____	4._____
h._____	8._____	8._____	8._____	5._____
i._____	9._____	9._____	9._____	6._____
2._____	10._____	10._____	10._____	7._____
3._____	11._____	11._____	11._____	8._____
4._____	12._____	12._____	12._____	9._____
5._____	13._____	13._____	13._____	10._____
6._____	14._____	14._____	14._____	11._____
7._____	15._____	15._____	15._____	12._____
8. a. _____	16._____	16._____	16._____	*Total*_____
b. _____	*Total*_____	17._____	*Total*_____	
c. _____		*Total*_____		
d. _____				
e. _____				
f. _____				
g. _____				
h. _____	*Total Score for Parts I–V* _____			
i. _____				
9._____				
10._____				

Total _____

middle-range score suggests only a moderate likelihood that you are an addictive person.

This means that the Individual Addictiveness Profile test will separate people into three large groups. Early experience with the test suggests that if you score under 50 on this test it is very unlikely that you are addictive, and this book probably will be of major interest to you only if other people close to you happen to be addictive. If you score between 50 and 100, you should definitely be on guard and read this book for further information, because you may well be an addictive person with present or potential problems with addiction. If you score above 100, it is extremely likely that you are an addictive person and probably already have one or more active addictions whittling away at your vitality and reducing the quality of your life. People with a high score may or may not have known that they are addictive or addicted, so the test results may well come as a surprise to them.

It has been my experience that addictive persons are very likely to have a number of qualities or traits in common, and the more such qualities or traits that a person exhibits, the more likely it is that he or she is an addictive person. It is these qualities and traits that the Individual Addictiveness Profile is designed to reveal or identify — the more of them identified, the higher the score.

It is very important to evaluate the partial scores as well as the total score. It's conceivable that a score lower than 50 could be misleading and the person could be addictive or even addicted. For example, if the person eats little sugar and is unaware of depression, but has a heavy family history score and uses no alcohol or drugs, his/her total score could be below 50. He or she could well be addictive and should understand the risk present of becoming addicted to sugar, alcohol, or drugs in the future because of the heavy influence of family history.

Another person could have a score around 50 or less with the points coming primarily from consumption of sugar. Even though there is low scoring in family history and alcohol and drug use, one should take a serious look at the addictiveness risk if large quantities of sugar are being eaten.

If the depression score is 12 or higher, regardless of the total score, the person should be evaluated for depression by a trained health professional. If the depression score is high, addictiveness is a risk even without any known family history.

Occasionally, low scores may be obtained by persons with alcohol or drug problems if (1) those taking the test do not have adequate information about their family history, (2) depression is masked by regular alcohol and/or drug use, and/or (3) sugar intake is low because of alcohol consumption. In these cases low scores may result despite addictive use of alcohol and/or drugs.

In chapter 3, let us consider in more detail exactly what addictiveness is and how this condition comes about.

3

Addiction: A Working Model

WHAT IS ADDICTION? Where does it come from, and why does it affect one person and not another? Although solid answers to these basic questions must be at the root of any serious attempt to understand and treat addiction, until recently there weren't any.

Most doctors, when starting to explore some completely unknown territory in clinical medicine, can at least find some reasonably familiar territory from which to start. When I first began to explore addiction, however, there wasn't any solid ground in sight. At the time, almost nothing was known about either the nature or the treatment of addiction. Addictions to different substances seemed to have little or nothing in common with one another: addiction to heroin, for example, seemed to be a totally different entity from addiction to alcohol. Addiction to such common prescription drugs as tranquilizers or sleeping pills wasn't acknowledged at all, and a large number of experts maintained that such drugs as marijuana and cocaine were definitely *not* addicting.

Now, after specializing in addiction since 1977, I would like nothing better than to say that I have found answers to the basic questions about addiction. I would like to be able to tell you precisely what addiction is, exactly what biochemical changes in the body are associated with it, and, above all, how those biochemical changes could be reversed by proper treatment. Unfortunately, I can't, because I still don't know the answers — and neither does anyone else.

I *have* developed a completely hypothetical, speculative *working model for addiction,* however, to guide me in my treatment of addicts. It is a new and practical way of looking at addiction based upon years of observing addicted patients and the many research fragments that have appeared in the medical journals.

As far as I know there are, as yet, no scientific studies demonstrating the validity of this model for addiction. I make no apology for this. I know the model fits a multitude of addictive characteristics that I have observed in my patients; it works as a valuable guide in successfully treating addicted people and helping them become and stay chemically free regardless of the form their addictiveness takes. It helps me to recognize as addictive not only the nurse who steals narcotics from hospital supplies to support her addiction, but also the teenager who hides candy bars or cookies under her bed, just in case she should happen to run short one evening, or the young executive who has two or three stiff drinks before leaving for an evening cocktail party or dinner gathering. As a tentative working model, it isn't sacred. When new knowledge or information appears, I delete an old piece of the model and put a new piece in.

What is this model for addiction? Its basic premise is that addiction in any form has little or nothing to do with moral weakness, psychological flaws, or lack of willpower. Rather, addiction arises primarily from physiological or metabolic flaws built into each addict's biochemistry, much as diabetes or hypothyroidism results from built-in metabolic flaws.

Specifically, according to my model, addiction is the direct result of a biochemical error, as yet unidentified, that is passed down genetically from generation to generation and that affects a surprisingly large number of individuals. Although the precise nature of this biochemical flaw has not yet been identified, a considerable body of suggestive scientific evidence convinces me that it results, among other things, in a deep-seated and pervasive disturbance in carbohydrate metabolism.

According to my model, people who harbor this biochemical flaw are by nature *addictive* — that is, they are vulnerable to addiction and are capable of becoming addicted to a wide variety of chemical substances, including sugar, alcohol, nicotine, caffeine, speed, marijuana, myriad prescription drugs, and opiate narcotics. People who do not have this biochemical flaw are nonaddictive, and they may well use various of the addicting chemicals from time to time without becoming addicted.

Addictiveness Is Physiological

My observations of many of the patients I have treated convinced me of the truth of this concept. The first glimmer came years ago when I saw the dismal results of "traditional" modes of treatment for narcotics addiction. Heroin addicts were supposedly cured of their addiction by withdrawing from heroin and substituting another highly addicting narcotic — methadone in decreasing doses. The vast majority of patients treated that way continued to remain vulnerable to heroin and became addicted to methadone as well. The actual cure rate was only 1 or 2 percent.

What struck me as most distinctive about such people was the degree of compulsion — the appearance of being driven — that they demonstrated regarding their addiction. One way or another, they arranged their lives to fulfill their addictive needs, and absolutely nothing — pride, economics, health, or relative values — was allowed to get in their way, ever. They always took care of their addictions first — even when the addicting substance no longer gave them any pleasure.

It seemed to me that this compulsiveness had to result from more than just a mental quirk or psychological flaw. These people really had to be suffering from some kind of recurring, insatiable, built-in physiological hunger for the addicting substance that simply had to be satisfied. It was the physiological hunger that caused the addiction and made the person's life unmanageable.

What kind of a physiological hunger? I had also noticed in many addicted patients a strong correlation between the use of alcohol or other addicting drugs and a strong craving for sugar. I could hardly believe the amounts of sugar the heroin addicts would eat when they were in treatment. They would stuff down staggering quantities. If they ate enough sugar and simple carbohydrates, they could satisfy their physiological hunger and postpone or alleviate withdrawal for prolonged intervals. As an alternative to sugar, there was alcohol; many heroin addicts trying to kick their habits drank heavily, even though very few of them were alcoholic. At the same time, I began to realize that many alcoholics I had treated had reacted to alcohol deprivation by gorging on sugar — and often, their gorging on sugar seemed to be connected with relapse. They'd eat sugar and then start drinking again, as though the sugar and the alcohol were interpreted by their bodies as "essentially the same thing."

The pieces began to fall into place as my model for addiction took shape. Addictive people suffered from a built-in biochemical disturbance, a real physiological hunger temporarily satisfied only by an addicting substance. There was a "carbohydrate connection" — something gone awry with the way sugars were handled in the body — behind all forms of addiction. People who had this biochemical disturbance were addictive, and extremely vulnerable to becoming addicted; those without the disturbance were not.

The Link with Depression

In developing my model for addiction, I soon became aware of a striking connection between addiction and another very common phenomenon: depression. Many addicted people I have treated recall being depressed as children or adolescents, but simply assumed at the time that that was the normal way to feel. Then when they experimented as teenagers with alcohol or various other addicting drugs, they experienced sudden, temporary relief from a depression they didn't even know they had. They suddenly felt great, happy, relieved of gloom for a while. It wasn't surprising that they returned to the addicting substance again and again. If they tried to stop using it, the depression came back in a flood, driving them on to further use. Others found that as their addiction developed, their depression was no longer relieved, or even became worse. Only when they successfully stopped using their addicting substance were they able to get the depression under control — but sometimes this required long, diligent treatment and antidepressant medication.

No one knows precisely what causes deep or chronic depression, but mounting evidence points to the interaction of chemicals in the brain, the pituitary gland, and the adrenals. Depression often runs in families — and many members of those families become addicted. The DST, or dexamethasone suppression test — an experimental blood test I will describe later — seems, so far, to identify many people with depression. I performed this test on hundreds of my addicted patients and found that one out of three tested positive for depression — yet many of them had been so used to living in a depressed mental state that they couldn't recognize their depression until it was pointed out to them.

All addicting substances, from sugar to narcotics, seem to provide temporary relief from depression, at first, and then later actually aggravate it. I am convinced that it is depression that helps encourage many addictive people to become addicted in the first place, makes it so difficult for them to break free, and causes so many relapses.

Finally, I believe that the degree of "normalcy," "relaxation," or feeling of well-being a person experiences from an addicting substance probably is related to the degree of depression the person has. With little depression, there is less of this "positive" reaction to addicting substances. With much depression, the sense of relief may be striking. In addition, different persons may have "positive" reactions to different substances. Some may get such a reaction from only one type of drug — which becomes their "drug of choice." It may be sugar, alcohol, nicotine, painkillers, or any other of the addicting substances.

So far, little is clearly understood — or even recognized — about this link between depression and addiction. But I am certain that the link exists and plays an important part in the overall pattern of addiction and addictive behavior.

Testing for Addictiveness

It would be extremely convenient if there were some kind of laboratory test we could use to identify an addictive person for certain — one simple blood test and we'd have the diagnosis. There is no such lab test yet, however.

There are, of course, certain laboratory tests that I do order for each new patient who comes into my office.

Routine blood count, urine analysis, and blood chemistries. These don't tell me whether or not a patient is addictive, but they do help assure me that no other illness is muddying the waters. In selected patients a urine examination for traces of certain addicting substances such as marijuana or heroin may also be done, usually for medico-legal purposes. Positive findings, of course, suggest strongly that the patient is addicted.

Glucose tolerance test. This rather complicated test most commonly is used to help diagnose diabetes or hypoglycemia. Since it provides a general picture of how a fasting patient's body handles carbohydrates over a period of six hours, I run it on my new patients in search of consistent evidence of a disturbance in carbohydrate metabolism — that is, of addictiveness.

So far, these test results have been impressive, but not conclusive. Some addictive patients have perfectly normal glucose tolerance tests, while most have test results lower than normal with increased symptoms but no pattern as yet has emerged that can serve as a reliable diagnostic flag for addictiveness.

DST, or dexamethasone suppression test. This is a new and experimental blood test first developed by psychiatrists to help identify certain kinds of depression in patients. Because of the strong link I have observed between addictiveness and depression, I have been ordering the DST on my new patients since 1981. Initially I found that at least two out of every three of these patients have had abnormal DST results, indicating the presence of depression. Recently it has dropped to one out of three of those tested.

None of the lab tests provides hard, conclusive chemical evidence of addictiveness. I have had to rely primarily on the patient's history to determine who was addictive and who was not.

Addiction and Sugar

What is the nature of the physiological hunger that drives addictive people to use addicting substances so compulsively? We do not yet know the precise biochemistry behind it, but we can observe what it does to people.

A nonaddictive person who is hungry and feels in need of an energy boost will often eat some "sugar-food" — food containing added sugar, white flour, or other refined carbohydrate (see the list of sugar-foods, in chapter 5, p. 44). After eating a reasonable portion of sugar-foods — candy or pastry, for example — this person will feel satisfied for a prolonged period of time, perhaps for several hours. He or she will not feel any need to go back for more immediately. A normal physiological hunger has been met and satisfied in a normal way.

In contrast, the addictive person finds that something else happens. Feeling hungry, he or she eats a reasonable portion of sugar-food, but immediately wants more. The physiological hunger is not quieted and continues to signal for more for some time. Some such people will proceed on a veritable sugar binge, gorging on sugar or simple carbohydrates even when they know it is going to make them feel terrible.

Why this striking difference between one group of people and another? Some recent scientific studies suggest at least part of the answer. According to research done at MIT's Laboratory of Neuroendocrine Regulation, a clue may lie in the behavior of certain chemical messengers in the brain that normally regulate our hunger for sugars.

One such brain chemical, known as serotonin, is intimately involved with our appetite for sugars and other carbohydrates. Normally, serotonin is released by cells deep in the brain, as a result of a long chemical chain reaction, as soon as we have eaten a meal rich in sugars.

Once released, serotonin has several chemical effects on the body. For example, it induces sleepiness and decreases sensitivity to pain. Most notable, the released serotonin also suppresses the appetite for more carbohydrates. Thus the act of eating carbohydrates ordinarily triggers a kind of natural, biochemical "feedback mechanism" that shuts off the craving for more carbohydrates.

In some people, however, this carbohydrate-serotonin feedback mechanism may not work properly. Eating a little sugar doesn't end up suppressing their desire for more, as it normally should.

No one yet knows exactly why or how this carbohydrate-serotonin feedback mechanism gets out of adjustment. It is not hard to see, however, that an inborn flaw in it could result in a disturbance of carbohydrate metabolism that is expressed as addictiveness of the sort I hypothesized in my model.

Addictiveness and Other Addictive Substances

There is reason to believe that the biochemical defect in addictive persons involves far more than a sugar-regulating mechanism in the body resulting in addictiveness to sugar alone, or to sugarlike substances such as alcohol. Endorphins, the body's natural opiatelike substances, appear to play an important role in addiction and many studies are being done in this area. Recent research has suggested that addictive people may have a disturbance in the function of the hypothalamic-pituitary-adrenal axis — the great interwoven system of body-regulating hormones that not only affect carbohydrate metabolism but also control other appetites, feelings of well-being, emotions, body urges, desires, and physiological hungers. Because of this broader involvement, it is not only sugar or sugar-foods that can temporarily satisfy the addictive person's gnawing physiological hunger. Alcohol, caffeine, nicotine, narcotics, speed, cocaine, and Valium affect the central nervous system as well. Any or all of these substances can temporarily satisfy the addictive person's physiological hunger just as sugar can, and thus the addictive person can become addicted to them. Some, such as alcohol or nicotine, because of their chemical effects on the body, are highly addicting substances — they are easy for the addictive person to become addicted to and hard to break away from. Others, like caffeine, may be only moderately addicting. But addiction is addiction. Whatever the addicting substance may be, the body, including the central nervous system, becomes accustomed to it, and when it is withdrawn the central nervous system generates withdrawal symptoms, as if in prot--t.

Indeed, many addictive people become so accustomed to staving off physiological hunger with one of these nonsugar substances that they have forgotten — or never even knew — that they had a sugar addiction, and sugar-craving doesn't appear overtly in their behavior. They may not care for sweets at all.

Addictiveness Is Hereditary

Where does the biochemical flaw that results in addictiveness come from? It doesn't seem to be acquired late in life, for even young children can be addictive. We know today that most biochemical reactions in the body are governed by specific genes transmitted from generation to generation. We also know that genetic accidents can produce biochemical malfunctions that are transmitted genetically. A biochemical flaw resulting in addictiveness, then, could be passed down from parents to children.

My practice experience to date suggests strongly that the "genetic connection" in regard to addictiveness is true. A large number of addicted people I have treated over the years had strong family histories of addiction. Time and again I encountered heroin addicts, cocaine addicts, or speed addicts with one or both parents addicted to alcohol, for example, or with one or more brothers or sisters also addicted — though not necessarily to the same drug. It is known and acknowledged that many alcoholics have one or more alcoholic parents; the large number of children of alcoholics who are *not* alcoholic but instead are addicted to other substances, however, is not so well recognized.

Here, perhaps, we can see the surface manifestation of addictiveness — the ways it reveals itself in different people — most clearly. The idea of pan-addiction — addiction to anything as a manifestation of an inheritable biochemical flaw — is borne out by my repeated clinical observation that addiction to one substance is basically the same as addiction to another. The underlying pathology is the same in every case.

I look closely, then, at a person's family history to help determine whether he or she is addictive. The affected people may be the patient's forebears (parents or grandparents), family contemporaries (brothers or sisters) or own children. (Probably aunts, uncles, and cousins should be included, too, but until more studies are done I recommend considering only the immediate family.) In such a family review, we are looking not only for specific addictions, but for evidence of addictiveness as well. The children of a severe alcoholic, for example, may well be teetotalers — no alcohol for them, they've seen enough of it — yet still may be addictive persons who are thoroughly addicted to sleeping pills, tranquilizers, sugar, or even heroin.

Of course, the most careful studies of family histories do not necessarily prove that addictiveness is hereditary, but they do raise serious questions and force us to consider what might be possible. In recent years researchers have demonstrated beyond doubt that a number of different biochemical flaws are linked to specific genes and result in specific, inheritable diseases. Phenylketonuria (PKU), for example, is one such hereditary disease caused by a gene-related defect in one particular enzyme system. There is reason to believe, then, that another inheritable biochemical flaw could lead to a subtle disorder of carbohydrate metabolism.

Addiction and Withdrawal

As we have seen, addictive people become addicted, whether to sugar, caffeine, nicotine, alcohol, narcotics, or a variety of prescription drugs, because they are satisfying an inner biochemical craving. The addicting substance is used because it temporarily makes the addictive person feel better or "normal," and allays tension, anxiety, depression, or other distressing symptoms. And when the addiction is not fed, even more aggravating symptoms begin to appear — symptoms commonly known as withdrawal symptoms.

We don't know precisely why withdrawal symptoms occur when an addicting substance is withdrawn, which is why they're so difficult to treat. And different substances cause different types of withdrawal symptoms, some far more severe than others.

Of all withdrawal symptoms, perhaps the most universal is a vague, pervading sense of restlessness, unease, and fear, a sense that something terrible is about to happen. Addicts in withdrawal are frightened. Often this distress is accompanied by swiftly rising anxiety and tension, and by a severe emotional "crash" or depression. Withdrawal from some drugs, notably the narcotics, also brings physical symptoms — abdominal cramps, profuse sweating, chilling, and so forth. In some cases of alcohol or sedative drug withdrawal the individual may even have convulsions or lapse into coma.

Addiction to a substance exists when withdrawal from that substance, whatever it may be, causes predictable unpleasant responses. Whether or not the substance is classed as "narcotic" or "habit-forming" doesn't matter; addiction exists when withdrawal causes pain, discomfort, unpleasantness, ill-feeling, or distress, whether physical, mental, or emotional.

Fear of withdrawal affects the addict's behavior. Alcoholics typically gravitate to places and situations where alcohol is appropriate and available; they become irritated when forced into situations where they can't drink. Sugar addicts typically are the first to ask about dessert after a big, satisfying meal. And the nicotine addict is invariably the one who complains most bitterly about customs and regulations that don't permit smoking in certain places.

The Meaning of Addictiveness

What does it mean to be an addictive person? Essentially it means that you are excessively vulnerable to or at risk of becoming addicted to a variety of addictive substances. If you drink alcohol, you are at much higher risk of becoming alcoholic — addicted to alcohol — than the nonaddictive person, even though he or she may drink more, or more regularly, than you do. You are at much higher risk than the nonaddictive person of becoming trapped in a compulsive pattern of sugar-food consumption. If your doctor finds it necessary to prescribe sleeping pills, painkillers, or tranquilizers for you, you are at much higher risk than the nonaddictive person of becoming hooked — addicted to — those medicines.

Does being an addictive person mean that you are already addicted to something? Not necessarily. Yet the plain fact is that the vast majority of addictive persons either *are* actively addicted to some drug or chemical at the present time or have a history of such addiction in the past.

Indeed, most addictive people become addicted to their "chemical of choice" fairly early in life. Patterns of addiction often can be extremely difficult to pin down, however. In some cases, such as addiction to sugar-foods, the idea that you are addicted may come as a shock; only when you recognize the thoroughly unpleasant ways that sugar addiction can affect your life and health will you understand how real the addiction is and how important it may be to you to recover from it.

Similarly, alcohol addiction is often notoriously hard to identify — but if you are an addictive person who is already using alcohol to excess, merely recognizing your vulnerability to a life-threatening addiction may enable you to cut through the fabric of denial and rationalization that so commonly surrounds alcoholism.

Many people who are not overtly addicted to any of the widely recognized addictive substances may nevertheless be addicted, without even knowing it, to prescription drugs such as sleeping medications, tranquilizers, or allegedly non-habit-forming pain pills such as Talwin or Darvon. Since it is my clinical observation that nonaddictive people usually do not become addicted to anything, the existence of an addiction, even an unrecognized one, or just the suspicion of a possible or probable addiction, is a suggestive marker to help identify the addictive person.

A Definition of Addiction

People who are, or may be, addictive need a clear statement of what addiction is. Most definitions I have seen fall short of usefulness because they define addiction in terms of the addictive substance; they are based on the notion that addiction occurs only in response to one of a few specified addicting substances. My experience indicates that addiction can exist in relation to any number of different substances, whether or not they are allegedly habit-forming, and that addiction can best be defined according to how the substance is used by the individual and what happens when its use is discontinued.

I have developed what I believe to be a good working definition of addiction. *An addiction is the compulsive and out-of-control use of any chemical substance that can produce recognizable and identifiable unpleasant withdrawal symptoms when use of the substance is stopped. Such addiction is driven by an inborn physiological hunger in the addictive person, and is frequently intimately related to depression.* This is, admittedly, very broad. It covers not only the acknowledged habit-forming drugs, and the recreational drugs such as cocaine and marijuana, but a wide range of seemingly harmless substances and "safe" prescription drugs as well. With such a definition as a guide, addictive people can be forewarned — and forearmed. Knowledge of their addictiveness can, in some cases, enable them to avoid addiction altogether. Most important, such knowledge can motivate some people already caught up in the addiction maze to break the grip of existing addictions.

In summary, according to my model for addiction, addictive people — those capable of becoming addicted to a wide variety of chemical substances — have a built-in, inherited biochemical flaw that results in their addictiveness. The flaw underlies a disturbance in the way their bodies metabolize carbohydrates, and creates a physiological hunger that can lead to addiction. The presence of addictiveness can be identified by discovery of symptoms suggestive of sugar dysmetabolism, by examination of family history, by pinpointing existing addictions, or by recognition of withdrawal symptoms. The presence of depression can be another important clue. The Individual Addictiveness Profile self-administered test presented in chapter 2 offers a new, accessible way for individuals to measure the likelihood of their own addictiveness.

Questions about Addictiveness

WHENEVER SOMEONE suggests a new and different way of looking at an old problem, questions arise. Here are some questions I am frequently asked about my concept of addictiveness. The answers are the result of my clinical experiences.

Question 1: Can you inherit alcoholism, or is it learned?
Answer: Alcoholism is not learned. The trait of addictiveness is inherited from the parents through the chromosomes and genes. Some addictive persons become alcoholic; others acquire addictions to other substances. Some remain addiction-free. Nonaddictive persons cannot be made into alcoholics.

Question 2: Isn't everyone addictive for some things?
Answer: No, people are born either addictive or nonaddictive, depending on the genes inherited from their parents. If both parents are alcoholic, the odds are great that the child will be addictive. If one parent is alcoholic, the odds are about 50-50 that the offspring will be addictive. Sometimes the parents are neither drug- nor alcohol-addicted but produce mostly addictive children because of their parents' addiction patterns and their own addictiveness manifested by addiction to sugar, caffeine, or cigarettes.

Question 3: Do all addictive people become addicted?
Answer: A few manage to escape entirely; some never get past sugar in their addiction; many others go on to alcohol or drugs. The person's environment can have a great influence on the actual addic-

tions that develop. For example, many addictive people who were raised by an alcoholic parent are determined never to become alcoholic. They may drink very little or not at all. However, they may fall victim to sugar or prescription drugs. If an addictive person belongs to a religious group that abhors the use of addicting substances such as caffeine, nicotine, alcohol, and street drugs, he or she may readily avoid those addictions but succumb to sugary substances or eventually to a prescription drug.

Question 4: Are there degrees of addictiveness? Are some addictive people more addictive than others?

Answer: I am convinced that the degree of addictiveness can indeed vary widely — that some addictive persons are moderately addictive while others are extraordinarily addictive. Why this is so is not known, but I have observed it repeatedly in patients I have treated, and I have seen it reflected to some extent in people's scores on the Individual Addictiveness Profile test. People who score relatively low in the addictive range (50 to 100) tend to be more mildly addictive and may become addicted to only one substance — caffeine, for example, or nicotine, or even alcohol — but nothing else. People with very high scores (110 and higher) tend to be extremely addictive and may become addicted to any available addicting substance.

Just how these varying degrees of addictiveness are expressed can depend heavily on such factors as the degree of depression present or the social controls that are at work in a person's life. A severely depressed person may easily fall prey to addiction in pursuit of the temporary relief from depression that the addicting substance provides. On the other hand, even an extremely addictive person might moderate his addictions very rigidly in order to conform (or seem to conform) to prevailing social standards.

I believe that the degree of addictiveness also will affect the addictive person's ability to get off an addicting substance once an addiction is recognized. Mildly addictive people may be motivated early to seek treatment because addiction is offensive to them, whereas extremely addictive people may exhibit strong denial that they are addicted and need professional help. The addiction becomes so important that they cannot imagine giving it up, at least not until tremendous pressures from the outside build up against it.

Question 5: Are some addicting substances more strongly addicting than others?

Answer: Yes, some certainly are more strongly addicting than others. This may be a result of the basic chemical nature of a given substance and the way it interacts with the body. Frequency of use may also be an important factor. Sugar, caffeine, or nicotine may be used many times a day, or repeatedly every hour, sometimes together. It is extremely easy to become addicted to these substances if you are addictive. Even a mildly addictive person with a low addictiveness score may become addicted to cigarettes. Public acceptance and availability of the substance in our society also encourages addiction. Sugar is everywhere and widely condoned; many times I have stopped at a gas station to get a snack only to find that all available food contains sugar.

The degree of addictiveness of substances may depend on the individual's response to the drug. If a substance makes a person feel much better, or different, he or she is apt to return to it whenever possible. The improved feeling may stem from alleviated depression or satisfied physiologic hunger.

Question 6: How does the "addictive personality" fit in with your concept of addictiveness?

Answer: Since addictiveness is determined by the physiology and biochemistry a person inherits at birth, it is clear to me that any "addictive personality or behavior" must be the *result* of addiction, and not the *cause*.

Question 7: Don't people get addicted because of problems they are trying to escape from?

Answer: Again, the problems often are the results of addiction rather than the cause. All people have problems, but only about 10 percent of the population is alcoholic. Wouldn't everyone who drank be alcoholic if problems caused alcoholism? Treatment aimed at solving the addicted person's problems has a poor track record of success. Amazingly, one's problems do not have to be dealt with directly to treat one's addiction successfully. Stopping the use of the substance is the first step. As the person becomes chemically free, his or her problems seem to solve themselves or at least get better. The answer to alcoholism is, clearly, *stop drinking*.

Question 8: Some people seem to be addicted to nonchemicals such as work, exercise, gambling, hyperactive behavior, or listening to music. How does this fit into your addictive concept?

Answer: Addictive people frequently have some amount of genetic depression, which may not be readily visible. Since the addictive activities listed above may give considerable relief to depression, some addictive people pursue them.

Question 9: What is genetic depression?

Answer: Genetic depression is a chronic physiological and biochemical depression that is transmitted from generation to generation in some families, although not necessarily to every family member. It is closely related to addictiveness, possibly stemming from the same physiological defect.

Genetic depression may be manifested in infancy or childhood, or it may not appear until the teens or even adulthood. It may even go unrecognized because it has been present so long that it seems normal, and the person has become an expert at living with it.

Question 10: Do you always know when you have genetic depression?

Answer: No. I have had many patients tell me that they had never had depression, and then when I questioned them further, tears poured forth uncontrollably, much to their surprise.

The signs of genetic depression are many and varied. Physical pain is the number one symptom and frequently cannot be diagnosed. Headaches, backaches, and stomachaches are common. Sleep problems, appetite changes, lack of energy, and constant fatigue may be present. Changes in sexual response may be related to depression. (Depression may wax and wane constantly, and the depth of depression may be reflected by the degree of interest in sex.) Anxiety and worry are common symptoms. People often blame their fears on external factors, but when depression is relieved and their physiology becomes balanced, the anxiety and worry disappear, even though the external factors remain unchanged.

Question 11: Is genetic depression treatable, or do you just have to live with it?

Answer: Genetic depression is very treatable. There are many things we can do, not only to relieve it but prevent it from coming back. Some of my patients have responded dramatically to my prescribed program of diet, exercise, proper rest, and vitamin and mineral supplements. However, often it is necessary to use antidepressant drugs in the early stages of treatment in order to break down this long-standing wall of depression. Once it is down and the patient becomes stable, the prescribed health program is often effective in maintaining a depression-free state.

Question 12: Is an antidepressant just another addicting drug acting as a substitute for the addicted person's drug of choice?
Answer: No, antidepressants are not addicting. They are, however, very long acting and must be introduced slowly and tapered off slowly. Even when an addicted person stops using the addicting substance, he or she may be in jeopardy of relapse if depression has not been dealt with adequately.

Question 13: What is the most common cause of relapse back to the addicting substance?
Answer: Addiction is a disease of denial and relapse, and this is what makes it so difficult to treat. I am convinced that relapse is closely related to depression. If depression is not adequately treated, the person will eventually return to his or her addicting substance.

Question 14: So much treatment fails. What are the most important factors in a successful treatment?
Answer: Abstinence, and relief from the underlying depression, are both vital, and diet and supplements are important factors. It is essential that all treatment be given out with generous amounts of love and dignity. Treatment must be tailored to each individual, enabling the patient to apply it to his or her unique set of needs.

Question 15: Can addicted people be helped if they don't want to be?
Answer: Yes, many a person has been taken to residential treatment in a stupor and stayed on to become sober and grateful. Those who love an addicted person can help by putting pressure on the addict to get treatment — many addicts finally get the help they need when loved ones threaten to or actually do leave, the job becomes at risk, or the courts make an offer they can't refuse.

Question 16: Can a recovering alcoholic learn to be a social drinker?
Answer: No, absolutely not! Sooner or later, the alcoholic will succumb to the full addiction. Many have tried — and died.

Sometimes a nonaddictive person in a heavy drinking environment is mistaken for an alcoholic. After leaving that climate and returning to normal social drinking, he or she is mistakenly identified as an alcoholic turned social drinker.

Question 17: In college, almost everybody seems to drink a lot. How do you know who is alcoholic and who isn't?

Answer: That is a very good question. Some of the identifying signs of alcoholism will give you important clues.

- Tolerance — a person's ability to consume large amounts of alcohol without getting sick, sleepy, or nonfunctional.
- A preoccupation with and attraction to alcohol.
- Avoidance of activities and people who do not use a lot of alcohol.
- The need to use alcohol on a frequent and regular schedule.

Question 18: Prescription addiction is frightening. If my doctor orders a medicine for me, can't I assume it's not addicting if I take it as prescribed?

Answer: No, many doctors do not understand addiction, nor do the drug manufacturing companies. Valium has addicted tens of thousands of people, even at very low dosages; and Xanax, also an addicting drug, may be tomorrow's Valium, because it is now widely prescribed for anxiety and depression. Meprobamate is another addicting tranquilizer. Withdrawal from these drugs can be most unpleasant and prolonged.

Question 19: I have a nineteen-year-old son who uses alcohol and marijuana to excess daily. What can I do?

Answer: Don't contribute to his addictions either financially or emotionally. Let him know how you feel. Give him this book to read. Offer to help him get the proper treatment. If he refuses, you must separate yourself from his problem but continue to love him.

Question 20: How can you tell the difference between habit and addiction?

Answer: Sometimes it's difficult. Of course, many everyday habits — brushing your teeth at bedtime, having eggs for breakfast, eating butter instead of marmalade — have nothing whatever to do with addicting substances, so there isn't any question. But some habits do involve addicting substances, and here the distinction can get sticky. Consider the person who always has three cocktails before dinner, but says, "It's just a family habit, we're certainly not addicted to the stuff." Or take the person who smokes just five (or maybe ten or fifteen) cigarettes a day who says, "It's purely a nervous habit when I'm under pressure. I don't really need to smoke."

Habit or addiction? Checking against our definition of addiction perhaps can provide us with the best answer. Many habits may appear compulsive — the same thing is done in the same way at the same time without variation — but few are out of control in the sense that people rearrange their lives to accommodate them. True habits simplify people's lives by providing repetitive behavior pathways that require no thought, but they don't result in real, unpleasant withdrawal symptoms when the pattern is broken; temporary annoyance, perhaps, but nothing more.

Question 21: I thought people got addicted to the "highs" they obtained. Isn't this true?

Answer: People certainly do obtain pleasurable highs from taking addicting substances, but it's not the high that causes addiction. Even nonaddictive people can experience highs or relaxation from addicting substances — from a couple of martinis, say, or from smoking pot. The addictive person, however, is likely to experience a far more intense high, because the addicting substance is feeding a built-in physiological hunger that the nonaddictive person doesn't have.

Most, if not all, addicting substances perform some type of action on the central nervous system. They stimulate it (as does caffeine), depress it (as do sleeping pills or tranquilizers), or alter perceptions in some way (as do narcotics or marijuana). Often that central nervous system effect is pleasant, at least for a while, and this may indeed lead a person to repeated or frequent use. (For example, it is the intense high from cocaine that induces many users to take dose after dose all evening long, until they run out of the drug or money to buy more.) But addicts become addicted not because of the high, but because they need their substance to satisfy their physiological hunger, to relieve the symptoms of depression, and to stave off withdrawal symptoms.

Question 22: You say nonaddictive people never become addicted to anything. If a person is hooked on one thing and only one, like cigarettes, does that mean the person is addictive, even if he or she scores very low on the Individual Addictiveness Profile test?

Answer: Yes, I'd say the person is addictive. He or she may be at the "mildly addictive" end of the addictiveness spectrum, or may have extremely strong and rigid behavior controls and just doesn't allow him- or herself to become addicted to anything else. Often, both of the above are true. Bear in mind that the Addictiveness Profile test is not infallible; it is merely suggestive.

Question 23: Aren't there some heavy drinkers who aren't addictive — they just drink a lot?

Answer: I don't believe it. It's a contradiction in terms. Few, if any, nonaddictive people "just drink a lot." Why would they? The stuff doesn't even taste that good to most nonaddictive people, and they usually dislike the effects. It is addictive people who develop tolerance and can "hold their liquor." I suspect the heavy drinkers you describe are actually quite addictive and probably are addicted to alcohol. They are merely denying their addictiveness and addiction, an extremely common practice among addicts in general and alcoholics in particular.

Question 24: Are all drugs or chemicals addicting substances?

Answer: No, not by any means. Only a few select substances have the power to satisfy temporarily the addictive person's physiological hunger. Many widely used prescription medicines (antidepressant drugs, heart and blood pressure medications, nitroglycerine preparations for heart pain, or antibiotics, for example) are not addicting in any way. Many over-the-counter medicines are not addicting either — but you'd better check the ingredients, because many others do contain addicting substances.

In fact, most addicting substances fall into just a few broad families. These include sugars and refined carbohydrates, alcohol, central nervous system stimulants such as caffeine, amphetamines or cocaine, sedative sleeping pills, many tranquilizers, the opiate narcotics, and certain unclassifiable substances such as marijuana. We will discuss each of these groups in later chapters.

Question 25: You sometimes speak of drugs and chemicals in the same breath. Aren't they the same thing?

Answer: Maybe it's a fussy distinction, but I think of *drugs* as chemical substances that have (or once had) a legitimate medical use in treating illness, whereas *chemicals* are substances that never have had any legitimate reason to be put in the body. By this gauge, Valium and Demerol are drugs, and nicotine is a chemical. I guess I use both terms to be sure I'm not leaving something out.

Question 26: Why on earth would a nonaddictive person ever use an addicting substance if it isn't needed?

Answer: A nonaddictive person might choose to use an addicting substance in a casual or social fashion, such as accepting a glass of wine at a dinner party, because it makes the food taste better, because of peer pressure, or simply to bow to social custom, even though he or she doesn't really want the stuff or particularly care for it. Other possible reasons include ordinary curiosity or, in the case of a prescription drug, a legitimate need for medication. The important point is that the nonaddictive person makes the choice whether or not to use the substance; it is not forced on the person by his or her biochemistry.

Question 27: Can't an addict's spouse get involved in the addict's addiction even if the spouse isn't addictive?

Answer: Yes, indeed, the spouse can get involved — the whole family can — but not necessarily as addicts. Typically, any addict wants things to coast along quietly, but people who live with the addict come to feel beaten down and emotionally trapped, maybe just sick and tired of fighting, because they're living in the constant presence of a sick person, and *they* have to change *their* lives to fit into the addict's sick life.

One distorted way such families often cope is to become enablers, who, far from encouraging the addict to stop, make it as easy as possible for the addiction to continue. They make excuses for, cover up for, and support him or her. They may even openly encourage the addict to use the drug of choice, because it makes his or her behavior, although sick, at least predictable.

Obviously, a family caught up in this sort of trap is deeply involved in the addiction, whether or not they themselves have any addiction. When the addict comes to treatment, these people may need vigorous support or counseling themselves to help them reconstruct their lives with a recovering addict. Organizations such as Al-Anon and Naranon exist specifically to help such nonaddicted spouses or families make their own recoveries.

Question 28: Can addiction be cured?

Answer: No, it cannot be "cured," but it is very treatable. The risk of relapse is present throughout life no matter how long the recovery.

5

A Program for Treatment

ONCE IT BECAME clear to me that all addictions arise from the same underlying cause — an error in metabolism that creates an abnormal physiological hunger — then it followed logically that any pattern of treatment that helps overcome one form of addiction ought to be effective for any other form of addiction.

Over the years, my experience has led to the development of my working model for addiction and to a basic program of treatment that works for any addiction. In many cases the program works best, at least at the start, when it is supervised by a doctor; in some of those cases the doctor's guidance is imperative. However, my treatment program depends in large part upon the patient.

In the long run it is the patient who must make the commitment to recover from the addiction and do the hard work necessary to achieve that goal.

The Patient's Self-Help Program

There are several steps you can take to help yourself. No matter what substance or substances you may be addicted to, the simple, basic self-help program outlined below will help any addicted person break free of any addicting substance.

1. *Education.* Before seriously embarking on any treatment program, you first must have an understanding of your own addiction.

You cannot comprehend addiction if you don't understand what addictiveness is: how and why you fell into the addiction trap in the first place. You also need to be educated out of many destructive and enslaving misconceptions — that you've done something to feel guilty about, that there's something wrong with your mind, that you're a weak, unworthy shameful person — all the useless debris piled up on the doorstep of addiction, making you feel helpless and hopeless about ever getting rid of your problems.

You must understand clearly that addictiveness is a built-in, inherited condition that exists through no fault of your own. In many cases, recognizing the biochemical basis of addictiveness seems to alleviate much of the guilt and fear of craziness that so many addicted people are carrying when they approach treatment. Your underlying addictiveness can't be eradicated, but knowing it for what it is can help immeasurably in avoiding future addiction once the current problem is under control. Why go through the hard work and distress of eliminating one addiction, only to fall right into another one a little later? Understanding the nature of addictiveness is a powerful safeguard against that possibility.

By reading this book carefully and taking the addictiveness test in chapter 2, you will obtain a great deal of the information you need for a rational approach to treatment. There are many other resources available as well. For example, many communities provide educational lectures at addiction treatment centers, addiction awareness hours, and so forth.

2. *Commitment.* After education, your commitment to treatment must come first: you must commit yourself to stop using the addicting substance. This is the bedrock on which the treatment of any addiction must rest, and until you have made this commitment you cannot go forward. Don't consider tapering off. It doesn't work. It would work only if the patient actually had control over his or her use of the addicting substance, and we know that's not true: addiction, by definition, means uncontrolled or out-of-control use of the substance. My experience with patients bears this out. The vast majority who tried tapering off never made it; they remained addicted until they stopped completely.

3. *Abstinence.* Once you have committed yourself to terminating the addicting substance, pick a date on which you will stop, and then do so, immediately and completely. One important caution: *If*

SUGAR-FOODS TO AVOID

bagels*
baking powder biscuits
breath mints
cakes
candies
canned fruit in sugar syrup
chewing gum
chocolate
chocolate milk
cocoa
cookies
corn sweetener
corn syrup
Danish pastries
dessert toppings
dextrose or dextrin
diet candied appetite suppressants
dinner rolls*
doughnuts
English muffins*
fruited yogurts
fruit juices (sweetened)
glucose
honey
ice cream
ice cream toppings
jams
Jell-O (various kinds)

jelly
ketchup
Kool-Aid (sugar-sweetened)
laxative candies or caramels
lemon- or limeade
malted barley
maple syrups
mayonnaise
pancakes
pancake syrup
pasta (spaghetti, macaroni, etc.)*
pastries
pies
pizza
popsicles
preserves
pretzels
relishes
sherbets
sodas
soft drinks
sweet and sour sauces
sweet pickles
sweet rolls
Thousand Island dressing
white bread*
white flour croissants
white rice

* Bread and pasta products made from whole wheat flour are acceptable.

the substance you are terminating is alcohol, a sleeping pill, or a tranquilizer, you should stop only under a physician's supervision, because withdrawal symptoms from these can be life-threatening. Consult the later chapters on each individual addiction for more information on this subject.

Stopping completely and immediately might seem to be doing it the hard way, but actually that's not true. It is, in fact, the easiest way there is, and in most cases, the only way. Attempting to taper off is far more difficult, especially because after all the agonizing struggle it fails, and the patient ends up starting over. Terminate completely, and you have to terminate only once. After that, the recovery phase of treatment can begin.

4. *Avoidance of New or Substitute Addictions.* During the difficult period immediately after termination of the addicting substance — the period of detoxification and withdrawal — the possibility of becoming addicted to some other substance is a major danger. Your addictive thinking may tell you that you deserve a reward for not using your drug of choice. After all, as we saw in chapter 3, all addictions are associated with a deep-seated physiological hunger; if you are removing an addicting substance that has been partially fulfilling that need, it is hardly surprising that the body should seek out some other addicting substance to serve as a substitute. There is a variety of drugs, perhaps some already in your home or medicine cabinet, that you might be tempted to turn to, on your own, to help you get over the rough spots of withdrawal or early treatment — tranquilizers to help "quiet your nerves," for example, or alcohol or sleeping pills to help with the insomnia that may bother you. If you use any of these other addicting drugs for "help," however, you run a grave risk of becoming addicted to *it*. Substances to avoid include the following.

- *Alcohol.* There is no place for this dangerously addicting substance in the treatment of addiction. Even a person who has "never had trouble with alcohol" should discontinue its use during treatment.
- *Sugar-foods.* This refers to the sugars and refined carbohydrates, which are addicting substances to the addictive person — sugars, honeys, syrups, and jams; cakes, pies, and sweet pastries; white bread or rolls; sweet desserts; nondiet soft drinks; and so

forth. (For more detail, see the expanded list of sugar-foods, p. 44.) Bear in mind that prohibition of sugar-foods does not necessarily extend to all foods containing carbohydrates, but specifically to those containing added sugar or those made from white flour or other refined carbohydrates.

■ *Caffeine.* This includes not only regular coffee and tea, which are loaded with caffeine, but also the decaffeinated coffees (which still contain 3 to 7 percent of their caffeine), cocoa and chocolate, and a large variety of soft drinks (including many cola drinks and fruit-flavored sodas), which contain varying amounts of caffeine. (For more detail, see the list of caffeine-containing beverages, p. 132.)

■ *Drugs.* Since neither prescription nor over-the-counter drugs generally carry labels indicating whether they are addicting, dispense with any drugs that are not specifically prescribed for you by a doctor for some important medicinal purpose. Naturally, if you are taking a drug for some condition such as arthritis, high blood pressure, or heart disease, you should not just stop taking such a medication on your own. Talk to your doctor first, explain that you are undergoing treatment for an addiction, and ask if the prescribed drug needs to be continued.

In general, drugs to avoid include tranquilizers, sleeping medicines, diet pills, cough syrups, and any narcotic-containing painkillers. This refers to over-the-counter products as well as prescription drugs. Read the labels and avoid any product that even hints at tolerance, physical dependence, or habituation under any circumstances. For instance, many over-the-counter diet pills contain phenylpropanolamine, a compound similar in many ways to the highly addicting amphetamines. Other drugs, such as Alka-Seltzer, for example, or over-the-counter sleeping pills such as Sominex, which contain an antihistamine as the active ingredient, are not addicting. Since you may not know in any given case, the best course is to discontinue anything that is not specifically prescribed and necessary.

5. *Nutritional Treatment Plan.* Nutrition is the foundation of my treatment program, which emphasizes frequent sugar-free feedings to stabilize the blood sugar and large doses of vitamins and minerals to reverse the body's long-standing depletions.

Your malnutrition must be dealt with. The more preoccupied a patient has been with feeding an addiction, the less time and attention he or she has spent on obtaining adequate, balanced nourishment — good basic nutrition is often one of the first things to go. In my experience, almost all addicts are malnourished in one way or another, whether underweight, overweight, or merely lacking in a variety of nutritional basics. Since an addict in treatment is in the process of healing an illness, and a malnourished body does not heal well, restoration of proper nourishment during treatment is important for healing the addiction and is good for the patient's body in general.

In a recent study of patients receiving inpatient treatment of alcoholism, half received the regular treatment plan and the other half received a nutritional program along with the regular treatment. Six months after discharge, only 33 percent of the patients in the regular program remained sober, whereas 81 percent of the nutritionally supported group remained sober.

What is proper nourishment? Nutritionists and other authorities differ on this, but the nutritional program I have developed has worked successfully for my patients. The program is always customized to each patient's individual needs.

The elements of treatment listed below are ones that I often use, although not all patients receive all parts of the program. You may use these guidelines to plan your own self-help program. I have used the vitamin supplements for many years with consistent effectiveness and no significant problems. It is important to listen to your body, however. Body protests are occasionally seen in the form of gastric upset, best handled by adding vitamins in gradually increasing doses. Diarrhea and headache often are side effects of the detoxification process as the body expels toxic substances.

A. *Body detoxification.* Vitamin C is the most essential ingredient in the treatment of addiction, and I recommend that almost all my patients take high doses during the withdrawal period.

Vitamin C is valuable to your treatment in three significant ways. First, it is perhaps the best and safest detoxifier known, helping to clear the body of any residual addicting substance as rapidly as possible. Second, vitamin C can eliminate or modify many of the withdrawal symptoms associated with addicting substances. Third, it is a powerful aid in rebuilding the nutritional status of the patient's body.

The easiest way to take vitamin C during the treatment period is

RESOURCE LIST*

JCM Research
222 Nineteenth Avenue East
Seattle, Washington 98112

Supplies: NutraBalance Multivitamin and Minerals
ProBalance Protein Powder supplement
Adrenal Balance
vitamin C crystals — sodium ascorbate and buffered C
Free Form Amino Acids
calcium-magnesium-potassium (Trispartate)
Write for product list

Bronson Pharmaceuticals
4526 Rinetti Lane
La Canada, California 91011-0628
(818) 790-2646

Supplies: vitamin C crystals as sodium ascorbate
vitamin C crystals as calcium ascorbate — buffered
multiple vitamin supplements
Write for catalog

Phelps/Nourse Individual Addictiveness Profile
(tests and score sheets)

Janice Keller Phelps, M.D.
1110 Harvard Avenue
Seattle, Washington 98122
(206) 325-9095

* These products may be available from some health food stores as
well as from the manufacturers. Prescriptions are not necessary.

in crystalline or powder form. It can be purchased by the pound or
kilo at most health food stores, at many supermarkets or drugstores,
or by direct mail from pharmaceutical suppliers (see the resource
list above for addresses).

Vitamin C in crystalline or powder form may come as buffered
vitamin C (ascorbic acid), as sodium ascorbate, as calcium ascorbate, or as ascorbyl palmitate, as well as in other forms. All are es-

sentially tasteless powders containing approximately 4,000 mg of vitamin C per teaspoon. I ordinarily recommend that my patients take the sodium ascorbate, one teaspoon every two to four hours while awake during the detoxification period. Sodium ascorbate powder is easily dissolved in fruit juice, milk, or plain water. Usually the sodium is rapidly excreted by the body and does not add to the total body content of sodium.

You may develop diarrhea on this dosage of vitamin C. If you do, cut the dosage in half but maintain the same frequency. Remember, however, that diarrhea is a common symptom of narcotic withdrawal and more likely is a result of the withdrawal. In addition, diarrhea is helpful in cleansing the body of its toxic substances. Rarely, an individual's body collects fluid or the ankles start to swell. Should this happen, switch to an ascorbate containing calcium, magnesium, and/or potassium instead of sodium. If you develop any other unusual negative side effects (skin rash, itching, nausea, urinary distress, and so forth), discontinue the vitamin C immediately and consult your doctor. Very rarely, a patient has some undesirable reaction unique to that person. If there is any question, consult your physician at once.

You should continue to take vitamin C for three to seven days, depending on your addicting substance, since the length of time needed for detoxification varies from one substance to another and from person to person. Continue to take vitamin C every two to four hours until you are stabilized and without craving, then reduce the frequency to twice daily, and the amount to 4 to 8 grams daily.

B. *Restoring vitamin and mineral deficiency.* Since all addictions cause serious vitamin and mineral deficiencies, a potent supplemental schedule is an important part of the restorative nutritional program I recommend for any addicted patient in withdrawal and recovery. Since the very high doses of individual vitamins and minerals that I prescribe are not generally found on the drugstore shelf, or are not available in the proper balance, I give my patients individual instructions for the specific vitamin products and amounts I want them to take. For the multivitamin I usually recommend a specially designed preparation called Nutrabalance supplied by JCM Research (see the resource list on p. 48). The proper ratios allow me to prescribe it safely in varying amounts up to nine capsules a day. One capsule provides the following.

VITAMINS

beta carotene	2,778 I.U.
vitamin D_3	11 I.U.
ascorbyl palmitate (vitamin C)	5.5 mg
vitamin B_1 (thiamine)	16.6 mg
vitamin B_2 (riboflavin)	11 mg
niacin	2.8 mg
niacinamide	16.6 mg
pyridoxal 5' phosphate (active vitamin B_6)	2.8 mg
pantothenic acid	83.3 mg
folic acid	89 mcg
PABA (para aminobenzoic acid)	11 mg
biotin	33 mcg
vitamin B_{12}	111 mcg
choline (citrate)	55 mg
bioflavonoids	22 mg
vitamin E (d-alpha tocopherol)	22 I.U.

AMINO ACIDS

glutamine	55 mg

MINERALS

calcium (aspartate and oyster shell)	55 mg
magnesium (aspartate and oxide)	55 mg
zinc (picolinate)	3.3 mg
potassium (aspartate and chloride)	11 mg
manganese (aspartate)	2.2 mg
iodine (potassium iodide)	25 mcg
chromium (aspartate)	22 mcg
selenium (aspartate)	22 mcg
molybdenum (aspartate)	11 mcg
vanadium (aspartate)	2.7 mcg

DIGESTANTS

betaine HCl	36 mg
bromelain (1,000 mcu)	5.5 mg
papain	5.5 mg

I find the high levels of the B vitamins and the various minerals in this preparation particularly valuable. The relatively low content of vitamins A, D, and E is important for safety when giving multiple capsules daily.

C. *Body-building raw materials.* Many people need extra protein during the withdrawal phase to help the body repair damaged and malnourished tissues. Since you may not be able to eat much solid food, I recommend a protein drink using a protein powder made from special milk protein, with no added flavoring or sweeteners (although a synthetic sweetener may be added if desired). The most successful formula I've found is ProBalance, which has seventy calories per serving and a protein efficiency ratio of 2.5, with low carbohydrates and fat content (see the resource list p. 48). It is well tolerated and very satisfying, and mixes conveniently with fruits or juices, milk, or almost any other sugarless beverage. Added vitamins and minerals are not required since the multivitamin is prescribed daily. The protein drink helps stabilize patients' blood sugar levels so that they don't feel too hungry or crave sugar, and it contributes significantly to lowering depression episodes. Many patients report that it gives them energy. (See p. 56 for recipes and further directions for use of the protein supplement.)

There are protein supplements that are made from soy protein or contain sweeteners, flavorings, and sugar available in some drugstores and supermarkets. I advise my patients to avoid these preparations, but other flavorless, sugarless milk or egg protein supplements may be used. The quality of protein in soy protein powders is not as high as in products made from milk and eggs, but soy products without sugar may be used by persons who cannot tolerate milk or eggs.

D. *Specific symptomatic treatment with additional vitamins and nutrients.* In addition to the treatment basics outlined above — vitamin C, the high-potency vitamins, and the protein supplement — I may recommend a number of other vitamins or nutrients to help patients deal with specific problems. (See pp. 52–53 for a summary table of supplements and dosages.)

For *nervousness and agitation,* additional calcium (100 mg chelated) may be added with magnesium (90 mg chelated) and potassium (30 mg chelated) two or three times a day for withdrawal symptoms. Most addicted people gain a calming effect from these two minerals, although additional supplementation usually is not necessary if the Nutrabalance multivitamin is taken. (See the resource list, p. 48.)

For *depression,* niacinamide (1,000 mg) may be used three times a day for its natural antidepressant effect. The benefit is significant in

Supplements	Dosages	Before Breakfast	Breakfast	Mid-Morning	Lunch	Mid-Afternoon	Dinner	Bedtime
Vitamin C — Sodium ascorbate (4000 mg/tsp.) — Buffered ascorbate (2350 mg/tsp.)	1 tsp., two times per day		1				1	
Multivitamin — NutraBalance	3 capsules, 3x/day		3		3		3	
Protein supplement — ProBalance	2 tbsp. 1–3x/day		X					X
Niacinamide — 1 g (antidepressant)	One, 3x/day		1		1		1	
Pantothenic acid — 500 mg (for adrenal support)	One, 3x/day		1		1		1	
Vitamin B$_6$ — Pyridoxine — 100 mg (with free-form amino acids)	One, with amino acids	1		1		1		
— 250 mg (natural diuretic)	One, 2–3x/day				(1)		1	1

Supplement	Dosage							
Cortex (Adrenal — 125 mg and adrenal cortex — 30 mg)	One, 2x/day	1		1		1		
Lipotrepein (Thorne Research) (Liver detoxifier)	1–3 capsules per day	1		1		1		
Free-form amino acids — 750 mg. (multiple amino acids)	3 capsules, 3x/day	3		3		3		
Phenylalanine — 600 mg (amino acid for depression)	1 tsp. or 3 capsules in A.M.	3						
Tyrosine — 800 mg (amino acid for depression)	1 tsp. or 3 capsules in A.M.	3						
Tryptophan — 500 mg (amino acid for depression and sleep)	Three at bedtime							3
Glutamine — 500 mg (amino acid for alcohol and drug cravings)	2 tablets, 3–4x/day	2		2		2		2

This is a list of optional supplements. The reader may choose those that are appropriate to his or her needs. It is not intended that anyone take every supplement on the list. Consult your physician.

some people, and it has few side effects. I avoid using niacinamide in patients with liver damage or elevated liver enzymes. The amino acids phenylalanine and tyrosine may also help with some forms of depression. One gram of each is taken first thing in the morning without food, at least an hour before breakfast. B_6 (100 mg) taken at the same time promotes absorption of the amino acids. Depression often requires initial treatment with medically prescribed antidepressants. You may choose to consult your physician.

For *frequent changes in energy level and poor stress responses,* I give pantothenic acid, one of the so-called antistress vitamins, 500 mg three times a day. Signs of adrenal dysfunction may include sugar dysmetabolism, genetic depression, or inability to cope with stress. Whole adrenal extract (125 mg) combined with adrenal cortical extract (30 mg), taken three times daily, will add support to the adrenals.

If a patient needs special attention to swift *body-building nutrition,* free-form amino acid complex preparations are helpful at 500 to 1,000 mg three times a day, with 100 mg of vitamin B_6 (pyridoxine) given with the amino acid dose for better utilization. These should be taken on an empty stomach at least one hour before food is eaten. (See the resource list, p. 48.)

For *trouble sleeping,* tryptophan (1,500 to 1,800 mg) may be taken without other protein at bedtime. Tryptophan may improve sleep dramatically, and help the body fight off depression. (Some people, however, are stimulated by tryptophan and can't sleep when taking it. They should not use it.)

Finally, glutamine is an amino acid that *helps curb craving for alcohol, drugs, and sugar.* It is taken in doses of 500 to 1,000 mg four times a day between meals.

E. *Food plan.* The elimination of sugar from your diet is vital. Eat a basic complex carbohydrate diet, to which you may add animal protein and dairy products as you see fit. Eliminate all caffeine and alcohol, even if you don't consider them a problem; all sugar-foods, including honey; and white flour or enriched wheat flour.

Frequent feedings also are necessary. You should eat something about every two hours during the daytime, most conveniently by taking three moderate meals at regular mealtimes plus three small supplement snacks at mid-morning, mid-afternoon, and mid-evening. The protein supplement drink can be premixed and carried in a container for use at these times.

Controlling your diet carefully during the treatment period produces several different benefits at once. It breaks the pattern of sugar-food eating common to many addictive people, and introduces you to a practical, healthy alternative; it helps restore good nutrition and repairs the damage that addiction has done to your body; and, if you are overweight, it helps you begin to get your weight under control.

Most addictive people eat on a disorganized schedule dictated by when they happen to feel hungry — which may be all of the time. Their eating patterns often make little or no nutritional sense, skipping breakfast, snacking on sugar-foods at mid-morning, having a fast-food lunch, eating one huge meal per day in the evening, and so on. In my treatment program, you supply your body with food as it needs fuel in a series of small but nourishing meals throughout the day. For most patients a schedule like the following works out well.

8:00 A.M.	breakfast or protein supplement
10:00 A.M.	small mid-morning snack and protein supplement
12:30 P.M.	lunch
3:00 P.M.	small mid-afternoon snack and protein supplement
6:00 P.M.	dinner
8:30 P.M.	protein supplement or snack
11:00 P.M.	very small optional snack for "late-nighters"

The first goal of your eating program is to divide the day's calories more or less evenly among the three major meals (no huge meals and no skipped meals), while weeding out sugar-foods and refined carbohydrates and substituting whole grain breads and cereals, vegetables, salads, and fresh fruits. The latter contain complex carbohydrates, which are not quickly broken down by the body. As a result, the sugar from these foods enters the bloodstream in small amounts over a long period of time and does not cause a sharp rise in blood sugar.

What to eat. The three meals should provide approximately 70 to 75 percent of your caloric needs for the day. The supplements and snacks should be thought of as "little meals," or picker-uppers, which supply additional protein and complex carbohydrates. Between them, they will provide the final 25 to 30 percent of your calories. Once or twice a day the snack can take the form of a high-protein "milkshake" based on milk or unsweetened fruit juice to which a high-protein supplement such as ProBalance is added. Here is a recipe my patients have found tasty and refreshing.

HI-PRO MILKSHAKE

8 oz. unsweetened orange juice or 1 oz. frozen orange juice concentrate plus 8 oz. of water
½ banana
4 oz. plain yogurt
3 tbsp. ProBalance protein supplement
cracked ice
whirl in blender until smooth

Berries or other fruit, and skim milk instead of juice, may be used. A synthetic sweetener may be added (NutraSweet or Equal works well), as well as vanilla or other flavorings.

Below is a sample day's menu following the principles outlined above. The portions are merely guidelines and may be varied to suit the individual. Weight-loss efforts should be deferred until one is stable and in balance.

BREAKFAST

4 oz. fruit juice (unsweetened) or small serving fresh fruit
2 oz. whole grain cereal, dry or cooked, with ¼ cup 1% milk but no added sugar (raisin bran, for example, or other natural fruit-sweetened cereals, but not sugar-added cereal)
or
1 piece whole wheat or other whole grain toast with 1 tsp. butter or margarine
1 egg
4 oz. 1% milk

MID-MORNING SNACK
Hi-Pro milkshake

LUNCH

3 oz. chicken salad with curry dressing, in lettuce leaf, sprinkled with pine nuts
cauliflower and broccoli flowerettes with lemon juice or mayonnaise dip
½ toasted whole wheat English muffin

fresh fruit in season (apple, banana, peach, slice of melon)
6 oz. buttermilk or skim milk

MID-AFTERNOON SNACK

1 oz. Muenster cheese with 4 whole grain crackers
or
3 tbsp. protein supplement in juice
caffeine-free diet soda

DINNER

white fish fillet, steamed or baked
½ cup cooked brown rice
fresh vegetable, steamed
tossed green salad, oil and vinegar dressing
fresh fruit or berries
1 slice whole wheat bread with 1 tsp. margarine or butter
8 oz. 1% milk or unsweetened sparkling grape juice or sparkling apple
juice

EVENING SNACK

Hi-Pro milkshake based on 8 oz. 1% milk with a dash of vanilla extract
for flavoring and synthetic sweetener to taste.

LATE-NIGHT SNACK

piece of fruit

More than half of the calories in your diet should come from
complex carbohydrates, with the rest coming from proteins and
fats. See the list of "good" foods to choose from in planning other
menus, pp. 58–60. Note that not all carbohydrates are restricted;
unrefined complex carbohydrates are a necessary and beneficial
foundation for your diet.

Some notes about your nutrition program. As you can see, there is
no shortage of foods from which to choose. The above list is for
guidance only; it is not meant to be complete. With imagination you
will find many appealing ways foods can be prepared and presented. Bear in mind, however, what this nutrition program is intended to accomplish and what it is not intended to do. It provides
guidelines for ample nourishment with emphasis on complex car-

"GOOD" FOODS

Complex Carbohydrates

Fruits

(dried fruits are too high in sugar to be used regularly)
apples
apricots
bananas
blackberries
blueberries
cherries
fruit juices, fresh
grapefruit
grapes
guavas
mangoes
melons
nectarines
oranges
papayas
peaches
pears
persimmons
pineapples
pomegranates
prunes
raspberries
strawberries
tangerines

Whole grains, beans and legumes

barley
black beans
black-eyed peas
bran
brown rice
buckwheat
corn
dried split peas
garbanzo beans
gluten flour
grits
kidney beans
lentils
lima beans
millet
navy beans
oats
peanuts
pinto beans
popcorn
red beans
rye
sorghum
soybeans
wheat
wheat germ
white beans
whole grain (breads, cereals, crackers, pasta)

Nuts and seeds

(no added salt or addictives)
almonds
Brazil nuts
cashews
filberts
poppy
pumpkin
sesame
sprouted seeds
sunflower
walnuts

Vegetables

artichokes
asparagus
avocados
beans (green, yellow, snap)
beets
broccoli
Brussels sprouts
cabbage
carrots
cauliflower
celery
corn
cucumbers
eggplants

greens (collard, lettuce, turnips, beet tops, kale)
green peas
mushrooms
okra
olives
onions, leeks, scallions
parsnips
peppers
potatoes, white
pumpkins
radishes
sauerkraut
spinach
sprouts (bean, pea, alfalfa)
squash
sweet potatoes
tomatoes
turnips
vegetable juices, fresh
zucchini

Protein Sources

beans and legumes
cheese of all sorts
plain yogurt
fish of all kinds
meats: lamb, beef, pork, veal, rabbit, and so forth. Many people
want to limit red meat, since there is evidence linking some red

Protein Sources (cont.)

meats to degenerative diseases and cancer. The high fat content is also a negative factor.

nuts and seeds

organ meats: liver, heart, sweetbreads, kidneys. Many people avoid these foods because of their exceedingly high cholesterol content and their possible causative link with coronary artery disease.

poultry: chicken, game hen, turkey, duck, wildfowl

shellfish: crab, shrimp, oysters, scallops, squid, clams, mussels

Most foods contain an amount of *fat,* and some contain a great deal. Strive to keep your daily fat intake no higher than 25% of your total calories by simple measures such as trimming all meat of visible fat, avoiding frying or deep-frying, eliminating very fatty foods such as bacon and reducing butter or margarine intake.

Salads

tossed green salad (lettuce, tomato, onion, etc.)

caesar salad
crab or shrimp Louis

Waldorf salad (unsweetened dressing)

cottage cheese with fresh fruit on lettuce

tuna salad, chicken salad, egg salad on lettuce

dressings: oil and vinegar preferable, oil and lemon juice, blue cheese (*avoid* sweet-and-sour dressings, sugar-sweetened dressings such as French dressing, sweetened specialty dressings)

Desserts

fresh fruit and cheese are ideal

unsweetened fruit salads or the fresh fruits alone (e.g., fresh strawberries with synthetic sweetened whipped cream)

unsweetened canned fruit packed in water (*avoid* fruits packed in heavy syrups)

Best advice: Learn to live without desserts for four major meals out of five.

Beverages

1 percent milk or skim milk

buttermilk (occasionally)

chilled sparkling grape juice, apple juice (nonalcoholic)

diet soda, caffeine-free varieties (e.g., 7-Up, Diet Pepsi Free; *if a soft drink doesn't say it's caffeine-free, assume that it's not*)

unsweetened frozen, canned, or fresh juice in moderation (one to three 4 oz. glasses per day)

Condiments

avoid added salt; heavily salted, preserved foods such as ham, bacon, sausage, soy sauce, pickles, herring, and anchovies should be used only occasionally and in small amounts; *avoid* monosodium glutamate — sodium has been proven to have a negative effect on the body

virtually all spices, herbs, vinegars, may be used freely in food preparation

avoid sweetened, prepared sauces (e.g., ketchup, barbecue sauce, steak sauce)

---

bohydrates. Its goal is to bring a marginally malnourished and under-par body into balance nutritionally, and to eliminate dependence on sugar-foods. It is not intended as a high-fiber, low-cholesterol, diabetic, or reducing diet. In most cases, however, its overall effect will be to increase your dietary intake of fiber significantly and curtail your intake of cholesterol and other dietary lipids.

F. *Daily exercise* is an essential element of your self-treatment program. It is a basic premise of physical medicine that a regular, consistent program of daily exercise contributes greatly to the good nutrition and healthy conditioning of the body. Regular exercise tones the heart and vascular system, conditions the pulmonary system, stimulates appetite, and promotes mobilization of dietary fats, especially the high-density lipoproteins that are so important to healthy maintenance of the cardiovascular system. Perhaps most important of all, exercise tones and conditions cerebral circulation and, among other things, acts as a powerful antidote to the depression many recovering addicted persons encounter.

How much exercise? What do we mean by "regular" and "consistent"? For a person otherwise healthy and nonhandicapped (not crippled with arthritis or limited by severe heart disease, for example), an ideal program goal would be thirty to sixty minutes of moderate to vigorous exercise *daily*, seven days a week. Probably the easiest and most universally accessible form of moderate exercise is brisk walking, energetic enough to raise your before-walking pulse rate twenty to thirty points and sustain it until exercise is ended. Other moderate exercise modes might include swimming (serious swimming of laps, not just a dip in the water and then sunbathing), bicycling, or rebounding (mini-trampoline). The number of blocks or miles one walks or bicycles doesn't matter — it's the length of time of sustained, pulse-raising exercise that counts.

I emphasize that the exercise should be regular and daily; two or three times a week off and on will not do. This means that it must be planned in advance and carried out consistently at the same time (or times) each day so that it becomes as much a part of your daily schedule as eating or sleeping. Avoid scheduling exercise after meals. The best times are first thing in the morning before breakfast or late afternoon before the evening meal. Start slowly and build up duration as tolerated.

If you already are exercising — perhaps jogging, playing racquetball twice a week, or playing tennis — you need only add to your existing exercise program to bring it up to the thirty-to-sixty-minutes-daily, seven-days-a-week level. On the other hand, you may regard the ideal goal as virtually unachievable if you presently don't exercise at all. It isn't, if you approach it as a regular program.

■ Start by walking five to ten minutes twice a day. Don't worry about speed; walk at any pace that's comfortable. This stage of the program is aimed only at getting you out and moving.

■ On the third day, walk no less than fifteen minutes twice a day. Use a watch to time yourself. Look for landmarks along the way, and look ahead for landmarks you'll achieve later.

■ On the fifth day, walk no less than twenty minutes twice a day, and make a conscious effort to walk more briskly. Thereafter add five minutes total walking time every two days and continue to increase your pace. Time yourself to your landmarks, and watch the time decrease as your range increases.

■ Begin pulse-checking. Walk fast enough to increase your resting pulse ten beats a minute, then fifteen, then twenty. If you drop back one day, start building up again from that point the next day.

■ If you want to aim for one sixty-minute walk instead of two thirty-minute walks, make the jump in stages: forty-five minutes one day, with a shorter walk later, then sixty minutes altogether.

This "prescription" for increasing exercise tolerance is intended primarily either for people who are severely debilitated by their addiction or for those who have never exercised. Many of you may not need such a build-up program, or may already be partway there. Start at your own level, and bear in mind that sixty minutes of moderate to vigorous exercise daily is not a limit. Many patients find that regular daily exercise is not only tolerable, but pleasurable. If you want to set your goal higher, all the better; the only obstacles are the amount of time you can comfortably devote to exercise each day and the natural limits of fatigue.

G. *Activities.* As a final point in your self-help program, you will almost certainly need to find new and fulfilling things to do. Since tending to an addiction is time consuming, you will discover that you have much more free time once treatment has started. Consider, for example, the amount of time one might devote to preparing and drinking ten cups of coffee a day. A cigarette smoker can spend as much as an hour and a half a day just lighting cigarettes, puffing them, and snuffing them out. The alcoholic can easily lose hours a day to drinking. Whatever the addiction, it swallows up minutes or hours that suddenly become available as a bonus when the individual begins treatment and recovery. New activities can take advantage of that time in a pleasant and therapeutic manner, combating depression and opening up new vistas to the recovering addict. You must look into your own life and tastes to find them, and you may discover that old friends involved in addictive activities need to be excluded. Look for activities in two classes: *individual,* and *shared* or *social.* Each is rewarding in its own way.

Some individual activities might include:

■ reading — catching up on the books you've wanted to read but haven't;

■ starting a diary — and keeping it;

- sewing — perhaps recovering an old skill you haven't practiced for a long time;
- gardening — vegetables, flowers, arboriculture, landscaping, whatever piques your interest;
- painting, remodeling, redecorating — these can not only keep you busy but give you a new, more pleasant place to live, a break with the past;
- creative arts — watercolors, oil painting, photography, potting, things to do with your hands and your mind;
- music — listening and performing.

Shared or social activities abound in our society; you have only to seek them out. These might include:

- evening or extension courses in your community college or university;
- church guild work or other church work;
- volunteer work at local hospitals, food banks, or other charitable organizations;
- city council meetings, school board meetings, or other local political involvement;
- business or professional organizations — BPW, AAUW, Chamber of Commerce, professional societies;
- service clubs.

These lists, of course, are not in any way all-inclusive; they are intended to suggest possibilities that you might want to pursue.

The Physician's Contribution to Treatment

It is the doctor's job to make a knowledgeable assessment of the patient's addiction and general health; to be alert for special hazards that can arise during detoxification and withdrawal; to guide the addict's nutritional and physical rehabilitation; and to prescribe any medications that are appropriate. Let's look at each of these contributions in more detail.

1. *Assessing the Problem.* The first part of my initial visit with a new patient is devoted to careful medical history, physical examination, and laboratory tests, the basis for treating any disorder. I need to know the history of the patient's present addiction and details of any earlier addictions. I explore his or her family history, social history, occupational history, and relations with others, as well as the

history of any medical illnesses such as heart disease, diabetes, kidney disease, and so forth.

I obtain some answers from a questionnaire the patient is asked to fill out before our interview; others I elicit one-on-one, planning sufficient office time in advance so that we aren't rushed. In addition, I have the patient take the Individual Addictiveness Profile test. These steps provide me with a necessary baseline of information about the patient and the problem, and may forewarn me of any special difficulties he or she may encounter in the course of treatment.

Finally, I evaluate all the information I have gathered and form an impression and diagnosis, which I share with the patient. I also prepare an individual treatment plan, including input from and choices made by the patient. Then I have a specially trained nurse spend further time with the patient, going over the treatment plan and explaining why each item is an important component of treatment. If the patient brings a spouse or relative, whenever possible I include that person — who may provide invaluable support to the patient and even be the key to success — in the entire process.

2. *Abstinence.* As the first step of actual treatment, the patient must exercise his determination and commitment by discontinuing all use of addicting substances immediately and completely. In many cases I can provide powerful reinforcement and support to help the patient get over this difficult hurdle.

3. *Detoxification.* As soon as the addicting substance has been terminated, the patient must be detoxified and supported during withdrawal. In every case, even in sugar addiction, the addicting substance is a harmful chemical that has been having a highly damaging effect on the patient's body. Sugar, for example, affects the patient's carbohydrate biochemistry, and probably the function of neurotransmitters in the brain. Alcohol's damaging effect may be more protean, literally whittling away at cells all over the body: brain cells, liver cells, peripheral nerve tissue, and so forth. Other addicting substances can have equally destructive effects on other tissues or biochemical systems. As we know, the only way to break an addiction is to eliminate the addicting substance, and this primary goal can be achieved only by ridding the body as fast as possible of any residual amounts of the addicting substance — detoxifying — and building the body back up with strong nutritional support.

The goal is to remove all traces of addicting drugs from the body as quickly as possible, and to keep them out; with sugar, the goal is to reduce the intake of sugars and refined carbohydrates and substitute complex carbohydrates to provide nourishment. At the same time, the body must literally be nurtured back to health. My potent vitamin and mineral treatment plan works quickly to bring the body into complete nutritional balance.

Time and a functioning body are the greatest detoxifiers of all. Stop adding an addicting chemical to the body, any addicting chemical, and with time, the body will eventually get rid of whatever part of it remains in the bloodstream or tissues. It will metabolize the chemical and excrete its breakdown products, since most of them do not belong naturally in the body. Treatment of addiction during the detoxification phase entails finding ways to help the body detoxify itself faster.

Vitamin C is perhaps the best and safest detoxifier known. I prescribe large doses of sodium ascorbate for all my addicted patients during the detoxification period.

4. *Withdrawal.* The moment we terminate the addicting drug and begin detoxification, we face withdrawal — a problem that must be tackled head-on.

There are ways to modify or minimize the distress of withdrawal. Since each patient is unique, what works for one may not work for another, but there is a variety of supportive substances that can help the patient fight severe withdrawal symptoms. I differ sharply from many people treating addiction in that I do not hesitate to prescribe appropriate nonaddicting drugs to help cut the edge of severe withdrawal when it seems medically advisable to do so.

With some addicting substances, withdrawal can mean anything from a few days to weeks of acute symptomatic discomfort if left untreated. Sometimes there are real problems that should be anticipated and addressed. If the addicting substance was alcohol or other sedatives, for example, I urge my patients to call me immediately at the slightest sign of jitteriness, shakiness, or anxiety. If untreated, these symptoms can progress to tremors, disorientation, hallucinations, and delirium tremens. Without prompt medical care, the patient could have seizures or even die.

Many alcoholics can abstain from alcohol without serious ill effects, whereas others cannot — it is difficult to predict in advance.

Seizures take time to develop and are preceded by nervous activity, tremors, jerking of the arms or legs, and marked fear and irritability. Chlordiazepoxide is the generic drug of choice for treating alcohol withdrawal symptoms and can be obtained only by prescription from a medical doctor. When taken properly it prevents severe alcohol withdrawal symptoms.

Other addicting substances that can lead to withdrawal seizures are sleeping medications such as Dalmane, Seconal, or Nembutal, and tranquilizers such as meprobamate, Valium, Tranxene, Azene, and Xanax.

Substances such as sugar, caffeine, nicotine, marijuana, cocaine, and speed, and narcotics such as heroin, morphine, and codeine, do not cause life-threatening withdrawal, although the person may *feel* as if death is imminent, especially if he or she goes cold turkey — abstains abruptly without treatment of any kind.

Some people who have used a lot of cocaine for some time develop a severe depression when they quit its use. This could be dangerous if not treated medically.

How long will the withdrawal period last? There is no magic range of time that applies to all addicting substances, and there is no way to predict in advance how any given individual will react. Withdrawal can occur for a day or two for caffeine, three to seven days for alcohol and sugar, five to ten days for heroin, and many weeks for withdrawal from tranquilizers and methadone if untreated. Some people experience no withdrawal, even though they are addicted. Motivation may be a contributing factor in these cases. However, the absence of withdrawal does not mean there is no addiction present.

In many cases, withdrawal proves to be more of a dreaded fear than a real problem. Almost all addicts facing the prospect of treatment feel certain that withdrawal is going to be a terrible ordeal. This is not surprising, since a major reason they have remained addicted so long to their drug of choice has been to evade or prevent withdrawal, rather than to achieve any particular pleasure or gratification. When actually encountering withdrawal after beginning my treatment, however, many addicts are amazed at how little trouble they have — either practically none at all, or far less than they imagined they were going to have. It varies greatly from patient to patient and from drug to drug.

Special prescriptions for specific types of withdrawal will be discussed in individual chapters in Part 2. An example is clonidine, an antihypertensive, which is especially helpful in softening narcotic withdrawal.

5. *Specific Treatment for Depression.* The patient's depression is a major contributor to relapse and must be treated immediately. A great many addicts are severely depressed long before they come to treatment, and many more become depressed during detox and recovery. It is only recently that I have begun to recognize what a profound part depression can play in the whole spectrum of addictive behavior, as I outlined in chapter 3. Depression must be guarded against and vigorously treated when and if it appears. If it isn't recognized and treated it can lead to relapse or, even worse, to suicide.

This aspect of treatment is at least as important as any other, and is possibly more important than all other aspects put together. First, it is necessary to determine when depression is present, and, if possible, to determine what kind. Since I started using the DST (dexamethasone suppression test) for genetic depression as part of the initial lab workup of my patients, I have found it to be extremely helpful in pinpointing depression and helping to identify its nature. Faced with depression, I have no hesitation in using appropriate

---

COOKBOOKS

Baker, Elizabeth and Dr. Elton, *The Uncook Book,* 1980.

Davis, F., *The Low Blood Sugar Cookbook,* 1974.

Ewald, E., *Recipes for a Small Planet,* 1973.

Ford, J., *Deaf Smith Country Cookbook,* 1973.

Katzen, Molly, *The Enchanted Broccoli Forest,* 1982.

Katzen, Molly, *The Moosewood Cookbook,* 1977.

Lansky, Vicki, *The Taming of the Candy Monster,* 1978.

Lappe, F., *Diet for a Small Planet,* 1975.

Robertson, Laurel, *Laurel's Kitchen,* 1976.

antidepressant medicine while treating addiction. If the depression is mild and situational, i.e., clearly accounted for by the depressing circumstances the patient's addiction has gotten him into, the antidepressant effect of the niacinamide and tryptophan along with the sugar-free diet may be all that is needed. But if it is the usual long-term physiologic genetic depression, then major antidepression medication may be indicated. Regardless, depression should be watched closely. Specific details of this treatment are outlined in chapter 14, "To the Physician."

6. *Treatment with Vitamins and Minerals and Special Diet.* This makes up the foundation of my treatment plan for recovery from addictions. I have outlined it in detail earlier under the self-help section. The exact plan is individualized to each patient's needs with frequent adjustments or additions as we go along.

Basically, we use high doses of vitamin C both intravenously and orally to achieve detoxification from the addicting substances. Potent multivitamin and mineral supplements help achieve a calm stability early in the withdrawal period. The protein drink helps the blood sugar level to remain even throughout the day and night and thereby helps stabilize the emotions.

It is vital that I see the patient daily during the initial phase so that any signs of difficulty can be dealt with. The injections of vitamin C are combined with other vitamins and minerals and adrenal cortical extract as indicated, and given daily during the withdrawal phase.

The diet must be free of sugar, honey, and other similar sweeteners. A basic diet of complex carbohydrates with added lean protein is the perfect stabilizing formula, when eaten in six or more feedings a day. The absence of sugar calms and soothes the body and helps prevent depression.

7. *Exercise.* A regular and effective exercise program is essential to any patient's recovery. Although the exercise program is part of the patient's contribution to treatment, as discussed in the patient's self-help section of this chapter, it is the doctor's responsibility to help the patient set rational limits and goals based on the person's individual physical condition.

8. *Counseling and Group Support.* Finally, the patient must have all the support that is available to him. My team includes a highly skilled addiction counselor who does both individual and group

counseling. She is also available for family counseling and interventions. We emphasize the biochemical basis underlying addiction and that addiction does not occur because of psychological pressures or mental flaws. Treatment is primarily biochemical and physical, not psychotherapeutic, so it is easy to overlook or underrate the very real psychosocial factors that are also present with most addictions. The social impact of one's addiction on oneself and others can be overwhelming, leading to shattered personal relationships, damaged marriages, broken homes, destroyed jobs, or wrecked business relationships. Addicts need support in recovering from such damage, and so do others around them.

Some of this support can be provided by the doctor and a supportive office staff, but not all of it by any means. It can also be sought from the surprisingly active support network that already exists in most communities. Organizations such as Alcoholics Anonymous or Narcotics Anonymous are made up of people who are already journeying on this path and want to reach out to others like themselves. Support can also be found in the family, in the church, sometimes from employers, and from psychotherapists of varying disciplines.

The treatment measures we have outlined — both the self-help program for the patient and the doctor's contribution — together form a valid foundation for the successful treatment of virtually any kind of addiction. As might be expected, variations or alterations in treatment may become necessary in dealing with individual addictions, some of minor importance, some major. In the later chapters addressing individual addicting substances in detail, we will discuss such variations or alterations in treatment where appropriate. For a solid and rational attack on any addiction, however, the program presented here is the place to start.

Part Two

The Many Faces of
Addiction

6

Sugar — The Basic Addiction

SUGAR ADDICTION is the world's most widespread addiction, and probably one of the hardest to kick. Because it is shared by so many addictive patients, I believe it is the "basic addiction" that precedes all others. Most of my addicted patients tell me that at one time they craved sugar almost daily. Furthermore, few people recognize their sugar addiction.

Sugar dysmetabolism is a major factor in my model for addiction. Sugar addiction can last a lifetime, or the sugar addict may progress to other addictive substances such as alcohol, street drugs, or prescription drugs.

Sugar addiction means addiction to *refined* sugars or carbohydrates, not to all carbohydrates or complex carbohydrates. Refined sugars, notably sugar, corn syrup products, honey, and white flour, have been broken down or processed from multiple sugar chains (polysaccharides) to single sugar molecules (monosaccharides), which when eaten are readily absorbed into the bloodstream without further digestion. On the other hand, complex carbohydrates (fruits, vegetables, whole grains, nuts, seeds, beans, and legumes) have not been "predigested" and therefore require a lengthy period of digestion before the polysaccharides are broken down into monosaccharides for absorption into the bloodstream. As a result, the sugar from complex carbohydrates enters the bloodstream slowly and does not trigger the physiological hunger described in chapter

3. This is the crucial difference between refined carbohydrates — "sugar-foods" — and complex carbohydrates.

Sugar addiction causes many insidious symptoms that are not recognized right away. Gradually, addicted people recognize that they do not feel as good as they should. Some typical profiles of my patients with sugar addiction follow.

Susan was a beautiful young woman in her twenties who suddenly realized that she hadn't felt good for a long time. She was tired when she woke up and remained tired all day long. Everything seemed hard. She noticed that she was turning down social invitations after work so she could go home and collapse.

Dan seemed to have undergone a personality change. He used to be easygoing, but then he became irritable and withdrawn. The fun had gone out of his life, and although he hadn't recognized the change, because it had been so subtle, his wife had.

Gail had a hard time sitting still. She was hyperactive and had to be constantly in motion. She couldn't sit down and relax or read a book. If she tried, it was over in a few minutes. She stayed up late until she finally collapsed into bed. She was never able to go to sleep at the regular time. Getting up in the morning was a real struggle. Her weight gradually slid upward unnoticed for a long time. She wondered if she was going crazy.

George was a foreman at an aircraft company. He used to receive frequent commendations and increases in responsibility, but then his evaluations started slipping and he was told his work was not up to his usual effective style. His concentration seemed to be affected, and he was anxious from worrying about his performance.

Mary suddenly realized that she had been having a significant number of severe headaches, two or three a month. They were of migraine intensity and each one wiped her out for days. She became fearful of the next headache, and even canceled activities because of the possibility.

Bob was an eighteen-year-old high school senior who began having fainting spells over the course of the year. He used to work hard and was an outstanding leader as well as student. A complete medical exam and tests were negative.

Fred had been evaluating his life and saw that he was having trouble in many areas. He was in his twenties, and work had become all work and no fun. His relationship with his live-in woman friend had begun to deteriorate, and he was tired and irritable. At one time he thought he had the world by the tail, but now it all seemed to be slipping away. At one point he even contemplated suicide.

Bobby, at age seven, was having a roller-coaster life. Much of the time he was relaxed and congenial, but at unpredictable moments he would turn into an angry, unhappy child who liked nothing and nobody around him, striking out at his little brother or his parents for no apparent reason. At other times it seemed that he could not sit still; he was in constant motion and talked incessantly.

All of these patients were found to be eating large amounts of sugar. When they were withdrawn from sugar and supported with frequent feedings of complex carbohydrates and the proper vitamins, minerals, and protein, they showed remarkable improvement. Life became harmonious once more and they realized how insidiously a sugar addiction could take control. Just because these symptoms may be hard to match up with any laboratory-measurable abnormality does not mean that they don't exist or can be written off as "all in the mind" and ignored. The symptoms are real, physical, and often immobilizing. Some people simply seem to feel "knocked out" or fatigued all the time. Some are constantly hungry, or feel shaky, sweaty, sometimes confused. Although some are of normal weight, many others range from slightly overweight to obese. They complain of low energy, difficulty getting going in the morning, trouble concentrating, or trouble accomplishing their normal everyday tasks. Some can't sleep at night, while others can't stay awake during the daytime. Some suffer from a variety of physical and mental symptoms: stomachache, headache, backache, or indigestion, for example. Some find themselves subject to angry outbursts for no reason, have trouble getting along with people, or find a great deal to criticize in others. Wide mood swings are common.

According to physical examinations or lab studies, these people seem to have fairly normal health. Indeed, the symptoms they describe may be so numerous and varied that one is hard-pressed to pinpoint any single symptom as the major one. Yet they feel generally miserable, depressed, and drained of energy, sleep poorly, feel down when they get up, and feel down when they go to bed. Many are concerned about their mental stability. When I take a careful dietary history, the typical findings reveal a large amount of sugar-food interspersed with attempted fasts and caffeine for a pick-up when sugar no longer gives the initial burst of energy. Typically, a great many of these people are constantly fighting their weight, because a large part of what they eat, in total, consists of sugar or refined carbohydrates.

Why do they eat so much sugar? Because it makes them feel momentarily better. It temporarily relieves the symptoms of depression and low energy, anger, headache, and backache they frequently suffer. For normal people, a very modest amount of sugar or refined carbohydrate will merely make them feel full and satiated, uninterested in consuming any more sugar. But for those with an inborn error in their carbohydrate metabolism, the more sugar they eat, the more they crave, often to the point of gorging. Gradually they feel worse and worse.

Taking sugar or some substitute for sugar is one way a person suffering from this disturbance — an addictive person — can temporarily quiet his or her physiological hunger and feel "normal" or "relaxed" for a while, however briefly. Most addictive people suffer at least some overt symptoms as a direct result of their disturbed carbohydrate metabolism. Due to overeating of sugar-foods, many are obese or are constantly "fighting their weight," almost invariably without success. Some are distressed by difficulty sleeping or suffer low energy levels almost all the time. Others have trouble getting a task started or concentrating on the work at hand, like my patient Jan, who couldn't read more than two pages of a book at a time because her attention span was too short. Others have recurrent, unexplained, and undiagnosed symptoms such as stomachache, backache, headache, or indigestion related to uncontrolled sugar-eating. Some have spells of daytime faintness, sleepiness, chilliness, or shakiness. Others become angry or hyperirritable for no apparent reason.

You will notice that almost all of these symptoms are rather vague and difficult to pin down, nothing a doctor could ordinarily base a diagnosis on, but they are present in these people so frequently and consistently that you could write a book about it. And these are not withdrawal symptoms following abstinence from sugar; they are symptoms these people may suffer virtually all the time due to disordered carbohydrate metabolism. Whatever other sugar-related symptoms addictive people may have, almost all display one sign very prominently: they don't like to go without their sugar-food for long, not even when they are taking extreme measures to diet, because sugar withdrawal is painful and distressing.

Are They Really Addicts?

We *are* talking about a pattern of addiction. Sugar addicts can be either "maintenance" sugar-eaters (who eat sugar in some form all day long) or binge eaters. A special category of sugar addiction is the bulimic who binges on sugar-food and then induces vomiting or uses a powerful laxative purge. There are bulimics who follow this procedure daily, or even two or three times a day or more interspersed by fasting.

Some describe a druglike euphoria upon stuffing themselves with carbohydrates, and then fall into depression and guilt immediately after vomiting it all up. Bulimics I have treated respond extremely well to the plan outlined in chapter 5. Antidepressants may be vital to their recovery, and Bonine (O.T.C.) helps control vomiting.

Finally, with many sugar addicts, there is a mixed addiction present. Their eating of sugar, for example, may be accompanied by daily consumption of large quantities of caffeine or the whole pattern may be mixed with cigarette smoking as well, or they may be caught up in a chain reaction of addictions, such as diet pills to help overcome the overweight, and then tranquilizers to help overcome the diet pills, and so on.

The people we are describing are addictive people who are indeed addicted to one of the most powerful substances to be found anywhere — the refined sugars. Their addiction to sugar is a real, harmful, highly damaging health problem, just as debilitating as addiction to any other substance. Like any addiction, when their chemical isn't supplied, they suffer identifiable withdrawal symptoms; like any addiction, the process of feeding their physiological hunger with a chemical is destructive to the body; and like any addiction, the point may be reached when supplying the chemical becomes as painful as withdrawing from it. The cycle of chemical dependence becomes both entrenched and intolerable.

Perhaps the greatest tragedy of all is that the vast majority of such people — and there are many of them — have no idea that they are addictive and may not recognize that they are addicted. Yet because of this one unrecognized chemical addiction, they have lost control over their lives. Some go on to become addicted to other substances more widely recognized as addictive and dangerous: alcohol, one of the benzodiazepine-type tranquilizers, or maybe even a hard drug like heroin. But in most cases, the initial addiction was to sugar.

Sugar addicts demonstrate in their life, behavior, and physiology all of the unmistakable signs and invariable hallmarks of entrenched or firmly established addiction. Sugar addicts eat sugar compulsively; it is in control of their life. They go to great lengths to obtain their sugar, and if they don't get it, they experience predictable withdrawal symptoms.

The withdrawal symptoms vary from person to person, from the merely annoying to the absolutely agonizing. Perhaps most universal of all, and indeed, a symptom highly characteristic of any type of withdrawal, is the pervading sense of physical uneasiness, an irrational, almost visceral sense of being vaguely frightened, a sense of impending trouble that can be shaken off only with the greatest difficulty. More than anything these people feel that something bad is going on, but they can't quite put their finger on it. Other symptoms are more specifically identifiable: they feel hungry; they develop headaches; they feel nervous and tense; they keep thinking about eating, to the extent that they're distracted from thinking about anything else. They even dream about eating.

Obviously, this kind of withdrawal pattern can be exceedingly uncomfortable and disruptive of everyday activities. In many cases it is accompanied by a deep depression, a sense that something is totally out of balance. Also, typically, it is relieved abruptly and dramatically, often within a few minutes, by eating sugar. For sugar addicts, as with other addicts, the use of the addicting substance ultimately becomes actively distressing, and still the substance must be used to prevent or relieve withdrawal. This is more characteristic of addiction than most people realize.

Many addicts continue to use a certain more or less fixed *amount* of the addicting substance for months or years, without increasing it. But *symptoms* of their addiction escalate, because addiction in any form is a progressive disease. As the disease develops, addicts no longer get a lift from their substance. Although they may try hard to stay out of withdrawal, sugar addicts begin to feel miserable much of the time. For one thing they aren't getting adequate nourishing food, because they haven't got room for it after all the carbohydrates they have been eating. They feel miserable because the body is literally malnourished. Also, they may be obese and don't like it — even feel guilty about it — but they haven't been able to change it, because every time they try a weight loss program the addiction wins. Lose to yourself enough times over a chocolate bar, and your sense of self-worth declines. Somewhere along the line it evolves to the point where the sugar addiction is clearly hurtful, and the addict finally knows it.

Sugar addiction fits my working definition of addiction: "the compulsive and out-of-control use of any chemical substance that can produce recognizable and identifiable unpleasant withdrawal symptoms when use of the substance is stopped." The addictive person has dysmetabolism of sugar and some degree of depression. The sugar addict responds to the same treatment plan, outlined in chapter 5, that other addicts do.

Diagnosing Sugar Addiction

Sugar addiction must be clearly identified in order to deal successfully with it. Not everyone who enjoys sweets is a sugar addict. A nonaddictive person likes a bit of sugar now and then as a supplement to his balanced diet, a dessert from time to time, a little ice cream on a hot day, a chocolate bar perhaps once a month. That's fine. There is a vast difference between the person who likes a bit of sugar occasionally and the person who has to have quantities of sugar as a major part of the daily diet.

For diagnosis, I use the six-hour glucose tolerance test (GTT) to evaluate the patient's carbohydrate metabolism; it may also give some clues to adrenal function. Besides being helpful to the physician, the GTT is a useful educational experience for the patient, because a great many of them may actually experience during the course of the test some or all of the telltale symptoms of which they complain. I have them write down how they feel as they go through the test.

Patients often feel better early in the GTT after drinking 100 g of glucose in a carbonated flavored liquid, but after the first hour and a half they begin to fade. They often complain of being fuzzy-headed, having a stomachache, and feeling apprehensive. By the third hour they are often asleep. Sometimes they experience fatigue, confusion, and a headache. They may become irritated over little things and blow them out of proportion.

I rarely repeat a GTT since it can be a traumatic experience for the patient. One man, about fifty years old, was having a GTT done as an inpatient in a local hospital, and became so irrationally angry in the middle of the test that he signed himself out of the hospital and went home. "I don't know what got into me," he apologized later. "I just got so sore about everything that was going on that I got up and left." What actually happened was that the way his body handled sugar caused him to become irrationally angry.

The interpretation of GTTs varies from doctor to doctor. One investigator of the body's handling of sugar, H. L. Newbold, M.D.,* of New York, offers five criteria for the interpretation of the GTT. According to Dr. Newbold, low blood sugar (which I have found often to be present in sugar dysmetabolism) exists when a six-hour GTT shows one or more of the following.

■ The blood sugar level fails to rise more than 50 percent above the fasting level.

■ The blood sugar level falls at least 20 mg percent below the fasting level.

■ The blood sugar level falls 50 mg percent or more during any one hour of the test.

■ The blood sugar level falls to 50 mg percent or lower at some point in the test. Anything below 65 mg percent is suspicious.

■ Clinical symptoms such as dizziness, headache, confusion, sleepiness, depression, vomiting, or fainting occur during the test regardless of the blood sugar reading.

Figure 1 demonstrates different GTT results. It shows a shaded area where normal blood sugar curves fall. A diabetic curve is shown at the top of the graph. Also shown are two common types of curves I often find in patients with sugar dysmetabolism. Both insulin and adrenal involvement play a role in these curves, rendering

*Dr. Newbold, formerly of Northwestern University Medical School, is now in the practice of medical nutrition in New York City. The five criteria are quoted from H. L. Newbold, M.D., *Meganutrients for Your Nerves* (New York: Wyden Books, 1975).

Figure 1.   Six-Hour Glucose Tolerance Test

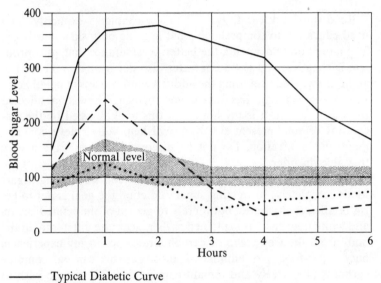

———— Typical Diabetic Curve
– – – Common Double Curve Found in Alcoholism
······· Low Blood Sugar Curve

the GTT somewhat controversial; it is important to understand that the GTT should be used only as an indicator, not as a final diagnostic procedure. Whatever the cause, low blood sugar is a finding, not a disease.

How, then, is sugar addiction diagnosed? The results of the GTT test, the patient's description of symptoms, a careful medical history (especially in regard to the patient's sugar consumption), and the results of the Individual Addictiveness Profile test presented in chapter 2 all will point toward a diagnosis of sugar addiction.

Treating Sugar Addiction

The program for treatment outlined in chapter 5 is essential and basic to the treatment of any addiction, including sugar addiction. The sugar addict, however, may face special difficulties in treatment that make his or her problem different from all the others.

What You Can Do

Read this book carefully, and follow chapter 5 explicitly. You need education to comprehend what is going on inside your body. The more you understand, the better. Reassurance that your problem is chemical and not a character disorder is vital. You are not going crazy. Understanding the addictiveness process in detail helps you to see what sugar has done to your body and how it has affected the way you feel. It is my hope that this book, backed by the discomfort of your present situation, will help you achieve commitment and motivation. Do not be discouraged. You have a very treatable disorder.

The first and most important step is that you stop eating sugar-foods completely. In treating sugar addiction the goal is not to get rid of all carbohydrates, but merely to get rid of the refined sugars and white flour that, as explained earlier, act quite differently in the body from the way complex carbohydrates do. In my experience, once sugar-foods are eliminated, most patients can eat complex carbohydrates freely and remain comfortable. Those who wish to lose weight should select the complex carbohydrates that have the fewest calories.

In some ways, treating your sugar addiction is much more difficult than treating drug or alcohol addiction. With the latter, you stop the addicting substance completely. But with sugar, since you must continue to eat food you are constantly at risk of eating the wrong foods — namely, sugar-foods. This makes recovery from sugar addiction especially difficult, and you need all the support you can get.

In following the treatment plan in chapter 5, your greatest aid to getting through withdrawal will be vitamin C: take it every two hours during the day and whenever you crave sugar. Withdrawal will last about three to five days. You may even dream about sweets. Once you eliminate the sugar from your body, however, you'll stop craving it. Then it will get easier.

The other most vital factor is frequent feedings. Eat something every two hours so that you don't get ravenously hungry, which usually is caused by sugar causing an appetite for more sugar. Carry the right food with you, because you can't count on finding it wherever you go. There's plenty of sugar out there in the world begging you to eat it!

Each of the vitamin and mineral supplements plays an important role, as does the protein drink. Use a potent multivitamin and mineral. If you experience depression, take niacinamide and one or more of the amino acids indicated for depression. Tryptophan at bedtime improves sleep while it fights depression.

One patient said to me, "Just what makes you think you can get me off the sugar? No one has ever been able to do that!" She returned the following week, after starting my treatment program. "I've not eaten any sugar all week. I can't believe it." Ordinarily, sugar withdrawal would be uncomfortable with strong cravings for sugar. When the nutritional program is followed, however, withdrawal is surprisingly tolerable or even nonexistent. As the sugar is eliminated from your body, you will feel increasingly better. The foods on the acceptable lists will taste more delicious, and you will discover a whole new world of eating as you combine vegetables, whole grains, beans, and legumes with fruit, nuts, and seeds, and fish, poultry, and dairy products.

Problems with withdrawal or depression or both can be helped immensely by the exercise program discussed in chapter 5, and by support from others. It can be extremely helpful, for instance, if others in the patient's family choose to join the special diet and exercise regimen as a family program. However, you must not expect others to get off sugar just because you do. In addition, there are other kinds of support groups in the community. Overeaters Anonymous, for example, is a noncommercial support group with chapters in most major cities. The group support program is based on the twelve steps of Alcoholics Anonymous. A person need not be obese to join this organization; it is enough to recognize that you have lost control over your eating and seek to bring about changes. The support the organization provides for the recovering sugar addict can be extremely helpful.

I have found that drugs of any kind usually are not called for in treating sugar addiction. Sugar addicts are, as we have seen, highly vulnerable to alternative or substitute addictions and should avoid so-called diet-aid medication at all cost. Alcohol should also be eliminated, not only because it is a powerful addicting substance in its own right, but because the body uses it in much the same manner it would use sugar and thus the risk of developing alcohol addiction is great. In addition, alcohol in any amount may cause sugar craving. In some cases the magnitude of withdrawal symptoms or depression may make antidepressant medication necessary to enable the patient to withdraw from sugar successfully. Underlying genetic depression usually is present in such cases.

So be of good cheer. Have courage, and you will find that the rewards are great as you enter your new sugar-free life and the real you emerges!

SUGAR CONTENT OF SUGAR-FOODS
Calculated from tables by Bowes and Church, 1956

12 oz. sugar-containing cola drink	8 tsp.
12 oz. ginger ale	6 tsp.
8 oz. chocolate milk	8 tsp.
12 oz. chocolate malt shake	18 tsp.
6 oz. cocoa	5 tsp.
8 oz. eggnog	6 tsp.
10 oz. lemonade	7 tsp.
1 regular ice cream soda	12 tsp.
1 average cinnamon roll	8 tsp.
1 cake doughnut, plain	4½ tsp.
1 brownie	4 tsp.
1 small piece angel food cake	8 tsp.
1 chocolate cupcake with fudge icing	14 tsp.
1 chocolate eclair	10 tsp.
1 small fig bar	3 tsp.
1 small serving sugar-containing fruit gelatin dessert	4½ tsp.
1 small serving pudding	8 tsp.
1 chocolate cookie with frosting	2 tsp.
1 cup vanilla ice cream	7½ tsp.
1 piece apple pie	15 tsp.
½ cup chocolate pudding	9 tsp.
1 tbsp. pancake syrup	4 tsp.
1 2 oz. candy bar	9 tsp.
2 oz. penny candy	10 tsp.
2 oz. candied apricots	13 tsp.
2 oz. chocolate fudge	12 tsp.
2 oz. milk chocolate	8 tsp.
2 oz. jelly beans	8½ tsp.
2 oz. lollipops	14 tsp.
1 tbsp. jam	3½ tsp.
1 cup sugar-coated cereal	8 tsp.
1 slice white bread	3 tsp.
1 baking-powder biscuit, small	4 tsp.
1 white flour pancake, plain	2½ tsp.
1 hard roll	4½ tsp.
1 white flour waffle, plain	5 tsp.
1 cup whole grain cereal flakes, sugar added	5½ tsp.
1 saltine cracker	½ tsp.
1 cup pasta, cooked, macaroni or noodle	10 tsp.

7

Alcohol

ALCOHOLISM IS NOT a bad habit, a weakness, a sign of moral decay, or a character defect. It's a physiological disease that affects every part of the body, mind, emotions, and spirit. Alcoholics drink because they must. Most alcoholics die without ever knowing they have the disease and they often die prematurely. What a terrible waste of human potential.

On January 17, 1985, one of my closest friends died of alcoholism. He shot himself to death shortly after learning his wife had cancer. He was forty-eight years old and the finest psychotherapist I have ever known. For years he had been a recovering alcoholic helping hundreds find their way to a rewarding sobriety. Then he decided he was not really an alcoholic and began separating himself from the recovering alcoholic community. He started having a cocktail in the evening and then two, telling his wife that he was in perfect control. Unknown to me, he started drinking heavily and getting drunk. His depression became more severe and constant. He agreed to take the antidepressant I ordered for him but he never picked it up from the pharmacy. He refused to meet with me for our weekly breakfast as we had done for years. He made up excuses and kept his friends at a safe distance. He couldn't seem to reach out for the help he was so talented at giving to others. And then he was gone.

* * *

Ethyl alcohol, or *ethanol* — the ordinary "drinking alcohol" found in every alcoholic beverage from the finest scotch or cognac to the cheapest beer — is the most commonly encountered and dangerous addicting drug in our society.

In earlier chapters, I referred to a connection between sugar and alcohol, speaking of alcohol as similar to sugar or describing it as an addictive substitute or alternative for sugar. Such statements are acceptable in a very broad sense. As an addicting substance, alcohol does indeed behave much like sugar, and it is true that abstaining alcohol addicts can often relieve their withdrawal symptoms by gorging on sugar. Furthermore, alcohol, like sugar, can be used by the body as a source of energy for the brain and other organ systems.*

Alcohol and sugar are not, however, by any means the same or even similar chemical substances. Although both are composed of carbon, hydrogen, and oxygen atoms, alcohol is not a simple sugar. It is one of a totally different family of compounds known as alcohols, chemically similar to hospital ether or chloroform. Alcohol is broken down in the body differently from sugar and produces vastly different physiological effects. Because alcohol itself and its major breakdown products, acetaldehyde and acetate, are poisonous to the body's cells, continued abuse of alcohol can lead to long-term damage to virtually all the body's major organ systems, quite aside from its addicting properties.

Above all, alcohol is a powerfully addicting substance in its own right. Addictive people become addicted to alcohol for exactly the same reason that they become addicted to any other addicting substance: they have a hidden, inborn, inherited metabolic error or flaw that affects the way their bodies metabolize carbohydrates. As a result of the hidden error, these people live with a continuing physiological hunger that addicting substances, including alcohol, can partially and temporarily satiate. Many, if not most, addicts also suffer some element of depression, recognized or unrecognized, which seems to be relieved for a time and to some degree by use of addicting substances, including alcohol. All addicting substances

---

*Thus, in a very limited sense, alcohol has to be classified as a food, but at best it is a "crippled" food since it provides no vitamins, no minerals, and no protein — just empty calories.

act at least temporarily as an effective antidepressant. This explains the term "high" — it's the opposite of depression.

On this basic level, addiction to alcohol, commonly known as alcoholism, is exactly the same as addiction to any other substance. It meets all the criteria of addiction outlined in chapter 3. Our definition fits perfectly: alcoholism is "the compulsive and out-of-control use" of alcohol, producing "recognizable and identifiable unpleasant withdrawal symptoms" when use of alcohol is stopped.

In certain ways, however, addiction to alcohol is not entirely typical of other addictions. For one thing, addiction to alcohol can, in some people, be insidious. Even highly addictive people may use alcohol "socially" for a time, perhaps years, before the addiction becomes firmly established and clearly visible. Unlike some addicting substances, alcohol is legal, readily available almost anywhere, cheap, and socially approved. As we will see, addiction to alcohol can be exceedingly difficult to recognize; multitudes of addicts simply can't or won't accept the fact of their addiction. And of all the addictions, there is probably none that is so difficult to treat effectively and permanently. Relapse is the rule and long-term sobriety the exception.

Portrait of an Alcoholic

Of all the patients I have encountered in my practice, Jan K. is probably the one I have come to know best, and she presents one of the most interesting and illuminating case histories I could possibly find to illustrate alcohol addiction.

Jan K. was a busy professional woman and mother who had everything going for her, or so it seemed. As an attractive, bright woman from a high-achieving family, she had gone to medical school at a time when few women had chosen to go, completed a demanding period of hospital training, and established an active medical practice in Seattle. Although she had been drinking occasionally as early as age seventeen, she had always associated drinking with fun and relaxation, the enjoyment of social gatherings or the chance to reward herself by relaxing with a drink or two at the end of a long day of clinics and office patients.

For years her drinking was occasional, but she often drank more than she intended, and was puzzled by her lack of control. Sometimes she even set out to get drunk as a reward for hard work. Over the years, as her income rose, her drinking became a daily event and the quantity had crept up to the heavy drinking range, more than four drinks a night. But she thought of herself as a social drinker. After all, she drank just like many of her friends, so it must be social drinking. Occasionally, she asked herself if she was alcoholic. Her honest answer was always "no" — she was not like the picture of the alcoholic she held in her mind. She was too responsible.

Indeed, Jan K. considered herself a social drinker in every sense of the term, trying to exercise control over herself and her drinking. She never allowed her drinking to interfere with her professional work (she didn't think so, anyway) and indeed enjoyed a good reputation among her medical colleagues. She never missed a patient appointment, never smelled of alcohol in her office, never appeared in any way out of control at a medical function; and yet every evening after work she drank to "unwind" from the day's tensions. On weekday evenings she often drank one or two fifths of champagne while she fixed dinner. After dinner she'd retire to the television room with a Scotch and soda where frequently she fell asleep, only to awaken around midnight and retire to bed. On weekends, free from professional constraints, she drank even more heavily. Often she had one or two large drinks to relax her before going to a party. Frequently she blacked out in the late evening before going to bed, and in the morning retraced her steps, trying to piece together the last hours. Often she could not remember greeting her teenagers when they came in.

It was not until Jan was in her mid-forties, when she happened to begin treating alcoholics and other addicts professionally, that she learned enough about alcoholism to evaluate herself more realistically. Was alcohol preventing her from realizing her highest goals? She wondered if her thinking and emotions were constantly distorted by her drinking, and decided to quit for a couple of months just to see. She was sure they were not, but sober, she began realizing the rewards of a clearing mind and knew that she was alcoholic and had been for the past thirty years. Alcohol had been a primary focus in her life for a long time. That confrontation did not come easily, but her recovery from a crippling and ultimately life-threatening addiction began. Once she had recognized it for what it was, she set about the long process of reaching out for help to make the vital change from being an active alcoholic to a successfully recovering alcoholic. It was the hardest thing she had ever done in her life, but the rewards continue to unfold, year after year. She has gained a new sense of wholeness and freedom, and she realizes now that she can attain any goals that she chooses. Perhaps most important, she has written this book. Yes, *I* am Jan K.

Alcoholism: A Major Killer

If you were to check the many statistical tables listing the major causes of death in the United States, you would find accidental death, heart disease, stroke, diabetes, and cancer prominent on every list. You would not find alcoholism listed on any such table, however, and this is a travesty; there is good reason to believe that alcoholism outstrips all the other causes of death put together as the number one major cause or contributory cause of death throughout the world. Let me hasten to add that I cannot support this statement with statistics, for there aren't any. Presently we will see why.

I've learned a great deal about alcohol use and alcohol addiction in the years since I started working in the addiction field, and I'm convinced that alcoholism is a major unrecognized killer-in-waiting for millions of people. Alcohol probably follows sugar as the two most widespread addictions in existence, and because of the long-term physical damage it does to body tissues, alcoholism has a truly murderous potential. It is a baffling, powerful, cunning disease that hides its presence so skillfully that it is not even recognized by the vast majority of its victims or by their doctors. It is a disease of *denial* (that any problem exists) and *relapse* (once it has been identified and treatment started). Perhaps the saddest thing that can be said of this disease is that most alcoholics die of alcoholism without ever knowing they have a disease, without ever knowing that they are alcoholic.

Alcoholism has been with us since the fermentation of sugar was first discovered, certainly long before the beginning of recorded history. Drunkenness has played some part in the social or religious life of virtually every major civilization, and an important part in some civilizations. It has been studied, after a fashion, ever since the Renaissance, and that study in modern times has been reflected in the proliferation of scientific journals devoted to problems and questions about alcoholism. Millions of published sociological, biochemical, and psychodynamic studies deal with the effects of alcohol on the human body. Still, there are great gaping holes in our knowledge of the disease, a multitude of questions we simply cannot answer, and, most unfortunately, a whole realm of misconceptions about alcoholism — beliefs that are flatly untrue but continue to guide a great majority of the medical professionals trying to grapple with the disease.

Chemically, alcohol is a poison that is toxic to virtually all the cells and organ systems of the body. It can cause damage and symptoms related to any or all of these organ systems, from brain to heart to liver to gastrointestinal tract, and so on down the line. Although we know what alcohol can do to these systems, we do not know how fast it can do it — this is one of the great variables of alcoholism. In most cases, alcohol-related damage begins to appear, in terms of symptoms and dysfunction, only after years of alcohol use, but there are those in whom the same damage may appear comparatively quickly.

We also do not know some of the most fundamental and basic facts about the incidence and epidemiology of alcoholism. How many active alcoholics are there, and how many people have recovered from alcoholism? Nobody knows. In almost every major book written about alcoholism you will find statements to the effect that 10 percent of the population of the United States is actively alcoholic. (Some authorities modify this by saying that 10 percent of the population is composed of "problem drinkers," but essentially they're saying the same thing.) Such statements have a solid ring, as if they are backed up by verifiable statistics, but actually they are nothing but guesswork. On what basis can such statements be made? Alcoholics don't register their names with any authorities. They couldn't; most alcoholics don't even know they're alcoholics. By whose definition is this 10 percent supposed to be alcoholic? How, precisely, does one define alcoholism in the first place?

You might, as a blind guess, say that one out of every ten people has a drinking problem, but you would almost certainly be falling far short of the mark. One might more reasonably guess that 70 percent of the population drinks alcohol more or less regularly in some volume or another somewhere. Of that group a certain percentage, say 10 percent if you wish, are obviously heavy, abusive drinkers of alcohol and are probably (though not necessarily) alcoholics. Another percentage, say 10 percent, are infrequent drinkers who clearly and inarguably are not alcoholics.

It is the great mass of people somewhere in between these extremes that raises the question. Alcoholism is a subtle disease, hidden and denied, unrecognized by those who most need to recognize it. The truth is that nobody has the slightest idea how many alcoholics there are in this country; beyond that, nobody knows how many once-active alcoholics are now recovering. Where would one go to find such statistics? Most authorities assume, correctly or incorrectly, that of all organizations dealing with alcoholism and helping alcoholics recover, Alcoholics Anonymous has the highest degree of success. It is not a research organization, however. Alcoholics Anonymous is concerned with the individual who comes to an AA meeting, and nobody else. They do not take roll at AA meetings. They do not compile statistics. They engage in no follow-up. A given AA group may know how many people attended a given meeting on a given day, but these figures are not sent anywhere and they wouldn't mean anything if they were. An individual may, and a great many do, attend three, four, or more separate and different AA group meetings per day. Thus the organization that may well know alcoholics and alcoholism better than anyone else has virtually no statistics to share, deliberately and by choice.

Defining Alcoholism

Developing a solid definition of alcoholism against which everyone could measure him- or herself might seem to be a good place to start, but here, too, we fall into traps. It is difficult to define alcoholism as a disease, because alcoholism in any person can appear as any one of a multitude of diseases with a multitude of possible symptoms, all related or bound together solely by the fact that excessive or addictive use of alcohol is involved. So what is "excessive or addictive use of alcohol?" A number of arbitrary standards have been set up by various authorities to separate the alcoholics on one side of the fence from the nonalcoholics on the other side. All of them fail, because invariably some nonalcoholics get caught on the alcoholic side for various reasons, and a large number of alcoholics slip through the cracks to the nonalcoholic side. As part of the denial that is an integral part of the disease, alcoholics constantly scrutinize any such arbitrary scale for the limitations that apply to other people but not to them. They look for the chance to say, "Well! I never do that, therefore . . ."

The problem of a rigid definition of alcoholism is illustrated perfectly by one widely publicized scale based entirely upon the amount of alcohol an individual drinks. According to the standards of the National Institute on Alcoholism and Alcohol Abuse (NIAAA), the *moderate* drinker is defined arbitrarily as anyone who drinks no more than two 1½ oz. cocktails of hard liquor or the equivalent (two 4 oz. glasses of wine or two 8 oz. glasses of beer) every day, seven days a week, or averages this much per day over the course of a week. According to this definition, those who drink this upper limit or less week after week are regarded as nonalcoholic, whereas those who drink more than this upper limit are considered a potential problem drinker or alcoholic.

What's wrong with this definition? It's fascinating how widely individual reactions to this volume-based rating scale vary from one person to another. Many nonalcoholics look at the figures and say, "My goodness, that's an awful lot! I've never drunk that much in my life." The alcoholic is apt to look at the figures and say, "That's not very much at all!" The problem is that a large number of people in the middle find such a scale confusing or baffling. Some suspect they are alcoholic (and probably are) but rarely drink as much as the prescribed "moderate" limit; others have no idea that they are alcoholic (and indeed may not be) and consistently drink more.

The fact is that no scale based on rigid quantities of alcohol consumed per unit time, which arbitrarily assigns individuals into alcoholic or nonalcoholic groups on the basis of these quantities, can be anything more than an indicator. *Alcoholism does not depend on the amount of alcohol drunk. It depends on the way the individual drinks it, and the effect the alcohol has on the individual.*

Identifying Alcoholism

If rigid, arbitrary standards are not useful in defining alcoholism, then what is? Obviously, a large number of people who drink alcohol are not alcoholic. These people, who are virtually all nonaddictive individuals, make up the large proportion of people commonly referred to as social drinkers. When they drink, they almost always do so in a social setting, and there is usually a distinct limit (different for each individual) to the amount they want and do drink.

Some drink regularly or daily to "relax after work," to use the time-worn phrase. Others drink only at cocktail parties or dinner parties as a social event. Even under those circumstances, many drink only because it is the socially accepted thing to do and they don't want to seem different — not because they particularly want the alcohol. The limits that these people observe usually are not consciously determined or contrived; instead they equate roughly with the amount of alcohol these people feel comfortable with, which is generally not very much. They dislike the loss of control. These people are equally comfortable at a gathering where no alcohol at all is served, where only white wine is served, or where a fully stocked bar is available. Such people, when their own home liquor supply unexpectedly runs out, may not get around to going to the liquor store to replenish it for a week or two.

Another group of people distinguishes itself from this first group not so much by the amount of liquor they drink as by their attitude toward liquor and drinking and by the way they drink. These people are actively interested in drinking, to the extent that it occupies an important place in their lives. They use social events, and many other kinds of events, as excuses or justifications for drinking. They seldom are found at dry parties. As for their own home liquor supplies, they almost never run out, unexpectedly or otherwise. They are usually way ahead of any possible shortage.

Do these people recognize their addiction, or that they are in jeopardy of becoming addicted? I think the vast majority does not. Actually, if you were to take a poll of every actively drinking person in the country and were to ask each one individually if he or she was alcoholic, I think you would find that there were few, if any, alcoholics anywhere in the country. A great many of your respondents would know *other* people who were alcoholics, but not report themselves. Most individuals who freely and sincerely admit to being alcoholic are recovering alcoholics who have stopped drinking. A few individuals might say, "Sure, I'm an alcoholic, but I don't let it bother me," but they are the ones who are "only joking" (or imagine that they are). Some who deny alcoholism know perfectly well that they are alcoholic and simply lie when asked. A vast number, however, really do not know where they stand on the scale or what danger they may be in.

One way of identifying alcoholism is to look at some patterns of drinking that are highly characteristic of alcoholism or developing alcoholism. Another way is to consider certain telltale signals that alcoholism is or may be present.

Patterns of Alcoholism

Alcoholic drinking patterns can vary widely from individual to individual; no single pattern is always present, and no one alcoholic is likely to exhibit all possible patterns. But the following case histories will illustrate something of the range. Consider them and see what you think.

Mary S. was not a teetotaler, but she rarely had more than one drink on any one occasion. No one had ever seen her even remotely "under the influence." She was the mother of teenage children and the wife of a prominent businessman. For years she had been active in community affairs. Then, when the first of her children left home and the second was preparing to leave, she became depressed and sleep became a problem. To help overcome it, she began having a highball before bed several evenings a week. When this no longer seemed to help her get to sleep, she started staying up after everyone else had retired. Within a few weeks her original "nightcap" had turned into two or three stiff highballs, or even more. Sometimes she found herself staggering on the way to bed, and occasionally she would fall down, but once she got into bed, she would sleep.

Was Mary S. alcoholic? The pattern of change from light, occasional drinking to quite heavy, compulsive drinking was certainly an alcoholic pattern. She thought that her evening drinking was unobserved, but she was wrong. First her children and then her husband became aware of the amount she was drinking, and the children observed her lurching to bed more than once. She was stunned to discover that they thought she was alcoholic. When she sought professional help, her doctor diagnosed an underlying depression and began treating her for it. Under that treatment she was able to stop the alcohol at bedtime and sleep normally.

Mary was probably not an alcoholic. She showed few other signs of being addictive. If she had shown these signs, her drinking might have developed into alcoholism. *Alcoholic patterns of drinking are progressive and lead to alcoholism in addictive people.*

John L. seldom drank, but when he did let down his hair and have a few, he always drank until he was drunk. He never meant to drink that much and was always apologetic and remorseful afterward. Each time it happened he swore he wouldn't do it again. He just couldn't understand what happened on those occasions.

Was John L. alcoholic? We don't have enough evidence here to say for sure. But the pattern of "drinking out of control," that is, drinking to inebriation whenever one drinks at all without knowing how to stop or being able to stop, is a highly familiar alcoholic drinking pattern.

Paula K. drank on frequent occasions and drank quite a lot, everybody knew that, but she never got drunk. She always seemed the same to her friends no matter how much she had to drink, and she seemed to have an endless capacity. One night she was stopped by the police for weaving across the center line as she was driving home from a dinner party. Her blood alcohol level was .18, considerably above the legal intoxication level of .10, and she was arrested and booked for DWI (driving while intoxicated). That was the beginning of a long, mortifying ordeal for Paula K. — two court appearances, a heavy fine, temporary loss of her driver's license, and court-ordered attendance at drunk drivers' classes. But the worst part, for her, which she only mentioned to her doctor much later, was the fact that the morning after her arrest she couldn't remember being stopped or arrested at all. Her mind was a total blank from the time she left the dinner party.

Was Paula alcoholic? Her pattern of drinking suggests that she was. Frequent, heavy drinking is certainly suggestive. The evidence for her tolerance for alcohol is as well; the apparently endless capacity for alcohol without any appearance of getting drunk is a pattern highly suggestive of alcoholism. In addition, the appearance of blackout spells — periods of loss of memory while drinking — is characteristic of alcohol addiction.

Jean M. worked full time during the day and had three children and a husband to care for as well. She was always glad to have a relaxing drink when she got home from work, and she had several more while preparing dinner each evening, just to help her unwind. During the evening meal there was always wine, she never paid much attention to how much, and after dinner a bit of Kahlúa or some brandy with her coffee. The children always did the dishes, which was just as well, because by that time Jean M. was passing out in the living room over the evening newspaper. The children would ask each other, "Is Mommy asleep again?" Sometime around midnight she would wake up and go to bed, and the next morning she would feel extremely shaky and her thinking would be slow.

Was Jean M. alcoholic? Compulsive drinking, especially every day at some set period of the day, is a characteristic alcoholic drinking pattern; so is passing out at the end of a period of compulsive drinking. The precise amount of alcohol consumed during such a period is not necessarily significant. If we were to explore Jean's history in a little more detail, we would probably find two other alcoholic patterns present: a steady progression in the amount of alcohol consumed during the evening period over weeks or months; and occasional cutting back sharply in the amount she drank (but, characteristically, never actually stopping) as she realized the increasing amount of alcohol she had been consuming.

Jean M. was surely alcoholic. In all likelihood she did not realize it, or if the idea entered her mind she rejected it with the self-assuring notion that she "can control it." She might well have been able to terminate her addiction to alcohol if she had seen her drinking patterns for what they really were and called her condition by its real name. But she didn't recognize it.

Bill G.'s wife and children always knew when he'd been drinking, because whenever he did, his normally warm, loving nature seemed to disappear and he became distinctly hostile. They could tell the minute he walked in the door if he had stopped for a "few short ones" after work, or had hit the "bar car" on the way home. It wasn't that he lurched around or smelled of alcohol; he was simply a different person — angry, demanding, and malicious. If anyone mentioned it to him, Bill would deny this abrupt change of personality and, in fact, he was completely unaware of the contrast. He didn't *feel* any different. But then, without much warning, he would get into a big fight with his wife or one of the kids, and then later not understand what had happened. Finally, one night he began tormenting his wife about some unpaid bills and in a fit of anger knocked her down and broke her arm. A few moments later, when he realized what he had done, he was horrified and immediately sought help to get her to an emergency room. He was extremely remorseful and apologetic.

Was Bill G. alcoholic? The tipoff here is not the violent behavior toward his children or his wife. Many nonalcoholic men, including teetotalers, beat their wives. The clue is the change of personality that occurred when Bill had been drinking — a characteristic phenomenon or pattern of alcoholic drinking. Time after time, in talking to family or friends of alcoholic drinkers, I hear this same basic pattern expressed: "he changes when he's been drinking"; "he's like a different person"; "she's the nicest woman you could hope to know when she's sober, but as soon as she's had a few drinks she starts picking fights"; "he's a great guy, ordinarily, but when he starts drinking he turns into a real animal."

It takes most families a long time to recognize this pattern and identify it with drinking. Family members often equate it with "moodiness," "being upset," "a hard day at the office," "trouble at work," and so forth, but traced to its roots, the trouble is virtually always alcoholic drinking. In one of its worst manifestations, men or women who normally are excellent, careful, law-abiding drivers become irrational and dangerous on the road when they have been drinking.

Tom K. prided himself on being a social drinker, and so did his wife, Irene. Tom was determined not to be like his grandfather, who was (as everyone in the family knew) a falling-down drunk who embarrassed the family for years with his unpredictable behavior. Tom wanted no part of that, and reminded his close friends that he was nothing like his grandfather, never drank alone, never drank in the morning, didn't even ordinarily have cocktails before dinner. As he pointed out, he drank only socially and on special occasions; but Tom and Irene found an awful lot of special occasions. Birthdays, anniversaries, holidays, promotions, graduations, weddings, funerals, births, christenings, reunions, housewarmings, or any of the innumerable round of parties thrown by themselves and their circle of friends are just a few of the special occasions.

Tom and his wife loved to entertain. Everybody knew that the K's had really great affairs that were always well attended. There was plenty to drink, and the liquor never ran out. Besides cocktails before dinner and wine with dinner, there was alcohol in much of the food, especially the desserts. Irene was creative in her cooking.

Tom and Irene were loads of fun, and people were drawn to their magnetic personalities. They were the perfect host and hostess. As it happened, many of their guests unintentionally drank too much at their parties; some would get sick and have to go home early, and now and then a guest would pass out in a bedroom. Tom and Irene always poured drinks strong and big — as they said, "It saves time running back and forth to the bar." As for Irene herself, she always appeared the same, never drunk or sloppy. The same can be said for Tom, except that occasionally he got overseductive with one of the women at the party, or did something shocking like taking off his clothes and streaking through the middle of the party with the woman from next door — but everybody knew he was just clowning to liven things up a bit.

Was Tom K. alcoholic? Was his wife? Were any of the people in their circle of friends? Frequent, heavy drinking at social gatherings where some people are overcome by the amount of alcohol served and others begin engaging in inappropriate behavior is not necessarily demonstrative of alcoholism, but it certainly is symptomatic and suspicious. The basic purpose of such parties is not to gather together with friends to converse, dine together, share experiences, or discuss interesting things, because the alcohol soon obliterates meaningful conversation. The basic purpose of such gatherings is *to get together to drink*. Tom K. was not an obvious drunk like his grandfather was reputed to be, but his life was following an alcoholic pattern. In his own way Tom was probably just as alcoholic as his grandfather was, as was Irene.

How do you tell if someone is alcoholic? As you can see from the above case histories — only a few among dozens I might have selected — it often isn't easy. If a person's face is red and puffy with veins standing out on the nose, and he or she is always drunk and passing out, the diagnosis is clear to all. But most alcoholics are not lying face down in the street on Skid Road with a brown paper bag under their arm. The vast majority are reasonably successful, functional people, and most of them will die of their alcoholism without ever knowing they are alcoholic. Their denial of the condition and their ignorance about the killer disease that afflicts them may well be enough to prevent them from ever joining the ranks of "recovering alcoholics."

Certainly the most important first step in battling alcoholism is being able to identify it, in yourself or in someone you care about. Awareness of the disease is the single vital factor that can send a person down the path to recovery. With that awareness, it makes no difference how early or late in the progress of the disease the alcoholic may be. Alcoholics are never hopeless or beyond help unless they are dead.

I cannot produce a single, all-inclusive definition of alcoholism simply because there are too many definitions, dozens of them, and not a single one covers the whole ground. The best I know is "alcoholism is when your drinking causes your values and behavior to be separated by a wide gap." But most alcoholics would not admit it. As we have seen from the case histories above, there are many different profiles of alcoholics. The disease comes in many shapes and sizes. It is a progressive disease, one that does progressive physical, mental, and emotional damage and gets progressively worse as long as it continues untreated. There are many degrees and stages in its progress. Unfortunately, it is also a terminal disease. If an alcoholic does not stop drinking, he will ultimately almost certainly die from the disease in some manifestation or other.

Alcohol is one of the chemical substances to which addictive people — those born with a metabolic defect in sugar metabolism — can become addicted. Addiction to alcohol is called *alcoholism.* Like other addictions, alcoholism fits the definition of addiction provided in chapter 3; it is the uncontrolled or out-of-control drinking of alcohol and the associated occurrence of unpleasant withdrawal symptoms when alcohol is withheld. Nonaddictive people may drink alcohol, but do not become addicted.

Certain facts deserve reemphasis. Alcoholism is not a bad habit, a weakness, a sign of moral decay, or a character defect. It is a physiological disease that affects every part of the body, the mind, the emotions, and the spirit. *Alcoholics drink because they have to, not just because they want to.* As the alcoholic's body adapts to the continuing or recurring presence of alcohol in the bloodstream, the body cells become more proficient in burning part of the alcohol for energy. This may account for the fact that many alcoholics soon find themselves drinking more and feeling it less. Indeed, alcoholics must drink more in order to feel their drinks at all. As we have seen, an alcoholic often behaves differently under the influence of alcohol than when sober. Alcohol distorts the alcoholic's thinking and emotions even when he or she is not drinking. Certain broad patterns of alcohol use, however, offer some clues to help distinguish the alcoholic from the social drinker.

Most alcoholics drink in an alcoholic pattern beginning with their first drink. Some may be social drinkers for years before overt signs of alcoholism become apparent. Social drinkers can enjoy a party with or without alcohol; alcoholics can't. Social drinkers tend to have a drink or two, maybe even several, and then quit; alcoholics usually continue to drink until the party is over, the booze runs out, or they get drunk or pass out, whichever comes first. Social drinkers tend to drink slowly and often set their drink aside and walk around without it; alcoholics don't want to be that far from their drink.

Indeed, many alcoholics evidence a deep fascination with alcohol. They think a great deal about drinking, and they plan ahead for it. They love to talk about drinking and alcohol, debate about alcohol, discuss its merits. They want to be near it, and make doubly certain that their supply doesn't run out. They talk, think, and sometimes even dream about drinking. Alcohol lights up their world and makes everything better.

Characteristically, alcoholics drink more than they intend to and drink more often than they plan to. They drink more alcohol faster than their social-drinking friends, except that their "social-drinking" friends tend to be different from other social drinkers; alcoholics seek out friends who drink the way they do, a great deal, and then speak of them all, themselves included, as "social drinkers." Equally characteristically, alcoholics have memory blackouts, times when they have no recollection of certain events that took place while they were drinking. Such blackout spells can be inconvenient, annoying, joke-engendering, or downright frightening. Often the following morning may be spent tiptoeing around, carefully and craftily trying to piece together clues about what actually happened the previous evening.

Loss of control over one's drinking — inability to stop drinking once one has started — is another characteristic of alcoholism. Drinking to inebriation almost every time one drinks is one example. Tolerance, or the ability to "hold one's liquor," is also typical of alcoholics whose bodies have become adapted to the presence of large quantities of alcohol. Much more alcohol is required for the alcoholic to get drunk than for the nonalcoholic, under most circumstances. Such behavior as hiding bottles or hoarding a supply of alcohol is an obvious symptom of alcoholism, as is frequent surreptitious sipping from a small pocket bottle. Early morning drinking and drinking alone are such commonly recognized characteristics of alcoholism that they are practically clichés but, of course, they are not necessarily present in all alcoholism. The mere fact that one does not drink alone, in the morning, or before five o'clock in the evening is no guarantee that one is not alcoholic.

Physiological reactions can also be clues to alcoholism. For example, tremors of the hands, repeated severe hangovers, or acute anxiety attacks are such clues. These are reactions that draw some alcoholics to early morning drinking as a way to calm down the shakes or get rid of hangovers or anxiety attacks. Although far less well recognized, sleeplessness is common among alcoholics, particularly a pattern of insomnia in which one awakens in the middle of the night and then can't get back to sleep. More severe physiological evidence of alcoholism — delirium tremens (or DTs), loss of tolerance, or the facial changes of alcoholism come later in the disease. Heart disease (alcoholic myocarditis), liver disease (cirrhosis), portal vein hypertension and esophageal varices, alcoholic organic brain dysfunction, and various forms of alcohol-related cancer — any or all of these may make their appearance eventually.

Signals of Alcoholism

Of course, not all alcoholics necessarily fit one of the broad patterns or profiles of alcoholism discussed above. The disease is protean. It can take as many different forms as there are individual alcoholics, so it can be extremely inaccurate or even dangerous to say, "Well, I obviously don't fit any of those patterns exactly, so I can't be alcoholic." To further help you, or someone you care about, to focus in on an awareness of alcoholism or possible alcoholism, there are a number of suggestive signals that may help you clarify your own individual situation. Try answering the following questions.

Do you often (or almost always) drink more than you intend to on a given occasion? This is a positive signal of alcoholism. It actually has little or nothing to do with how often you drink, how much of the time you don't drink, or how little you drink on some occasions. *How* you drink when you are drinking is what matters.

Do your children think you are alcoholic? They may not rush forward to tell you, but they know. They may deny it, or insist that they don't know what you're talking about. It is often a well-kept secret among the alcoholic's children, but they almost invariably know, even very young children in grade school. They sense the sudden personality change that takes place so frequently in an alcoholic. For one thing, children are not readily fooled by excuses and rationalizations, nor are they fooled by the amount or type of alcohol you drink (it's just as easy to be an alcoholic on beer or wine as on hard liquor). If you can get your children to level with you about what they really think, not what they think you want to hear, they know the answer.

Do you find you can drink increasing amounts, really quite a lot, without feeling much effect? Do you have memory blackouts? These signals of alcoholism were mentioned earlier, but they deserve reemphasis. They are not necessarily experienced by all alcoholics. Tolerance — the ability to drink more and more without showing it or feeling it — is perhaps the most common signal, but tolerance may creep up on people so slowly that they tend not to notice it. Blackouts (memory loss following drinking events) can happen frequently and progressively and are usually associated with consumption of a large amount of alcohol on one occasion.

Have you ever been to Alcoholics Anonymous or had treatment for alcoholism? This might seem like a silly question, since one might think that nobody goes to Alcoholics Anonymous or gets treatment by mistake. But oddly enough, there are alcoholics who have been pressured by their families, their bosses, or courts of law to attend AA meetings for a period of time, attend alcohol classes, or even submit to alcoholism treatment who still steadfastly deny that they are or ever were alcoholics. I think such denials have to be taken for what they are: an integral part of the disease. From my experience, very few people go to treatment or organizations such as AA who don't belong there; the fact that a person has had such an experience is usually sufficient evidence of alcoholism.

Do you drink huge quantities of alcohol regularly? Although we cannot identify any specific quantity of drinking that separates the nonalcoholic from the alcoholic, we can say with some degree of confidence that nobody can or will drink large quantities of alcohol regularly without being alcoholic. For one thing, only an alcoholic likes alcohol that much. Nonalcoholics who try to drink large quantities over any period of time find it nauseating or tiresome. They don't like the inebriating effect of that much alcohol, and they don't like the cerebral depression, the hangovers, or the dehydration and other physiological effects that go with it.

Years ago an acquaintance of mine went to a weekend convention attended by many old friends, and deliberately decided to put aside his usual "one drink is enough" restraint and drink as much as the occasion seemed to dictate. As a result, he was either drunk or asleep virtually all of the three days of the convention, drinking gin at breakfast, going to the bar with friends at ten in the morning and belting away impressive quantities of alcohol. Throughout the weekend he got progressively sicker — sick to his stomach, sick to his head — and when he returned home it took him almost a full week to recover his normal balance. His overall reaction to the experience was "I certainly won't do that again!" He concluded that his original "one drink is enough" guideline was just fine. Now, twenty-five years later, he still drinks on a "one drink is enough" basis. He is not an alcoholic.

There is one other thing to say about drinking large quantities of alcohol. Although I won't try to define specifically how many ounces a large quantity of alcohol might be — 6 oz.? 8? 10? 20 oz. a day? — I will point out that a large quantity of alcohol is enough to do severe damage to body organs and tissues if drunk persistently and regularly, whether or not you are alcoholic. Even a modest amount of alcohol taken daily will chip away steadily at the cerebral neurones, liver cells, and peripheral nerve cells; larger amounts do it faster.

Do you carry alcohol with you when you travel? If your answer is "yes," it may mean nothing. Some nonalcoholics do. Alcoholics almost always do, however — a "little signal" of alcoholism.

Do you have persistent problems at home? Major interpersonal problems — marital problems or problems with children, for example — are often clearly recognized as being related to alcohol use, despite denial by the alcoholic. Certain other problems may not be identified with alcoholism at all but should be. Impotence, for example, is a common phenomenon among alcoholics, and it very often disappears as if by magic upon treatment of the alcoholism. Severe and persistent sleeplessness is another problem that occurs commonly with alcoholism, as is depression.

Do your friends drink heavily, get drunk, or pass out at your par-

ties? The host selects the guests, provides the alcohol, and creates the environment. Generally, the drinking party where almost everyone is too inebriated to enjoy the food by the time it arrives does not happen by accident. On the other hand, there are many parties where alcohol is offered but is lightly used. I have attended many cocktail or dinner parties where none of the guests, invited to pour their own drinks at the bar, drank more than one or two drinks. When I was an active alcoholic I hated such parties; whenever possible I had two or three drinks before I went, and looked forward to going home for some serious drinking. No hard-and-fast rules apply here, but a careful analytical look at the nature of your own parties, and your drinking at others, can provide a signal. Alcoholic hosts frequently push drinks.

Do you ever try to hide or disguise the amount you are drinking? Alcoholics usually try to please people in order to be able to keep on drinking without censure. They don't want their drinking habits to stand out in a crowd, and they often engage in various subterfuges to conceal how much they are really drinking. It is a sort of cliché of alcoholism when the hostess takes two or three fast extra drinks in the kitchen before returning to the party, or when a man or woman has two or three good stiff ones at home before going to the party in order to "float" at the social gathering without appearing to be drinking much. They may even refuse a second drink! We can suspect the host who pours himself doubles or triples while he pours everyone else singles of being an alcoholic. It may not be so apparent, however, in the female guest who says "Why not make mine a double so it'll hold me for a while," or in the man who asks for a dark-colored mixer like Coca-Cola so others won't notice how dark his drink is when he surreptitiously adds to it as he goes along.

Do you prefer to drink at home rather than in a social setting? Nonalcoholics generally don't. They may not drink at all, or only very little, except in a social setting. A wife, for example, may join her husband every evening for a cocktail before dinner in a setting of enjoying each other's company for a few moments, sharing the day's events and accomplishments, yet she may rarely, if ever, have a drink even at cocktail hour when he is away. Alcoholics often prefer to drink at home simply because they can drink as much as they want without the sense of condemnation or social scrutiny they might suffer at a social gathering.

Do you find alcohol leading to performance or behavior that con-

tradicts your basic values? This is very difficult to face honestly, but anyone who suspects that he or she may have a problem with alcohol might consider it. Everyone has a system of values. For many people, their value system dictates that they keep their word, appear when they say they will, maintain their personal integrity and veracity, recognize the rights of other individuals, and resolve interpersonal conflicts peacefully by discussion and diplomacy. It is common for conflicts to arise between the alcoholic's value system and his or her actual performance or behavior. According to one's values, one does not go to a gathering of people and drink oneself into a stupor, but the alcoholic sometimes does. According to one's values, one does not lie to one's wife about how many drinks he has had before he gets home from work, but the alcoholic does. According to one's values, one does not lie to one's employer about why he has been missing work, but the alcoholic will do so quite glibly. According to one's values, one does not break long-standing promises to one's children and lie about the reason, but the alcoholic does. Of course, this same type of conflict between values and behavior is highly characteristic of many other addictions as well.

Alcoholism, the addiction and disease, with its built-in elements of ignorance and denial, is clearly a formidable enemy. We all have a picture of the typical alcoholic in mind, but it never includes ourselves, because so much alcohol is used in our society and overdrinking is well tolerated and condoned. Alcoholism is a hidden addiction; vast numbers of people don't recognize it in themselves, and those who do (or at least suspect it) won't admit it. Many people are looking for a definition that doesn't fit them, which is why I have not offered a precise definition here. Many latch onto questionnaires in magazines and then say, "Well, that couldn't be me." Many tell themselves, "I can take it or leave it," or "I can quit any time I want to." (I personally never got past Wednesday without alcohol after resolving to quit on Sunday night, time and again. But I still denied the truth.)

Nothing can be done about alcoholism until it has been at least tentatively identified in yourself or in a loved one. Only then is there a serious chance of dealing with it effectively. Fortunately, once it has been identified and recognized or acknowledged by the individual, there are a number of more or less effective approaches to treatment.

Dealing with Alcoholism

Alcoholism, once identified, can be treated effectively. There are a number of ways of dealing with alcoholism. Some approaches work better than others, but any approach is far better than none at all.

When considering approaches to treatment, once again we find the pathway liberally booby-trapped with myths and misconceptions that do nothing but get in our way, hide the real problem, and obscure the only possible hope of achieving an effective treatment and lasting recovery.

One such misconception about alcoholism, perhaps the most common, is the completely misdirected notion that the alcoholic is an alcoholic because all kinds of terrible and deep-seated physical, social, or psychological problems have driven the person to drink. To enable the alcoholic to stop drinking, one must first unearth, identify, and solve all of those terrible, deep-seated problems.

I think of this idea as the "psychiatrist's life work" approach to treatment. Slightly restated, it is saying, "We can't do anything at all to help your alcoholism until we have first treated and resolved a whole string of complicated problems that we think are making you drink." This is sheer nonsense! I am convinced that this misconception has arisen because, for generations, almost invariably it has been the psychiatrist who ended up treating the alcoholic as a matter of practicality and tradition. General practitioners and internists traditionally have had a poor record of dealing with alcoholics, and many are convinced from their own experience that they can't treat alcoholism effectively. Some are reluctant even to try, because they believe that the alcoholic is going to cause them nothing but grief and consume an enormous amount of time and energy for nothing. Another attitude prevalent in the medical profession is that alcoholics (like heroin addicts) "bring this trouble on themselves" and don't deserve to be treated — "Look what you've done to yourself!" Eventually, by default, these patients reach the office of the psychiatrist, who, by training, invariably searches for the underlying psychological root causes of the presenting symptoms. Thus, in the psychiatric tradition, alcoholism is considered the *result* of some emotional or psychological condition, and the psychiatrist says, "We've got to get to the root problem that caused it all in order to enable this person to stop drinking."

This notion is completely backward; it simply isn't true. The best proof I have of that is that it doesn't work. You can't treat alcoholism successfully by treating social and psychological problems. On the contrary, you can cure such problems, sometimes almost miraculously, by treating the alcoholism. The truth is that *there is only one problem that matters in alcoholism, and that problem is drinking alcohol.* A disordered physiology, a genetically deranged metabolism, is causing the body to react addictively and alcoholically when alcohol is consumed, and that is the only cause of alcoholism. It is drinking the alcohol that results in many of the physical, social, and psychological problems the alcoholic is likely to have. True enough, he or she may have other problems, too, which don't necessarily bear on the alcoholism at all; or he or she may have problems, such as depression, that make it easier to continue drinking than not to drink. The basic problem in alcoholism is drinking alcohol, and the only way to eradicate the problem is to stop drinking! Many trained people working in the field repeat this, but they don't really accept it. They continue to look for problems fostering the alcoholism.

Another gross misconception that keeps turning up from time to time, even in otherwise responsible medical literature, is the notion that alcoholics can effectively resolve their problem with alcohol by cutting down the amount they drink, or that alcoholics can learn to drink socially again.

Alcoholism is entirely analogous to addiction to many other drugs or substances. No one tries to teach a recovering heroin addict to use just a little heroin now and then; the addiction would be back almost instantly and just as severely. Surely the recovering tranquilizer addict would not reasonably be advised to go back to using his or her tranquilizer from time to time, and the recovering sugar addict would return to a full addictive pattern the moment he or she decided to "give another try" to a diet heavy in sugar-foods.

The truth is that the recovering alcoholic who has stopped drinking can never again safely drink alcohol, socially or any other way. This is not just an artificial knee-jerk kind of dictum invented by a group of moralists somewhere, as is sometimes thought. In the world of the recovering alcoholic, it is simply a fact of life that has been substantiated innumerable times under innumerable sets of circumstances, and our concept of the underlying genetic and metabolic flaws that lead to alcohol addiction explains why. The alcoholic's addictive physiological hunger does not change when alcohol is not consumed for a period of time. He or she is vulnerable to addiction for a lifetime. Recovering alcoholics by the tens of thousands can bear witness to this. They know, often from bitter experience, that they can't take so much as a single drink. In rare instances, if the personality is rigid enough and other controlling forces are powerful enough, the alcoholic might manage to imitate a "social drinking" role for a period of time. Such a person is fighting constantly against a physiological hunger that is demanding something quite different, however, and the strain usually is overwhelming. Sooner or later, even rigid control breaks down. The idea that recovered alcoholics can engage safely in limited or periodic drinking only instills false hope. When an "expert" proposes it, some alcoholics want to try it, only to end in readdiction and perhaps death.

Approaches to Treatment

If the first vital step in dealing with alcoholism is to identify it, the second is to find an approach to bring the alcoholic to treatment. The only effective treatment for alcoholism includes abstinence, which sounds simple but can be very difficult. The alcoholic, in order to stop drinking, must break an addiction to one of the most addictive of all substances, and then find a way to cope with withdrawal symptoms and craving for alcohol, either alone or with medical help.

Once this essential first stage of treatment is under way, the alcoholic is faced with the task of repairing the myriad facets of life that alcoholism damages or destroys: health and nutrition, interpersonal relationships, value systems, and self-esteem. Genetic depression may be a significant factor to face, as well as emotional growth, which often is at a standstill throughout the alcoholic period. To accomplish this rebuilding, restoration, and growth during treatment and recovery, support systems are vital to the patient's progress. They can include tightly knit, highly supportive family and job situations, an outside group such as Alcoholics Anonymous, a medical clinic treatment program, or a combination of these.

The extreme difficulty of achieving success in treating alcoholism is reflected in the few studies done on long-term recovery among treated patients. Alcoholism is a disease not only of denial but of relapse. One of the major organizational approaches to supporting recovery from alcoholism, Alcoholics Anonymous, keeps no records or statistics, so we have no way of knowing what percentage of alcoholics who go to AA achieve permanent or long-term recovery. Rumor says one in thirty-five. Many private organizations and medical treatment centers boast of very high recovery rates, but on close examination one finds that their follow-ups tend to be very brief, perhaps only a year or two, and that the follow-up techniques they use are suspect, so it seems likely that they miss a great many relapsing patients.

In one eight-year follow-up study of 1,000 treated alcoholic patients, investigators found only 28 percent to be sober at the end of eight years, and many of those had experienced one or more relapses during the follow-up period. Among the 28 percent, however, almost all had the help of an excellent group support system. Either they had a solid, concerned, and loving family and a supportive job environment backing them up, or else they had found adequate support through Alcoholics Anonymous.

Obviously, just embarking upon abstinence and treatment is no guarantee of long-lasting results. How any given alcoholic responds to treatment varies greatly from individual to individual; it also depends on the way a person is brought to treatment. Some individuals make a completely unpressured, self-determined decision to terminate their drinking permanently with no one else involved. Some then actually do it, and never look back. But all too frequently this kind of self-determined approach proves of little value.

A number of readers, for example, may have come to this book already vaguely concerned about the amount they have been drinking and wondering if they might possibly be alcoholic. Such people might feel that if any question exists, now is the time to do something about it, and indeed, one of the purposes of this book is to raise and address such questions. Other experiences stimulate some people to come to such self-determined decisions. One patient who ultimately came to me for treatment had been drinking quite a bit one night and fell in the bathroom and cracked his head hard on the toilet bowl. The blow stunned him, and when he regained his senses his first thought was, "My God, I could have killed myself." Many other people suffer stumbling and falling accidents while drinking, slipping on the ice, tripping on the stairs, or other such accidents in which the protective reflexes are blunted by alcohol so that serious consequences could occur.

Near misses with accidents may provide enough incentive for some alcoholics to terminate their drinking. Although some alcoholics are able to make their own decision to quit, help is needed if they relapse. In my experience, self-determination alone is usually not enough to combat this physiological disease.

Nonstructured Intervention

Other patients approach treatment as a result of what we might call *nonstructured intervention.* As we have seen, many alcoholics don't recognize their alcoholism, or won't admit it, but others in the family see it clearly. Unfortunately, avoidance is the most frequent, highly instinctive reaction to someone else's drinking in the family: "Let's not talk about it; don't mention it and maybe it'll go away." Family members often become involved in elaborate prevarications designed to hide the fact that Daddy is alcoholic. When he's too hung over to go to work, his wife telephones the boss and says her husband has the flu. The children carefully avoid bringing their friends home because Daddy may be suffering from a hangover. All this denial, cover-up, and falsification actually has the effect of enabling the alcoholic to pursue alcoholism more readily, and the people who engage in this charade are spoken of as enablers. All the alcoholic has to do is sit in the middle of this milieu, drinking and behaving in any fashion desired, while everyone else scrambles around picking up the pieces and maintaining the façade. Inside, however, they often are crumbling; people who live with an alcoholic are sick too.

This pattern of family behavior clearly doesn't do the alcoholic any good. It doesn't move him or her toward treatment, and often things simply drift along, getting progressively worse until some sort of crisis is reached: if it's Daddy who has the alcohol problem, his wife decides to pack up and leave home, he gets a DWI and loses his driver's license, or he goes to work drunk once too often and finds his job in jeopardy. Simply by refusing to be enablers anymore, ceasing to cover up, lie, and maintain the façade, the family can begin a positive sort of intervention that could get the alcoholic moving toward treatment before things reach a crisis point.

The first step in such nonstructured intervention is talking about the problem. This does not necessarily mean angry accusations, finger-pointing, and recrimination for past deeds. It should be an honest confrontation. If the "short one" the drinker has before dinner is, in reality, 6 oz. of raw bourbon, call it a "6-oz. drink." One can discuss the fact that one person perceives a problem even if the other doesn't. The point is not to recriminate but to stop hiding and covering up. The second step is to introduce the idea that whatever the nature of the problem — whether it's drinking too heavily or alcoholism — it's still a problem, and something can be done about it. One can stop drinking, and if necessary there is help available. No problem with alcohol is hopeless or beyond help.

Occasionally, of course, things get bad enough, and the alcoholic's spouse or children reach a point that they are willing to lay it on the line, "do something or else!" Many co-alcoholics (those living with an alcoholic, particularly enablers of his alcoholism) either can't or won't actually bring themselves to do anything, and some alcoholics simply won't respond; but often an alcoholic will be sufficiently shaken up by the threat of imminent disintegration of a relationship that he or she will agree to approach treatment.

There are many pitfalls in attempting nonstructured intervention to bring an alcoholic to treatment. One is the appearance of a rescuer, an individual within the family or from outside who wants to ride in like a knight in shining armor and save the alcoholic from himself. Such a person, just another form of an enabler, proposes to solve all the alcoholic's problems, smother the alcoholic with possessive love, take the alcoholic away somewhere for a fresh start, do it all for him or her, and of course it doesn't work. The alcoholic must participate in treatment and eventually acquire motivation and commitment.

Structured Intervention: A Professional Approach

Sometimes the individual alcoholic cannot or will not achieve motivation to approach treatment and shows no sign of responding to nonstructured intervention on the part of spouse, family, friend, boss, or anyone else. Rather than having the family continue to cover up and enable the alcoholic to continue drinking, or precipitate a crisis in order to force the alcoholic's hand, there is another, more "sociological" means of persuasion that has achieved good results in skilled professional hands. This is known as *structured in-*

tervention. It is strong medicine for dealing with a cruel and relentless disease.

A structured intervention is a preplanned, rehearsed scenario guided and directed by a professional, in most cases a psychologist, sociologist, or case worker associated with a professional alcoholism treatment center (although professional interventionists may also be found in private practice). The intervention itself consists of close family members and friends telling the alcoholic at a preappointed time and place, without recrimination or accusation, how much they love the person and how specific elements of his or her alcoholic behavior have been hurting them, one by one, and to offer loving pleas to the alcoholic to go to treatment.

How might this intervention scenario work? One patient of mine, Vern C., provides a good example. Vern was an alcoholic for at least twelve years. Over the previous five years, his drinking had grown progressively worse until his family relationships, job position, and friendships had all disintegrated virtually to the breaking point. Everyone knew Vern was alcoholic except Vern, who considered himself far too clever and functional to be alcoholic. His wife, however, had long recognized the disastrous change in his personality when he was drinking. His two children both recognized that Dad drank too much. They were in high school and college and were often embarrassed in front of their friends by their father's behavior.

Vern's mother lived next door and knew of her son's drinking problem. His boss was a close friend, and they had worked together for over twenty years. The Johnstons, their neighbors, were also old friends, having lived next door to them for fifteen years.

Vern's wife finally sought help for his drinking problem one summer when she realized that his denial had become more than she could continue to combat and found herself thinking seriously, for the first time, about just packing up and leaving to preserve some of the remnants of her own life. On the advice of their family doctor she called an alcoholic treatment center in her city and made an appointment with John Arneson, an intervention specialist there. She told him that she knew her husband was alcoholic, but he refused to deal with it in any way.

Arneson explained that structured intervention techniques had succeeded in bringing many resistant alcoholics into treatment; for example, such a technique had persuaded Betty Ford, wife of President Gerald Ford, to enter treatment. He asked about all the significant people in Vern's life and arranged a time for all of them to meet together, without Vern, for an instruction session. Vern's wife then talked with each of these people and asked them to attend the instruction session in order to help Vern. They all agreed, including the two children, the oldest returning from college just for the meeting.

At the meeting John Arneson discussed what they would try to do: motivate Vern to recognize his alcoholism and agree to go directly into alcoholism treatment. He helped each person put into words exactly how Vern's drinking affected him or her. He helped them eliminate name-calling, but had each express clearly the feelings of embarrassment, anger, sadness, hurt, and loss that Vern's behavior caused them to experience. Even more important, he helped them get in touch with the feelings of love they had for Vern. These feelings often get lost under the anger and hurt.

On the designated evening, Vern's closest family members, his boss, and his close friends from next door all gathered at Arneson's office with their rehearsed speeches ready. Vern's wife had told him that she and his daughter were seeing a counselor and wanted him to come to a session. He had agreed and came with her on that special evening. When they walked into the room together, Vern was stunned. Arneson asked him if he knew why everyone was there. "It must have something to do with me," Vern said.

"That's right," Arneson responded, "it does. We'd like you to hear what each one of these people has to say before you speak."

At this point, one by one, each person in the room presented his or her personal plea to Vern. They expressed the pain, anger, embarrassment, or grief that Vern's drinking behavior had caused; they expressed the love, affection, or concern they felt for Vern; they pointed out the lost opportunities for full relationships because of Vern's drinking; and they urged him to recognize and confront his alcoholism and to seek help dealing with it. There were no threats, no name-calling, just the facts and a recurring urgent message. When it became Vern's turn, there was little he could say other than that he would go to treatment. Arneson then pointed out that arrangements had already been made for Vern's admission to the alcohol treatment center that evening and that a car was waiting outside at that moment for his wife and son to transport him.

This kind of structured intervention worked with Vern C.; he went to the treatment center for a four-week period and now, some two years later, is still maintaining a successful recovery. Of course, there are some built-in flaws in this intervention technique, and it does not always turn out the way it did with Vern. It is a highly emotional form of persuasion, and there have been patients so infuriated by it that they turned and walked out of the room, subsequently refusing angrily to have anything to do with any form of treatment. All this notwithstanding, structured intervention *does* work to bring even very resistant alcoholics to treatment in a high percentage of cases, and it is being used more frequently as we recognize how vital it is to break the alcoholic addiction by any means that *works.*

What Treatment? And Where?

Once an alcoholic has decided or agreed to confront his or her alcoholism and deal with it, there are several kinds of treatment that can be followed. First, the alcoholic can essentially "go it alone" without any professional help or formal outside support. Although this approach sometimes works, there can be danger in it, and it may not be enough for many alcoholics. Second, the alcoholic can choose to be admitted to a hospital or other alcohol treatment institution for an inpatient treatment program. Third, the alcoholic can go to Alcoholics Anonymous, for either major support or continuing support after treatment, or for both. Fourth, the alcoholic can seek the guidance of a private practitioner or an outpatient clinic. Each kind of treatment presents some distinct advantages, at least to certain alcoholics, and each presents some disadvantages.

Going It Alone

This is probably not the best choice for the alcoholic who has been actively alcoholic for years, whose life is disorganized by alcoholism, who has been in active treatment of one sort or another several times already and has subsequently relapsed each time, or who has reached such a point of desperation that something *has* to work. Such a person is probably going to do far better with a more formally structured and vigorously supportive approach to treatment — an inpatient treatment program of some sort, for example, or intensive outpatient treatment.

For the individual in the early stages of alcoholism who is motivated to stop drinking, a self-programmed plan may work. Good family support and stable job conditions make going it alone more feasible. The advantages of this route are that it is the least costly of all approaches to alcoholism treatment and it causes the least possible disruption in one's family life.

For such a person, the self-treatment program outlined in detail in chapter 5 is made to order. Begin with the first step, and commit yourself to quit drinking completely and at once. Whether or not you are actually alcoholic, giving up alcohol obviously will not harm you, and indeed, the cumulative toxic effect of alcohol starts decreasing as soon as you quit drinking it.

You will often find it difficult to maintain your commitment, since you will almost inevitably be faced with drinking opportunities. Rehearse your refusal of alcohol so you won't be embarrassed at the last moment and accept a drink to be polite. Plan to use substitute drinks: Perrier, soda and lemon, sparkling grape juice, or nonalcoholic beer, for example. As time goes on you will find contacts with nondrinking people to be increasingly rewarding, and the temptation to drink will arise less frequently. At the same time, quit eating sugar-foods, since these foods tend to make you crave alcohol. Follow the nutritional plan outlined in chapter 5. Be sure to add glutamine, 1 g three or four times a day, since it eliminates craving of alcohol.

Vitamin C for detoxification should be continued for at least five days. Start a regular exercise program and plan a variety of activities that don't include alcohol. Do some of the things you've always wanted to do but didn't have time for before. Buy yourself something special with the money you save by not buying liquor. (Even a very early alcoholic may be startled by how much money that is!) Without alcohol you will find it much easier to develop relationships with people you have neglected or passed by previously. You will find it much easier to enjoy people when much of your attention is not preoccupied with drinking.

If you have terminated your drinking abruptly and completely, within a day or two (sometimes within a few hours) you may become aware that you are feeling nervous, jittery, irritable, or depressed. Be prepared for it, don't be surprised. During this first period of treatment your body is in the process of detoxifying or unloading the last remains of alcohol and alcohol by-products still lingering in your tissues. This process is often accompanied by withdrawal symptoms, one of which is a sense of tension or even fear, fear of the unknown, fear that you won't be able to make it without alcohol. Many people try to rationalize this sense of fear and explain it away as related to job, spouse, or children, but it isn't anything of the sort. It's withdrawal.

In many alcoholics this sense of fear and other withdrawal symptoms such as nervousness, tremor, and irritability are merely annoying, coming and going for twenty-four to forty-eight hours but generally quieting down after a few days. This is what you can expect if you are going it alone, and anticipate that you will have little trouble with it after three or four days, in most cases. The vitamin C you are taking will help. If you are troubled for longer than three or four days, or find the withdrawal symptoms becoming exaggerated or, to your sensibilities, virtually intolerable, this is your clue to seek medical assistance for your withdrawal problem in an outpatient treatment program, or to opt for an inpatient treatment program with continuing medical supervision.

An alcoholic who follows a go-it-alone program will probably have a period of depression and nervousness, perhaps for just a few days, perhaps for several weeks. During that time you are going to feel much worse than you did before you stopped drinking. So why should you go on? What do you gain from all this? What good things happen, if any?

For one thing, you can expect to begin sleeping better, perhaps not immediately, but within a week or two. Most alcoholics have a difficult time sleeping, waking in the middle of the night and then not getting back to sleep. This sleep pattern begins to improve gradually after alcohol is terminated. Furthermore, your energy level will increase, and this can happen quite suddenly, within the first week. You will find you have more energy to do things and more interest in doing them. Relationships with people begin improving as well. You will find yourself with a strong drive to look and feel good. Your general attitude will improve, and your thinking will become less distorted. The edgy, hair-trigger temper of the alcoholic may disappear.

The longer you go without drinking, the better your chances for maintaining sobriety over the long term. Attendance at AA meetings can provide additional caring support from other recovering alcoholics, a support that powerfully reinforces not drinking.

But what about people who try to stop in this fashion and find that they can't? Where do they go from there? They will soon be drinking again and will be additionally depressed at their failed attempt to terminate alcohol. These people have learned firsthand that they need the intervention or assistance of others.

Alcoholism Treatment Centers

A wide variety of these institutions exists, available in or near most large communities. Almost all of them now treat drug addiction as well as alcoholism. In general, they are inpatient facilities — patients are admitted to the facility and remain there under close observation and control of the facility staff for a predetermined period of time, usually twenty-eight days (four weeks), although some operate programs of only ten days or even shorter duration. Most are voluntary facilities, and the patients have agreed to be there, whether they particularly want to be or not, for the prescribed course of treatment. Patients are not locked up, but they are not free to come and go as they please, either. In some states there are also certain legal commitment facilities in which people can be placed against their will. These are treatment centers to which the courts can order individuals for involuntary treatment of alcoholism, once it has been shown that they are endangering themselves or others.

All of these treatment facilities, voluntary and involuntary, provide alcoholics with an opportunity to stop drinking, and all follow relatively similar programs. For example, all of them terminate the patients' use of alcohol immediately and provide for three or four days of detoxification, if necessary, to clear the body of alcohol and its by-products. Librium or barbiturates are usually used to help get patients through the immediate distress of withdrawal, and the patients are under close observation for any evidence of impending convulsions.

Some institutions then follow up with a highly structured program of nutritious meals and vitamins, structured exercise, physical therapy, AA meetings, alcohol education classes, and group therapy throughout the remainder of the treatment period. Other institutions use a program of aversion therapy designed to condition patients to become so sick after drinking alcohol that they automatically associate alcohol with nausea and vomiting and stay away from it. In one such institution that I observed, on alternate days patients are given an intravenous dose of an emetic and then are given alcohol to drink precisely timed so that almost immediately upon swallowing the alcohol they become violently nauseated and throw it up. Others have experimented with programs using safe but highly uncomfortable electric shocks associated with drinking, so that any time patients drink anything, they do so in apprehension of being electrically jolted. The psychological conditioning process takes place regardless of what goes on in patients' conscious awareness, and has been shown to persist for a prolonged period of time in some cases. Various other forms of aversion therapy are practiced by other institutions, and some of these aversion therapy patients never drink again.

The question of the value of Antabuse as a means of outpatient aversion therapy is often raised. Antabuse, the drug disulfiram, is a chemical that blocks the oxidation of alcohol in the body at the acetaldehyde level and creates an acute negative physiological reaction any time alcohol is taken. It causes such symptoms as sudden sweating, nervousness, and jitteriness, and culminates in acute nausea and vomiting. The message is: "If you take Antabuse and then drink, you're going to be very sick."

This might seem an ideal way to keep an alcoholic away from drinking, but there are several problems associated with this kind of treatment. The major one is that Antabuse works only if it is taken, and many alcoholics on Antabuse simply neglect to take it on the day they plan to drink. Those who do drink in spite of the Antabuse become sick, but the sickness may become severe and require hospital treatment to help them recover. Many other alcoholics evade the effects of Antabuse simply by learning when its effects begin to wear off and waiting until then to drink. This drug works best with alcoholics who feel comfortable and confident in the morning and therefore take the Antabuse to guard themselves against the urge to drink later in the day. Although I have used Antabuse in my practice in certain selected patients, there is nothing magical or guaranteed about its results.

The real advantage of an inpatient treatment program, regardless of the precise approach to treatment, is that the patients spend four weeks without alcohol and with little or no opportunity to relapse along the way, and this is a long step forward in treating their alcoholism. Long-established patterns of drinking can be broken in that period of time, and new patterns of exercise and nutrition can be instilled. A major disadvantage is that these programs are expensive, with costs for a four-week program ranging from $2,000 to $10,000 or more. One might think that having invested such a sum of money in alcohol treatment would in itself provide powerful incentive to make the program work and avoid relapse after treatment is over, but this is frequently not the case. In addition, the cost alone prevents many people from considering such a treatment approach. Health insurance covers all or part of the cost of inpatient treatment for many people.

Perhaps the most serious drawback of inpatient treatment centers is the brevity of the treatment program. In some programs, when the prescribed period of treatment ends, it is over, and the opportunity for early relapse is ever-present. Other programs do better in addressing this problem. Some provide counseling and aftercare as a part of the program after discharge. Some also prescribe nutritional or diet advice, rules for the recovering alcoholic to follow, referrals for outpatient counseling, and perhaps even brief counseling for the family from time to time. Many relapse in spite of aftercare, possibly due to depression that has gone untreated.

Alcoholics Anonymous

For many alcoholics, Alcoholics Anonymous provides a much stronger support system for recovery than anything else available. AA is a vast organization with representatives and groups in virtually every community in the country, as well as throughout the world. It is not so much a form of treatment as it is a support system for sobriety, a group of recovering alcoholic men and women who share their common experience, strength, and hope with other alcoholics who desire to stop drinking, thus reinforcing their own sobriety along the way. Unconditional love is the real foundation of AA and makes it work: "Let us love you until you can love yourself."

Meetings consist of people taking turns talking about some aspect of their efforts to stay sober, and since one's view of sobriety changes from day to day, there's a great deal to talk about. The only requirement for membership is a desire to stop drinking; when you walk in the door you are automatically a member. There are no dues or fees. Donations of up to $1 defray the expenses of each group's meetings, all of which are self-supporting. Any extra funds are sent to an Intergroup office in the area to help the cause.

Among other tenets, AA emphasizes two important principles: don't drink, and keep coming to meetings. There are no officers or professionals heading the groups; a different person chairs each meeting. You need not speak up if you don't want to, but the benefits of the meeting derive as much from speaking out as from listening to others.

Sobriety in AA consists of not drinking at all. To help members achieve and maintain this, the organization has a strong spiritual foundation. Central to this foundation are twelve steps toward sobriety, articles of faith, which the members are encouraged to understand and follow. One of those steps is the recognition that alcoholics are powerless over alcohol, that they cannot handle it now or ever; another is that one accepts the need for the help of a higher power, however the individual conceives of such a power, to maintain sobriety. Some alcoholics are frightened off by what they construe as a religious bias in AA, but it is not really religion at all, merely a spiritual element of personal conviction or faith that has proven vital to countless recovering alcoholics. I have heard many AA members speak of coming to accept this aspect of the program only after being in AA for weeks, months, or years.

As its root, AA addresses the very practical reality that alcoholism is a continuing disorder and that for the alcoholic to stay sober one single day at a time is a thoroughly laudable achievement. The alcoholic in AA is not likely to declare, "I'm never going to drink again." Such statements are not even particularly encouraged, since relapse is the nature of the disease and we are all vulnerable daily to the possibility of taking a drink. In AA the alcoholic is more likely to say, "I'm going to try very hard not to drink today. I'll deal with tomorrow when it comes."

Along with the day-by-day attitude, however, AA does provide a continuing, long-term, and relatively unchanging avenue of support for recovering alcoholics. This support is *personal*, providing acquaintance and association with nondrinking people; *emotional*, combating depression; *inspirational*, providing the recovering alcoholic with examples of many people who have achieved what he or she is trying to achieve; and *spiritual*, reaffirming faith in a higher power to guide and help one achieve the goal of continuing sobriety.

My own association with AA has continued since 1980, and I find it just as helpful now as it was at the beginning — if not more so. For most of us, drinking was a major force in our lives, and it took a major force to help us replace drinking. AA has been that major force for many of us. Obviously there are recovering alcoholics who get along without AA, but I think the chances for a good-quality sobriety are much better with it. Relapse is always a threat, even with AA. I recently met a man who started drinking again after thirty-one years of sobriety. (I must keep in mind that the thirty-first year is dangerous!)

AA is criticized for many things, mostly for what it's not. It's not a medical treatment, it's not a nutrition center, it's not a health club, it's not psychotherapy per se, and it's not a church. All of these things can be helpful in addition to AA, but you won't find them there. Despite all this, AA has many members who are able to stay sober and were never able to before.

In addition to Alcoholics Anonymous proper, the AA umbrella sponsors two other support organizations: Al-Anon, an organization for the nonalcoholic families of recovering alcoholics, offering family members support and assistance in dealing with their own very real and difficult problems; and Alateen, an organization for teenage family members of alcoholics. Both Al-Anon and Alateen help the family members recover from the illness of living with alcoholism.

Certainly AA can provide long-range follow-up and support that almost no other treatment approach can offer, but not everyone who starts out with AA sticks around. During my years of experience in local groups I have noticed how many faces have disappeared, replaced by new ones. Some of these may have been people who decided that they "didn't need to go anymore" — that they had achieved sobriety and no longer needed AA. Maybe so, but it's my strong clinical impression that this "graduation attitude" can be dangerous and lead to relapse. Others surely are people who have relapsed into alcoholism again, and still others have doubtless moved or gone on to other groups in AA. I believe that continuing membership and attendance at AA is an important sustaining factor in maintaining sobriety, and despite the "short-termers," I know a number of people who have been attending regularly for twenty-five years or more and have remained sober all that time.

AA is available to almost everyone, since it exists in most communities, and reaches a lot of people who never are exposed to formal alcoholism treatment at all. But perhaps the best way that AA can contribute to the treatment of an alcoholic is by serving as one leg of a three-legged stool — as a supportive adjunct to a more comprehensive plan of treatment.

The Comprehensive Outpatient Approach

The plain fact is that no single approach to treatment works all the time. Although dependable statistics don't exist, there is ample internal evidence to indicate that all approaches yield relatively low-percentage permanent results, less than 50 percent, and my own clinical experience confirms this. Unfortunately, most treatment programs forget or refuse to accept the fact we have repeated more than once: alcoholism is a disease of relapses. Any treatment, to succeed at all, must accept that as a basic axiom, face the facts, and be prepared to accept relapse calmly and treat it as a major part of the disease.

It makes sense, however, that a comprehensive outpatient approach to treatment under a doctor's supervision may provide the best opportunity for success with many patients. This must involve positive identification of the condition in the first place and positive motivation of the patient to be involved in treatment. Attention must be paid to skillful detoxification with all the help medicine can provide and with protection against the more dangerous aspects of withdrawal. It should continue with attention to rebuilding the patient's body nutritionally so that he or she will be less likely to be drawn back into drinking. Active and vigorous treatment of depression is called for when it is a complicating factor; and drawing forth all of the personal, family, and emotional support that can be mustered is essential to success.

The treatment program outlined in chapter 5 for any addiction is the basis of the outpatient treatment program I follow in my office, and I believe the results surpass other treatment plans, but I have not been able to do a formal follow-up study. In addition to the basic program, I use a variety of prescription drugs and nutrients, described below, when I feel they are useful or necessary, according to each individual patient's needs.

For rapid detoxification, I not only direct the patient to use high doses of vitamin C powder regularly at home for the first four or five days; in many cases I also give patients even larger daily doses of vitamin C by intravenous drip under supervision in my office for the first critical days of detoxification. Most patients are over detox in three to five days. If patients develop problems with diarrhea or other side effects during this interval, I adjust the dosage.

To speed nutritional recovery, I sometimes prescribe higher doses of multivitamins and minerals under supervision than those outlined in the basic program. In addition to high-potency vitamins, I may add additional niacinamide, up to 1 g, three times a day, for its natural antidepressant effect, and pantothenic acid, 250 mg, three times a day for adrenal support.

As we have seen, *withdrawal symptoms* may vary from fairly inconsequential to extremely severe. Since it is impossible to predict who will have difficulty, I prescribe adequate amounts of chlordiazepoxide, to be taken for a period of up to a week. Although it could be an addicting drug, I have never had patients become addicted to it at the small doses and brief time periods required, and this dosage seems extraordinarily effective in preventing the severe withdrawal symptoms that alcoholics can experience. Indeed, it is the drug of choice.

Antidepressant medication is prescribed when the need arises. Although these are potent mood-altering medicines, they do not appear to be addicting substances. I have found that depression is a common and very destructive complication of recovery, but it can be effectively treated and relieved when necessary.

Counseling from a trained counselor is extremely valuable in recovery, and I recommend it for my patients in almost all cases.

Overall, a three-pronged approach to treatment of alcoholism — the patient's own self-treatment program, the doctor's supervision and prescription of medication as needed (whether at an inpatient facility or in an outpatient program), and the help of an outside support agency such as AA — offers the best possible hope for freedom from alcohol addiction.

8

Caffeine

FOR A PERFECT example of a supposedly "benign," "harmless," and exceedingly widespread addicting substance we need look no further than the caffeine in your morning cup of coffee or tea, your lunchtime soft drink, or myriad other sources. One hundred million Americans start their day with one or more cups of coffee. Many of these people drink six or more cups in a day, and a large number drink coffee more or less continuously from dawn until dark — ten, twelve, or fifteen cups daily. Add the millions of other coffee drinkers throughout the world, plus the multitudes of English and Europeans who start the day with tea, plus the millions worldwide drinking cola drinks, and you realize that caffeine is one of the most widely used addicting substances in the world. Don't overlook the many over-the-counter medications, such as Anacin or No-Doz, that contain caffeine.

Many people argue that caffeine is not addicting, but the observable facts are against them. Caffeine splendidly fulfills all the criteria of an addicting substance outlined in chapter 3. Great numbers of people use caffeine compulsively — when the time for their coffee comes, they want it then and there, before anything else happens — and their use of it is clearly out of control when they are drinking six or eight or a dozen or more cups of it a day. Furthermore, the drug produces clear-cut withdrawal symptoms upon abstinence. Perhaps the addictive nature of caffeine is reflected most convincingly in the economics of coffee sales throughout the world. This totally nonnutritive food commodity has increased in price from twentyfold to thirtyfold in the past ten years without any significant loss of purchasers or decline in sales. It is characteristic of any addicting substance that the addiction gets treated first, regardless of the cost. Only when the addiction has been taken care of can the addict get on with the other business of the day.

As for availability, caffeine can be found in many of our everyday beverages, either occurring in them naturally or present as an additive, as well as in other common sources. (See pp. 132–135 for a representative list of caffeine sources.)

Caffeine Effects and Addiction

Addictive people become addicted to caffeine in exactly the same way they become addicted to sugar, alcohol, or any other addicting substance. As we saw in chapter 3, according to my model for addiction, they have an inborn error in the way their bodies handle or metabolize sugar and carbohydrate. Caffeine is one of a variety of chemicals that can partially and temporarily satisfy a continuing physiological hunger that arises because of this metabolic error, but caffeine is particularly attractive for two reasons. First, it seems on the surface to have virtually no damaging effects whatever on the body — it appears remarkably "safe." (We will question this later.) Second, it is especially attractive because of its action on the body as a central nervous system stimulant.

Virtually any addicting substance can have distinct chemical actions on both the body and the mind. That is, it can have both *physiological* or "body-influencing" effects, and *psychoactive* or "mind-influencing" effects. In the case of caffeine, its body-influencing effects are familiar to most coffee drinkers. The drug produces an increase in heart rate, a rise in blood pressure, and an increased state of wakefulness and alertness. It stimulates insulin release into the bloodstream, causing a lowering of the blood sugar level. It prolongs the action of adrenalin, causing stimulation of heart muscle and increasing gastric acid in the stomach. It also elevates blood fats. In a pregnant woman it crosses the placental barrier, subjecting the fetus to caffeine levels equal to that of the mother.

In addition, caffeine stimulates the kidneys with a definite diuretic action, and for the multitudes of habitual morning coffee drinkers it serves as a distinct physiological bridge between sleeping and wakefulness. In very large or repeated doses it produces a state of hyperactivity or nervous jitteriness, a keyed-up, strung-out effect characteristic of all central nervous system stimulants or speedlike drugs. As for its psychoactive or mind-influencing effects, caffeine is a vigorous cerebral stimulant, raising the user's emotional tone or mood from the grogginess of sleep to a state of acute awareness during daytime activities, marked by a feeling of vigor and a sense of well-being.

In summary, in addition to its ability as an addictive substance to relieve temporarily the physiological hunger arising from the addictive person's carbohydrate dysmetabolism, caffeine can also speed up mental activity, counteract depression, and brighten the person's outlook, all at once. The drug can act as a stimulating jolt to a physiology that is experiencing the physiological hunger and depressive symptoms characteristic of addictiveness, and make the person *feel better* — at least for a short time. There is enough caffeine in one ordinary 6 oz. cup of coffee to produce and maintain these effects for half an hour or longer. Is it any wonder that so many caffeine addicts drink one cup of coffee after another all day long?

Caffeine can accomplish these things all by itself. In addition, a subtle aspect of caffeine's mood-altering effect is the way in which the drug fits in so neatly with other habits or addictions. As an addictive person, the caffeine addict is especially vulnerable to addiction to other substances. We see this, for example, in the way that coffee drinking and cigarette smoking are so firmly intertwined in many people's lives. Indeed, coffee time is notorious as one of the most difficult trigger situations for the cigarette smoker who is attempting to quit smoking (see chapter 9, "Nicotine"). One drug powerfully reinforces or encourages the use of the other. There is a similar connection, of course, between the pleasure of eating and the pleasure of drinking coffee — at breakfast, at morning break, at lunch, and so forth. Thus, in an addictive person, caffeine addiction and sugar addiction can become closely bound together. Indeed, the addictive ties between caffeine addiction and other specific daily activities — even nonaddictive activities — can become so strong that some people find they cannot get to sleep at night until they have had their final cup of coffee before retiring.

Like the craving for cigarettes, the craving for coffee at first glance might seem to be a fairly minor, relatively innocuous desire that costs little to satisfy and brings about no apparent or immediate ill effects. It is only when we stand back objectively and ask ourselves why a mature adult should need to gratify an emotional or physical craving eight, ten, or twelve times a day that we begin to see caffeine use in its true perspective — not as a pleasant, sociable habit, but as an entrenched addiction.

Caffeine Withdrawal

Like any other addicting drug, caffeine produces characteristic withdrawal symptoms when the supply is suddenly terminated. Most caffeine addicts take pains to avoid situations where they cannot get the requisite amount of caffeine to feed their habit at the right time. That's not hard to do in our society, but for those who do get into such a situation, or are deliberately discontinuing caffeine, withdrawal symptoms are subtle but distinctly recognizable. Most caffeine addicts, when deprived of caffeine for a few hours, first respond with a feeling of nervousness, irritability, and generalized vague discomfort. They usually develop a nagging headache, accompanied by a sense of just dragging around, or not being able to get started, and a feeling of blues or depression. The listlessness may be quite marked, far more than one might ordinarily feel on an "off" day. With continued abstinence these symptoms persist for a day or two in some people, for a week or more in others, before gradually subsiding. For some the headache may recur daily, to some degree or another, for as long as a week. A single cup of coffee will relieve it almost miraculously, within minutes.

It is interesting that most people who experience these withdrawal symptoms don't recognize them as such. They soon discover, however, that an appropriate dose of caffeine will clear up virtually *all* the discomforts in a matter of fifteen minutes or so. Thus it is accurate to say, for a caffeine addict, that taking caffeine at regular intervals is as much a matter of forestalling withdrawal symptoms as it is seeking any sense of well-being or pleasure from the caffeine-containing beverage.

Does caffeine addiction really matter? Is there anything serious to worry about — or to try to do anything about? It seems like such a trivial thing, at first glance. Surely if it were seriously dangerous or damaging, medical science would have told us by now. So people happen to enjoy a little lift from their coffee in the morning or throughout the day — so what? What is there to fuss about?

The answer, of course, is that we don't know what there is to fuss about — and that's the problem. We are talking about a widespread addiction to a drug that has a steady, relentless driving effect on heart rate, blood pressure, and cerebral activity as well as on blood sugar, fat levels, and gastric acid. No one knows how much the effect of that drug, in heavy, long-term use, may ultimately contribute to heart damage, pathological high blood pressure, or stroke; nor do we know what effect the recurrent cerebral stimulation of caffeine in high dosage over the long term may have upon people's minds. It is distressing to consider that there may be multitudes of people out there with significant drug-distortion of their thinking, ranging from mild depression to outright paranoia, related to heavy use of caffeine, which no doctor has ever really looked for or diagnosed. We do know that those two mental aberrations — depression and paranoia — are highly characteristic of continued use of the more potent central nervous system stimulants, the amphetamines and cocaine, as we will see in later chapters. Are they characteristic of caffeine too? Maybe yes, maybe no — but surely, heavy and long-term use of caffeine can't be beneficial. Who needs an addiction to a foreign chemical that alters our normal biochemistry?

So how much caffeine is too much, and who needs to worry? Probably the person who drinks only one or two cups of coffee or tea a day, or an occasional can of caffeine-laden soda, does not have a caffeine addiction worth worrying about. Most such people probably are not addictive at all, and aren't addicted to caffeine. On the other hand, those who drink caffeine beverages regularly each morning or all day, or take caffeine tablets in order to perk up, should at least consider that they are probably firmly addicted to caffeine and could do well without it. They might find that breaking this addiction pays off in less confused or distorted thinking, less depression, less paranoia, fewer headaches, and markedly lower levels of anxiety and tension. Surely they will be healthier in the long run without a drug that significantly affects blood pressure, heart rate, gastric secretions, blood levels of sugar and fat, and the functioning of the brain.

Treating Caffeine Addiction

Most people can eliminate a caffeine addiction by themselves without any outside help. The self-treatment program outlined in detail in chapter 5 will be helpful. Here are some additional pointers specific to caffeine to help make the process as easy and uncomplicated as possible.

1. *Make a list of the benefits you will enjoy* by getting off a caffeine-dominated daily routine. Everybody's list will be different, but yours will probably include most of the following:

- freedom from the tyranny of having to have coffee at a certain time of day no matter what;
- an end to nervousness, jitteriness, and the keyed-up feeling characteristically brought on by caffeine, and possibly less pain in the form of backaches or headaches;
- elimination of frequent caffeine-withdrawal headaches that pop up whenever caffeine is not fed into the system;
- a slower, steadier pulse and a lower blood pressure, and thus a decreased vulnerability to strokes;
- better sleeping at night;
- a feeling of quiet well-being and vigor unrelated to any chemical stimulant and relief from depressive episodes;
- easier weight control, especially if your coffee drinking is always associated with sugar-food snacks, heavy desserts, and so forth (in many people caffeine causes a craving for sugar and other foods because it lowers the blood sugar);
- a sense of self-satisfaction at having eliminated an addiction that was at best useless and at worst harmful;
- a considerable saving of coffee money that you can now spend for something you really want, need, or enjoy.

2. *Know your enemy.* Caffeine is present in so many common beverages and commodities that you will need to be knowledgeable about what items contain caffeine in order to completely avoid or eliminate it. Study the list provided on pp. 132–135 until you are thoroughly familiar with it, so that you will always know what to avoid.

3. *Discontinue the caffeine completely and all at once.* Pick the day that seems best — a day with as few anticipated pressures as possi-

ble — and do it. Alter your daily routine enough that caffeine at certain accustomed times isn't missed as much as it might be. The alterations can be simple. If, for example, you normally linger in bed in the morning with your first and second cups of coffee before getting up, change this by getting up as soon as you awaken and taking a hot shower; then, after dressing, have a cup of hot water with lemon juice. This will be just as stimulating as the coffee, and far more normal physiologically. If you usually have two more cups of coffee and a Danish for breakfast, change that to an egg and wheat toast and a glass of unsweetened grapefruit juice. Carry caffeine-free soda or milk or herb tea bags for your morning "coffee" break, and plan a brief walk at lunchtime to break the usual coffee-or-soda-and-chocolate-doughnuts routine. No rigid patterns can be set out for everybody — what you do will be up to you — but whatever you normally used to do, do something a little different, and have it planned in advance.

Patients always ask if they can have decaffeinated coffee, and I usually say, "Yes, for a short time." Certainly, 3 mg of caffeine is a vast improvement over 150 mg per cup. Many initially cannot imagine giving up coffee all at once, and decaffeinated coffee helps as a crutch. I point out, however, that they must eventually give up decaffeinated coffee as well, even though it has just a small amount of caffeine.

Withdrawal symptoms probably will bother you the first day or two, so don't be surprised if they do. They will seem to be demanding that you go back to your caffeine routine at once, without delay — but they are really telling you that your body is getting rid of the drug; if it weren't running short, it wouldn't be screaming. The vitamin C and glutamine help tremendously to reduce withdrawal and craving. For the nervousness and jitteriness of withdrawal, milk can be surprisingly helpful; it contains an amino acid, tryptophan, which acts as a gentle natural sedative. Or you may take 500 mg tryptophan tablets, three or four at a time. Bear in mind that most of the "nervous" withdrawal symptoms will be as bad as they are going to be by the end of the first day and will be absent or much diminished by the second and subsequent days. Fatigue, another common withdrawal symptom, will also go away with time.

Caffeine-withdrawal headache may be more bothersome. We know that certain kinds of headaches, such as migraines, occur when the small arteries in the brain become suddenly dilated; caffeine-related headaches are probably similar. Part of the effect of caffeine is to shrink or contract small arteries in the body, including the brain, and it is reasonable to assume that these vessels react by dilating when caffeine is withdrawn. Whatever the source of the headaches, they tend to appear daily for the first two or three days after caffeine is withdrawn, and in some people they can recur persistently for up to a week or so. These headaches are generalized and feel like your brain is too big for your skull; most people find them more annoying than severe, and they can be controlled with a mild caffeine-free analgesic, such as aspirin or Tylenol.

A few other pointers will be helpful during the withdrawal period. I think vitamin C is very important at this time. Obtain a supply of vitamin C crystals containing 4,000 mg (or 4 g) of vitamin C per teaspoon, and take one teaspoonful mixed in water or juice every two to four waking hours during withdrawal. Continue this dosage for a period of five days. If diarrhea should occur, as it occasionally does, cut the dosage in half but don't reduce the frequency of the doses. In addition, refrain from eating sugars and sugar-foods while detoxing from caffeine, but eat *small* snacks of protein foods, vegetables, or whole grain breads every two hours, as advised in the diet and nutrition section of chapter 5.

CAFFEINE CONTENT OF SELECTED ITEMS

	Average values (mg/serving)
Coffee beverage	
brewed, ground	85/cup
percolated	110/cup
dripolated	146/cup
instant	60/cup
instant, decaffeinated	3/cup

Tea beverage (bagged and loose teas, brewed five minutes)	
reg., bagged	46/cup
reg., loose	40/cup
green, bagged	31/cup
green, loose	35/cup
Darjeeling, loose	28/cup
Oolong, bagged	40/cup
Oolong, loose	24/cup
Japanese panfried, loose	21/cup
Japanese green, loose	20/cup
instant	30/cup
Cocoa, hot chocolate beverage	13/cup
Cola beverage	47/12 oz.
Coffee, instant or powder	
Brim, freeze-dried, decaffeinated	3/tsp.
Café Français	30/tsp.
Café Vienna	32/tsp.
Maxim, freeze-dried	61/tsp.
Mellow Roast (coffee and grain)	56/tsp.
Minicad, freeze-dried, decaffeinated American Hospital Supply	0/tsp.
Nescafé, Nestlé	59/tsp.
Orange Cappuccino	33/tsp.
Sanka	3/tsp.
Sanka, freeze-dried, decaffeinated	3/tsp.
Suisse Mocha	29/tsp.
Taster's Choice, Nestlé	59/tsp.
Taster's Choice, decaffeinated, Nestlé	5/tsp.
Yuban	56/tsp.
Coffee, instant beverage	
Hills Brothers	189/cup
Tea beverage	
Bigelow Constant Comment	31/cup
Boston's 99½% caffeine-free tea	9/cup
Brooke Bond Red Rose	54/cup
Canterbury	54/cup

Grand Union	48/cup
Harvest Day	45/cup
Jackson of Piccadilly Earl Grey	61/cup
Lipton, bagged	54/cup
Lipton, loose	51/cup
MJB	62/cup
Nestlé, instant iced with lemon flavor	42/cup
Our Own	60/cup
Pantry Pride	45/cup
Royal Jewel	44/cup
Salada	59/cup
Stewart's	53/cup
Swee-touch-nee	47/cup
Tender Leaf	66/cup
Tetley	61/cup
Twinings English	61/cup
White Rose	55/cup

Chocolate beverage, dry mix

choc. powder, instant dry, Hershey	10/tbsp.
cocoa, dry, Hershey	10/tbsp.
cocoa, instant, Hershey	10/tbsp.
cocoa mix, instant	9/tbsp.
cocoa mix, instant, Carnation	13/pkg.
Instant Breakfast, choc., Carnation	tr/pkg.
milkshakes, choc. malt, Delmark	tr/oz.
cocoa mix (water), Carnation	14/cup

Carbonated beverages

Coca-Cola	65/12 oz.
Diet-Rite Cola	33/12 oz.
Dr Pepper	61/12 oz.
Dr Pepper, sugar-free	54/12 oz.
Mountain Dew	55/12 oz.
Mr. Pibb	57/12 oz.
Pepsi-Cola	43/12 oz.
Pepsi-Cola, sugar-free	36/12 oz.
Pepsi Light	36/12 oz.

Royal Crown Cola	34/12 oz.
Royal Crown with a twist	21/12 oz.
Royal Crown Cola, sugar-free	33/12 oz.
Tab, sugar-free	45/12 oz.

Drugs

Anacin	32/tablet
Anacin 3	32/tablet
Maximum strength Anacin	32/tablet
DeWitt's Pill for Backache and Joint Pains	not specified
Dexatrim	200/capsule
Dristan Decongestant/Antihistamine/ Analgesic	16.2/tablet
Goody's Headache Powders	32.5/packet
No-Dōz	100/tablet
Vanquish	33/capsule
Vivarin	200/capsule
Cafergot	100/tablet
Esgic	40/tablet
Fiorinal	40/tablet
Soma Compound	32/tablet
Synalgos	30/tablet
A.P.C.	32/tablet
Midol	32/capsule
Excedrin	65/tablet

Miscellaneous (all contain significant amounts of caffeine)
  concentrated coffees (espresso, Greek, Turkish, Middle Eastern)
  coffee-chicory blends
  yerba maté — large quantities of caffeine in this common South American herbal tea

Note: Most cola drinks and other soft drinks, except those specifically advertised as "caffeine-free," are likely to contain significant quantities of caffeine, whether or not the label lists caffeine as an ingredient. This includes common carbonated fruit sodas, lemon-lime sodas, orange sodas, and so on, to which caffeine is often added. Because so many such beverages do contain caffeine with or without labeling, all should be avoided except those that specify they are caffeine-free. Brands currently advertised as "caffeine-free" include such products as 7-Up and Pepsi Free.

CAFFEINE-FREE BEVERAGES

Hot water with lemon juice — an absolutely safe alternative

Fruit juices — canned, frozen, or fresh unsweetened juices in small portions, as noted in chapter 5 in the diet and nutrition section

Milk

Many herb teas, but check the label to be sure they do not contain black or green tea as well as the herbs

Soft drinks labeled and advertised as "caffeine-free"

"No caffeine added" doesn't necessarily mean the same thing — the cola extract that goes into cola drinks may contain caffeine unless it has been actively removed. At present writing, 7-Up and Pepsi Free are the major soft-drink brands that are caffeine-free, but more are appearing on the market all the time because of their popularity.

Kool-Aid or other noncarbonated soft drinks with artificial sweetening, sugar-free

Sparkling grape juice, apple juice (nonalcoholic)

Nonalcoholic beer

The authors are grateful for permission to reprint the above chart from Bowes and Church's *Food Values of Portions Commonly Used.* Thirteenth Edition, revised by Jean A. T. Pennington and Helen Nichols Church, Harper & Row Publishers, New York, 1980.

9

Nicotine

Today, twenty years after the first Surgeon General's report identifying cigarette smoking as the major cause of lung cancer and other grave health conditions, there are still over thirty-five million active cigarette smokers in the United States and twenty times that number (or more) the world over. No single fact could speak more eloquently to the stubborn addicting power of nicotine, the main addicting chemical to be found in tobacco smoke. During the same twenty years, however, it is estimated that nearly as many Americans have *quit* smoking, most of them permanently, as the active smokers remaining. This fact suggests that multitudes of people can and do break their addiction to nicotine every year; and most of them do it completely on their own, without outside help from anyone.

Nicotine Addiction

Nicotine is not the only harmful ingredient in tobacco, but it is the major addicting substance present and accounts for the powerful addictive bonds that tie tobacco users of all sorts to their habits. Nicotine is most commonly taken into the body through the lungs from the inhaled smoke of cigarettes, cigars, or pipe tobacco, but it can just as well be absorbed through the mucous membrane of the nose, cheek, tongue, or mouth, or even dissolved in the saliva and

137

swallowed, as a result of pipe or cigar smoking, tobacco chewing, or snuff dipping. In any case, the nicotine absorbed from one source is every bit as addicting as that absorbed from any other source. Therefore, although for convenience we will be referring to "cigarette smokers" and "stopping smoking" throughout this chapter, we really mean "tobacco users of all sorts" and "abstaining from tobacco in any form."

Like other addicting substances we have discussed, nicotine is one of the substances capable of temporarily satisfying the physiological hunger an addictive person suffers because of an inborn metabolic error. Nicotine is an odd drug, however, with certain unique qualities all its own. Chemically, it is a plant alkaloid, similar in structure to the opium narcotics derived from the poppy, but in its physiological actions it resembles caffeine in certain ways. Even in small doses nicotine is a deadly poison — it is the major ingredient in a potent insecticide — but in the microscopically tiny doses obtained from cigarette smoking and other tobacco uses it is a powerful heart stimulant, a central nervous system stimulant, and an active blood vessel constrictor, all at once. It goads the heart into excessive activity while simultaneously cutting down the heart's blood supply and driving the blood pressure up. At the same time it has marked effects on the central nervous system, making the user feel momentarily more alert, brighter, more ready for action. Interestingly, none of these nicotine effects seems to diminish with continued use. The drug remains just as active after the smoker's ten-millionth cigarette as after his first. A beginning smoker often feels a "rush" of dizziness and a slight wave of nausea due to the poisoning effect of the nicotine, but the body adapts quickly to these small doses, so the smoker's awareness of these unpleasant effects passes very rapidly — within a couple of days — if he or she continues to smoke.

Nicotine, even in very tiny doses, is probably the most addictive substance known. No one knows why so little of this particular addicting substance can exercise such a firm grip on the user, but certainly nicotine's unique chemical nature must be part of the answer. Part may also lie in the fact that it is used so frequently each day by most users. It stands to reason that any addicting substance taken into the body ten, twenty, thirty, or more times a day is likely to have a potent addicting effect. Whatever the reason, nicotine's powerful addicting capacity is an indisputable part of nicotine addiction. Even a very mildly addictive person can easily become addicted in a very short time, and there is ample evidence that such a person can maintain just as active an addiction to nicotine on five cigarettes a day as on fifty. This addiction can be exceedingly difficult to break permanently; many smokers have stopped repeatedly over the years, only to have the same addiction pop up again and again, time after time.

Approaches to Quitting

Despite this singularly tenacious addiction, we know that millions of people have successfully quit tobacco use, so obviously it can be done. The question is how to go about it. As with any addiction, the key to freedom from nicotine addiction is to terminate the use of nicotine in any form immediately, completely, and permanently. There are many approaches to doing this, and all have proven at least reasonably successful for some people.

Traditionally, breaking a nicotine addiction is accomplished by the individual smoker acting on his own and unaided. The main drawback to this approach is that most of the resources for quitting have to arise from the patient, and many fail to carry through to success.

As one alternative approach, in recent years a variety of different commercial quit-smoking clinics and organizations have appeared, offering their services to help smokers quit. Some of these programs are modest in cost, others quite expensive. Most such organizations employ so-called behavior modification techniques in which a number of habit ties connecting the act of smoking with other pleasurable life activities (eating, drinking, coffee breaks, and so on) are systematically broken until smoking — at least theoretically — becomes an isolated and distasteful habit in the smoker's life. Some programs add aversion techniques deliberately intended to make smoking actively distasteful. One important advantage to these programs is that the quitting smoker usually is surrounded by a supportive group of people who are in the same boat, so that everyone is helping everyone else stay on course.

Other groups offer supportive programs as well. For example, the Seventh Day Adventist Church offers an inexpensive and effective program to quit smoking.

In addition to group approaches, various medical techniques

have been developed. Some, emphasizing the same sort of nutritional rehabilitation and vitamin therapy of value in treating any addiction, are based on valid medical rationale. Others, such as the acupuncture therapy practiced by various clinics, are available but as yet unproven.

Recently the use of a variety of antismoking aids has come into prominence. These products, in the form of lozenges or chewing gum, some sold over-the-counter and some by prescription, are touted as reducing the individual's "urge to smoke." Possibly they do, temporarily, but opinion is divided about their long-term value to the nicotine addict. The reason is simple: these products generally contain either lobeline, a close chemical cousin to nicotine, or nicotine itself. All that these substances can do is provide a substitute for the nicotine otherwise obtained from tobacco or smoking. According to one school of thought, it is not the smoking itself that the nicotine addict has to fear, but the nicotine absorbed from the tobacco smoke. Thus, it is argued, it makes little sense to use these products in order to combat nicotine addiction. Others argue that the long-established hand-and-mouth habit patterns of smoking itself are an extremely important part of the whole habit-addiction complex of tobacco smoking; these habit patterns must be broken before the patterns of smoking can be broken, and thus antismoking preparations can make it easier for the person to stop. Also, by chewing the gum instead of smoking, the person avoids the tar and all of the noxious by-products of smoke. Then, of course, the person must abstain from the gum or lozenge, which his or her addiction has readily accepted as a substitute for nicotine in the tobacco smoke. Should the smoker use cigarettes and gum at the same time, a bigger habit may be the result.

Other antismoking preparations contain ingredients to make tobacco smoke taste so bad that the smoker prefers not to smoke — or to overwhelm the senses of smell and taste so that smoking isn't enjoyable anymore. But since we know that the nicotine addict smokes not primarily for the smell or taste of the smoke but for the physiological effect of the nicotine, such products can scarcely be expected to deter anyone seriously.

One almost certain loser among the stop-smoking approaches is tapering. As we have seen with other addictions, tapering almost never works because the addicted person rarely if ever succeeds in tapering to zero — and this is certainly true of nicotine. At first glance it might seem that tapering could work well. Each dose of nicotine is very tiny, and by gradually widening the interval between doses and reducing the number, one might think the body would become progressively less dependent on the drug. Unfortunately, however, a full addiction to nicotine can easily be maintained with extremely tiny and relatively infrequent doses. Far from developing a declining dependence while tapering, the smoker, with each dose — however infrequent — merely reinforces the full addiction. The net result is that the addict who is tapering this drug virtually never actually terminates it. Somewhere along the line the smoker gets disgusted, stops tapering, remains at the low usage level achieved for a day or two, and then is right back at the former level, filling his or her waking hours with little doses of nicotine.

Some smokers accomplish some degree of tapering by using cigarettes with a lower nicotine content, but in the end they must still quit, no matter what brand they smoke.

A Program for Treatment

How well do these various approaches work? Nobody knows. Those who are "going it alone" don't sign up on any list and then report in later about how well they've done. The commercial organizations often have no long-term follow-up at all, and those that depend on telephone or mail surveys to determine their long-term success rate cannot expect to come up with statistically valid figures.

What we do know is that each of these approaches does work for some people, because people do stop smoking — probably those who develop the strongest internal motivation to terminate this difficult addiction.

Exactly which approach to quitting is likely to be best for any given person, only that person can decide. In my office, whether the person is going it alone, participating in one of the commercial clinics or programs, or actively seeing me as a patient, I have found that the patient self-help program outlined in chapter 5 is a useful guide. It is a treatment pattern people can follow on their own or with the guidance of a doctor, and there is nothing in it that will interfere in the least with any formally structured stop-smoking program. Here are some special aspects of that program as they apply specifically to treatment of nicotine addiction.

Patient Education. Probably the most important thing here is to recognize clearly and with open eyes exactly what you are dealing with. Smoking and/or nicotine addiction is not merely a messy, smelly habit, a minor annoyance, or a matter of no real significance. It is a very real addiction, and one of the most treacherous there is. The nicotine is crippling to the heart and vascular system. The tars in the smoke are a dangerous carcinogen. Don't approach treatment as a minor matter, because it isn't. You will find that your mind cooks up a lot of promises and fairy tales about "the pleasures of smoking" while you are in treatment. Ignore them and learn to laugh at them. Recognize that a little nicotine is as dangerous, in terms of addiction, as a large amount. As an addictive person, you may well have other addictions dovetailing with your nicotine addiction — caffeine addiction, sugar addiction, and alcohol addiction are perhaps the most common — and terminating those addictions simultaneously can be a great help in breaking your nicotine addiction.

Terminating. This means stopping immediately upon making your decision, completely and for good. This is by far the fastest, most effective, and most promising way to end your addiction. Don't try to make things "easier" by substituting or compromising — don't try switching from cigarettes to a pipe, cigars, chewing tobacco, or snuff; don't try "switching down" to a very low tar and nicotine cigarette. You already know why such maneuvers are traps; they all continue to supply nicotine to your system, and even the tiniest amount will simply maintain the addiction you are seeking to eliminate. Don't imagine that "sometime later" you may be able to smoke "socially," just one cigarette now and then when you want to; the pattern of nicotine addiction is stamped permanently on a template in your biochemistry, just waiting for the chance to revive again months or years later. You may control the addiction now, but that template doesn't go away and neither will your extreme vulnerability to nicotine. (This is exactly why so many nicotine addicts manage to stop their addiction for months or even years and then get right back into it again in three days after attempting "social" smoking.)

Many authorities recommend chewing gum or sucking lemon drops or treating yourself to rich meals as an aid to terminating smoking. A sugar-free gum may be helpful in this respect for a day or two, but I do not recommend candy, sugar, or sugar-foods, simply because these are also addicting substances and may serve only as a temporary substitute for nicotine. The nutrition and diet control part of the program outlined in chapter 5 is every bit as important in dealing with nicotine addiction as with any other — and will help you avoid the "inevitable" weight gain so often associated with stopping smoking. (You don't gain weight because you stop smoking; you gain weight because of what you tend to eat when you stop smoking.)

Should you keep smoking paraphernalia around the house? Why make things more difficult for yourself than necessary? Constant reminders of smoking and constant availability of smoking materials can only make termination more difficult. During those first few days you may have to deal with forty separate and distinct mini-urges to have a cigarette. I advise patients to get smoking reminders out of the house right from the beginning, even if it's only a short walk to the corner grocery to replenish them.

In picking your termination day, make things as easy for yourself as possible. Pick a time when you are not under external pressure: a weekend, for example, or between difficult jobs, or at the beginning of a vacation, but a day when you have plenty of pleasant, distracting things to do. The farther you can be from your "normal routine," which has smoking keyed into every move, the better. You are seeking to establish a *new* routine with no smoking in it at all, and the farther you can get into termination before encountering the old routines and smoking stimuli, the better.

Detoxification and Withdrawal. The detoxification program utilizing vitamin C that is outlined in chapter 5 is made to order for nicotine detox. Follow this program, using 4,000 mg (one teaspoon of vitamin C crystals) every two to four hours, for a full week, reducing the dosage to half if you are bothered by the diarrhea that sometimes occurs, but maintaining the frequency of doses.

As for withdrawal, although the nicotine will be cleared out of your body within about forty-eight hours, significant withdrawal symptoms can be expected to occur with decreasing frequency for a number of weeks. The first withdrawal symptoms, occurring within hours of your last smoking episode, include exactly the kind of internal discomfort that would ordinarily lead you to light up a cigarette: a feeling of vague distress, edginess, nervousness, and irritability. This feeling of coiled-spring tension is almost always associated with an intense craving to smoke, then and there. The best way to combat it is to forcibly turn your mind away from the thought of smoking and think of something else. These symptoms can be a recurring bother for the first two or three days after termination, but the very act of rejecting the thought, doggedly, again and again, begins to establish a new habit pattern. Within forty-eight hours or so this new habit of resisting the idea of smoking whenever it occurs will begin to pay dividends.

Other withdrawal phenomena may be less trying. Difficulty sleeping is common, but shouldn't persist for more than two or three days. Many smoking-connected activities (smoking on first arising or just before retiring, smoking with morning coffee, smoking at cocktail time, smoking after meals) can be defused by altering your routine as much as possible, perhaps radically, during this period of time. Go for a short brisk walk or take a hot shower in the morning when you would otherwise have had a morning smoke — and take another brisk walk instead of cocktail break. This would put the exercise part of the self-help program outlined in chapter 5 to creative use in combating this particular addiction. And following the nutrition and diet program to provide small meals of protein or complex carbohydrate every two hours without any huge meals so conducive to smoking will also help.

The withdrawal phenomena, especially the nervousness, discomfort, and irritability, will ease off within a few days after termination. Be prepared, however, for one characteristic aspect of nicotine addiction: the reappearance, without warning, of brief but intense episodes of cigarette-craving that suddenly may assail you weeks, months, or even years after your termination date. These episodes can be triggered by almost anything: the smell of cigarette smoke in a room, a particularly pleasant cocktail gathering where several people are smoking, returning to a place or a situation in which you always formerly enjoyed smoking, a card game, or an intermission at a play, to cite only a few examples. Fortunately, these episodes tend to be brief, passing within a few seconds or minutes at the outside, but they are treacherous. The only thing you can do is be prepared (so that such an episode doesn't shake you up when it occurs) and simply wait for it to pass, which it will do. Some ex-smokers of many years have told me that they have never been completely free of occasional such episodes and simply have to keep their guard up — living proof, I think, that the biochemical pattern of nicotine addiction remains in waiting in the body forever, ready to be revived at a moment's notice.

Complications. As a part of withdrawal from nicotine, many people suffer a period of depression after terminating. For most this is a fairly mild and transitory degree of gloominess that passes in a couple of days, with no need for special treatment. For some, however, it can be a severe depression that tends to hang on, actively interfering with normal life activities. If this happens, or if the depression doesn't clear up quickly, see a doctor for assistance. There are safe, nonaddicting antidepressant medicines that can be very effective in terminating such a depression. There is no reason not to seek assistance if you need it; the average person withdrawing from tobacco use has enough problems breaking the addiction without having to fight depression as well.

The Chances for Success

There are simply no figures available to indicate your chances for success, no matter what approach you choose for dealing with nicotine addiction. There are not even any figures to suggest that one approach might be better than another. Regardless of the approach, some people will succeed in terminating nicotine use permanently, and some will not. Failure in an attempt does not, however, necessarily mean that you have lost the fight permanently.

According to Dr. Arden L. Snyder, who directs the smoke-cessation program in the Department of Behavioral Medicine at the Mason Clinic in Seattle, most patients who come to his smoke-cessation program have already tried, and failed, to stop smoking at least once — and in his program, about 30 percent of these patients succeed. Dr. Snyder has this further encouraging message: "Although only a small percentage permanently succeed in any given effort to stop smoking, if a person really wants to stop, he or she *will usually succeed sooner or later* — if not this time, the next time, or the next."

Even the demonstration to yourself that you can stop for a day is a step in the right direction. The next time, at least you will *know* that you can make it for a day, which you didn't really believe the first time. A determination to stop this difficult addiction, and repeated efforts to do so if repeated efforts are necessary, will ultimately lead to success.

10

Marijuana

*U*NIVERSAL" IS the word to describe marijuana. You will find it virtually any place you look, from the secret closet Gro-Lite gardens of junior high school children to the executive suites of major corporations. And wherever you find it you will also find the hallmarks of physical and social disruption. As in every addiction, it is the drug that controls the addict and not the reverse, and where marijuana is concerned, there is a superabundance of evidence to support that statement.

Consider just a few of the addictive situations that I have encountered among patients in my practice in recent months.

Much to his disgust and apprehension, Jerry K., a young college professor, was recently forced to neglect his teaching in order to defend himself in court against criminal charges of marijuana possession. While fighting a small chimney fire in his home, firemen and police found a large bag of marijuana on Jerry's living room coffee table. He and his wife were arrested for illegal possession. News reached the papers, and Jerry's university superiors were not in any way pleased by the resultant publicity. In this case it doesn't matter whether Jerry K. was a heavily entrenched addict of marijuana or was merely an occasional "recreational user." What does matter is that this unfortunate incident could result in permanent damage to Jerry K.'s scholarly career.

Recently I was invited to an attractive-sounding dinner party.

The company was promising, the dinner conversation interesting, and the prospects for a stimulating evening assured. Then, after dinner, marijuana was produced for anyone who cared to partake — just about everyone present except me — and within thirty minutes I noticed the conversation disintegrating. People began talking all at once, with nobody listening to anything. A guest would start a long sentence, pause halfway through, then ramble on disjointedly about some totally different subject. One man who had earlier conversed quite rationally now seemed largely reduced to giggling, while another person spent long minutes trying to get hold of an idea he wanted to express and finally gave up. Very soon everybody gave up on conversation and sat torpidly listening to some music. Obviously, any kind of coherent conversation or meaningful social intercourse was over for the evening. When I bid my host farewell a few minutes later, nobody else seemed to notice I was leaving.

One evening recently Tanya M., the teenage daughter of a patient of mine, left home in her boyfriend's car to go listen to music at the home of another friend, with instructions to be home by midnight. At half past one in the morning, the mother discovered that her daughter was not yet home. A phone call revealed that she had never appeared at the home of the friend. At four o'clock, as the mother was preparing to call the police, the police called her from a town two counties away. The state patrol had just apprehended the car with Tanya at the wheel, driving north at sixty miles an hour in the southbound lane of an interstate highway. She had already sent two oncoming cars and a pick-up truck into the ditch before she was finally pulled over by the patrolman.

What had happened? The story was painfully typical. The young couple had shared a joint in the car on the way to the friend's house, then gone to a beer party instead. After mixing beer and pot in large quantities for several hours, they had agreed to drive two other couples to their homes, some 120 miles and two counties away. After delivering the couples, the young man began nodding off and turned the driving over to the girl. It was then that Tanya "got confused" and steered the car onto the wrong lane of the highway.

During his first two years in high school Tom E. was a busy, active, and basically happy teenager. Then his parents began to notice some distressing changes. The boy's relationship with his mother and father, once good despite occasional parent-teenage hassles, began to deteriorate rapidly. Old friends began to disappear in favor of two or three ever-present companions. The little time Tom was at home he and his friends spent closed up in Tom's bedroom, sitting on the bed or floor listening to rock and roll music. Gradually Tom seemed more hostile and withdrawn. Homework never got done; Tom's grades declined significantly; the part-time job he had held at the local supermarket was dropped.

Tom's parents knew what was going on. Tom's bedroom reeked of marijuana. There were reports that he was arriving at school in the morning so stoned that he could hardly talk, and he remained stoned throughout the day and into the evening. One teacher said the aura of pot smoke surrounding the boy at his first-period class made her eyes water. Worst of all, however, was the almost total apathy that seemed to have seized Tom. He appeared to be interested in absolutely nothing except the currently popular music and watching movies on television. By his senior year his grades were down to mostly D's, and he never got around to college applications. After graduation (which he did not attend) he left home to take a construction job and began drifting. Only after he had moved out could his mother admit to her husband that she had been missing sizable quantities of money from her purse for over a year and simply couldn't face up to telling him or confronting the boy about it.

Marijuana is an addicting drug, a fact that many users and "experts" alike either deny or simply don't understand. Marijuana is also socially disruptive, because possession is illegal in this country and many others and can expose its users to law-enforcement harassment and even prosecution. There is a saying that one thing marijuana can do to you is put you in jail, and although this may not be as true in America today as it was a few years ago, it is very, very true elsewhere, for example, in Turkey or Mexico.

Above all, marijuana is a subtle drug, widely misunderstood, and the subject of more fairy tales, misinformation, myths, and horror stories than any other addicting substance you can name.

What, then, is this drug? Where and how did it appear on the American drug scene? What is true about it and what is misinformation? Why the controversy about it? Above all, why is it so tragically disruptive to so many people?

The Second Most Popular Intoxicant

In its most common form, marijuana (also known as pot, tea, weed, grass, dope, or a dozen other more or less descriptive and colorful street names) consists of the dried flowers and resinous young leaves from the top of the Cannabis sativa or common East Indian hemp plant. In coarse lots of marijuana, small, round, brown seeds may be intermixed together with bits of stem; in more refined lots the seeds and stems are picked out. In any form it has a characteristic pungent odor and looks a bit like dried crushed parsley or oregano. In some parts of the world, notably the Middle East and North Africa, the leaves are crushed, pressed, and packed into a dark brown, gummy, concentrated material known as hash or hashish. In most cases marijuana and hash are smoked for their intoxicant effects, but these effects can also be obtained by mixing marijuana into various food preparations and eating it.

Since the import, transport, or sale of marijuana is illegal except for limited medical use, virtually all the marijuana available comes from the street market or illicit drug traffic. The active intoxicating and addicting substances in marijuana are a group of aromatic compounds known as cannabinols, the most active being delta-tetrahydrocannabinol, or THC. The THC found in hash is approximately ten times more concentrated than in dried marijuana leaves, so that hash represents a far more concentrated form of the drug. THC has been successfully synthesized and purified sufficiently to qualify for medicinal use, but the synthesis and production are so complex and expensive that there is little pure THC available on the street market. Products sold as THC on the street are almost invariably one or another of a dozen other compounds, including dextroamphetamine, PCP (angel dust), or even cocaine.

The marijuana plant grows and flourishes in virtually any temperate or subtropical climate where there is sufficient summer heat and rain. In the 1930s it could be found growing wild as a common weed in virtually any vacant lot in the midwestern or southern United States, and since most people didn't know what it was at that time, no one gave it any particular thought. The quality or potency of marijuana varies widely, however, according to its origins and subspecies. During the 1960s the most potent marijuana reaching the United States was grown in parts of Mexico. Today Colombia and other South American countries provide large quantities of marijuana of much-sought-after quality, and other sources, including Turkey, Algeria, Southeast Asia, and China, supply their share. In the United States today large quantities are grown in California, where marijuana is reputed, probably inaccurately, to be the number one cash crop in the state. Potency of U.S.-grown marijuana is steadily increasing to extraordinary levels.

Although precise documentation is hard to come by, marijuana has almost certainly been widely used throughout the world for centuries. There is reason to believe that marijuana was used in China as early as 2700 B.C., and in India for almost as long, as an intoxicant, a medicinal, and an adjunct to religious ceremonies. In the Islamic countries — with their age-long prohibition of alcoholic beverages — marijuana and hashish, together with heroin, have been virtually the only intoxicants generally available, whether or not legally condoned, and many of the wild myths about the maddening violence-inducing effects of these drugs, particularly hashish, have arisen from Middle Eastern folklore. (The word "assassin" arose from an Arabic term, *hashshashin,* meaning "eaters of hashish.")

By the early 1930s, United States authorities in charge of drug control saw a clear and present threat of wider marijuana use in our society, and took steps to stop it. Unfortunately, the steps they took were based almost entirely upon misconceptions and deliberately cooked-up horror stories. First of all, marijuana was declared and classified as a narcotic in 1937 under the Harrison Narcotics Act, despite the fact that it had virtually no opiatelike effects at all. This classification outlawed the use, sale, or possession of marijuana except for approved research. Unsatisfied with this, the narcotics authorities deliberately conjured up blatant scare stories of reefer-crazed men, butcher knives in their hands, prowling the streets after smoking marijuana, searching out women to rape and terrify. Women were depicted as becoming enslaved to pot, leaving home and family behind, and degenerating into mere sexual vassals or prostitutes for their suppliers.

Indeed, almost every "fact" presented about marijuana in those days was false. Addiction to marijuana was described in terms of unbreakable chains and physical slavery. Horror stories were circulated about stoned college students walking out of eighth-story windows, imagining they could walk on air. A propaganda movie called "Reefer Madness," produced during this time, embodied all the worst of this nonsense; the film remained in surreptitious circulation for years. During the 1950s and 1960s, young people who saw it roared with laughter, while the older generation was simply embarrassed and chagrined at the palpable falsehoods presented from beginning to end. Certainly this campaign of deliberate nontruth about the drug did as much as anything else to lay the background for the widespread marijuana use that flowered during the late 1950s and 1960s, until marijuana became the second most popular intoxicant in the country.

The Subtle and Bewildering Effects of Marijuana

In earlier chapters we had no particular difficulty describing the physical and psychoactive effects of various addicting drugs in a few simple sentences. With marijuana, however, we run into trouble, because the effects of marijuana are of a quite different order than those of many other drugs. If the effects of a large dose of alcohol, for example, tend to be direct, speedy, and impressive, those of marijuana are slower, more diffused, far more subtle, and often thoroughly bewildering simply because those effects vary widely from individual to individual or with the particular origin or batch of marijuana used. Many users insist that a person "gets more" out of marijuana the more experience he or she has had in using it, whereas a person using the drug for the first time may claim to have felt no effect at all, particularly if that individual's previous experience has been exclusively with alcohol intoxication. The effects of marijuana are there, all right; such a person simply may not recognize them. Indeed, the person who expects an alcohol-like intoxication from marijuana is likely to be disappointed; the effects of the two drugs in general are radically different.

In order to produce any effect at all, the active ingredient in marijuana must be absorbed into the bloodstream either through the lungs by means of smoking or else through the intestinal lining when the substance is eaten. In either case, absorption is relatively slow and the effects tend to appear gradually. There may be no sudden rush or high when marijuana is smoked; gradually, over a period of fifteen to thirty minutes or more, the individual develops a feeling of mild intoxication, relaxation, loosening of inhibitions, and often a relief of depression. Accompanying this intoxication is a willingness to talk, but often the talk tends more toward free association than toward connected, related sentences. Often there is an increasing sense of lethargy, of disinterest in going anywhere or doing anything. Unlike many people intoxicated on alcohol, who become very active and aggressive, people stoned on marijuana are generally uninterested in rushing out and driving a car somewhere. They are much more content to sit on the floor, "laid back," and nod away to whatever music is being played.

Strictly speaking, marijuana is not a hallucinogenic drug — it does not create illusions or sensory perceptions of things that are not there. What it does, and often in a very striking fashion, is to alter one's perception of things that are there, so that they appear somehow strange or different. For the person stoned on pot, for example, awareness of the past or future may be impaired temporarily, so that the individual seems to be existing from moment to moment in the immediate present. There is often a definite loss of memory of the immediate past — of the past ten or fifteen seconds — so that a person who starts expressing an idea gets halfway through a sentence and then can't remember what he or she started to say.

In addition, many people experience a sharp alteration of perception of the passage of time, as though everything had suddenly been changed to slow motion. Thus a song on the record player that actually lasts for only a little over a minute seems to take fifteen or twenty minutes to complete; the lyrics of the song, normally perceived as jumbled and slurred and shouted into the microphone, seem to be stretched out so that the individual understands the words much more clearly — or imagines so. To the marijuana user, then, the enjoyment and understanding of music seem to be greatly magnified.

The distorted time sense occurring under the influence of marijuana can extend to any mental or physical activity, including driving the car. You can be driving thirty miles per hour down the highway and have the sense of soaring along at ninety, or, conversely, feel that you are creeping along at five miles per hour when you are actually driving seventy, secure in the illusion that there is an infinite amount of time to lift your foot off the gas and put it on the brake in case of emergency. Obviously, the distortions of thought and time sense common with marijuana use can be an enormous threat to the stoned driver as well as to those who might have the misfortune of encountering one on the road.

Certain other effects of marijuana also are fairly consistent. Although in high doses this drug may make some people nauseated or even cause them to vomit, in more moderate doses it often induces a sense of hunger and, in some people, seems to make ordinary food taste extraordinarily good. An ordinary hamburger is as delectable as the tenderest steak, and a baked potato has flavors that one had never before tasted. Frequently, a ravenous hunger for sweets develops, and some regular users find they gain weight as a result of these binges.

Marijuana Myths

There are still many myths circulating about marijuana, some of which have a certain basis in truth and some not. For example:

Myth: Alcohol counteracts the effects of marijuana. This is a commonly held idea, and may in fact be true, at least for some people at certain times. The intoxication associated with alcohol and that induced by marijuana are not similar — they are completely different orders of experience, and marijuana intoxication is usually much more quiet and subtle. If a person has been drinking a great deal before or during a marijuana experience, the effects of the marijuana may simply be covered up or blotted out by the alcohol.

Myth: Some people suffer "flashback" experiences with marijuana. There is no convincing evidence to support this idea. The flashback phenomenon is familiar to users of some of the more potent hallucinogenic drugs, such as LSD, or acid. It is well documented that certain people, after using one of those drugs, at some later date return to the same state of mental aberration that they experienced while using the drug, except that the recurrent mental aberration occurs without taking any more of the drug. Since the 1960s there has been a rumor that marijuana users might also experience such flashbacks. These stories may have arisen in the period of heavy drug usage of the 1960s and 1970s, during which some marijuana users doctored the marijuana with PCP (angel dust) or LSD and actually did have psychedelic experiences related to these adulterant substances that later flashed back. With marijuana alone, however, there is no evidence of a flashback phenomenon, and considering the vast numbers of people using the drug, if any such phenomenon occurred to any significant degree, it should now be common knowledge. Flashbacks probably are related to a post-drug depressive episode that follows the new pathways found under the influence of psychedelic drugs.

Myth: Marijuana users automatically graduate to heroin use. There is no evidence to back up this scare story. It is true, however, that marijuana is an illegal drug that must be obtained from street sources, where heroin may also be available. There can be no doubt that many people using marijuana may be introduced to heroin or cocaine or both by the dealers they contact in order to obtain marijuana. In addition, as we have seen, addictive persons (including most heavy marijuana users) are much more vulnerable to becoming addicted to any addictive substance they may encounter than are nonaddictive persons. But the marijuana itself does not make the user "weaker" or more vulnerable to any other drug, nor is there any natural pattern of escalation.

Myth: Marijuana is a fantastic aphrodisiac. How much of this reputation is illusory and how much is valid is highly debatable. Marijuana, like alcohol, is a central nervous system depressant, and it ought to blunt or suppress the actions of the nervous system that transmit sexual sensations. Indeed, many marijuana users report exactly this effect. Like the alcohol user, the stoned marijuana user tends to be lethargic and slowed down and to drift off to sleep. On the other hand, the release of inhibitions, the stretched-out time sense, and the tendency to concentrate upon the sensation of the immediate moment can, in some persons, create the impression of enhanced sexual performance or response. Also, with temporary memory loss of the past and future, old sexual inhibitions may be eliminated, allowing more complete sexual enjoyment. Whatever the case, it is clear that marijuana does not act as an aphrodisiac consistently for everyone who uses it.

In discussing all these effects, we must bear in mind that people are different and marijuana is different from one lot to the next. Marijuana taken from different batches from different points of origin, or even from different parts of the same plant, can have greater or lesser effect in virtually any area, and individual users may well respond to one effect more than another. Even attempts to "standardize" marijuana effects by using purified medicinal grade THC have been largely unsuccessful. When used to combat the nausea and vomiting following chemotherapy, for example, responses to THC have been extremely varied. One person achieves excellent control of nausea and vomiting without any undesirable side effects, whereas another using exactly the same dose of the same preparation experiences little or no control of the nausea and vomiting and suffers a distasteful high as well. It is hardly any wonder that the individual responses to the raw product vary so widely from person to person.

Marijuana effects will last anywhere from an hour and a half up to seven or eight hours, depending on the quantity smoked and the amount of the active ingredient in the particular sample used. As the effect wears off, lethargy and torpor tend to overtake the user. Most people experience a period of sound sleep from which they awaken without any sign of hangover, a widely touted advantage over alcohol.

What about side effects and damage to the body? There is evidence to suggest that the use of marijuana produces permanent damage to various parts of the body, but the research is not complete or conclusive at this point. For example, the toxic effects of marijuana smoke on the lungs is believed to be much greater than those of cigarette smoke. The relationship of this drug to lung cancer is still being studied. There is evidence that it causes a decrease in sperm production in men as well. Many effects of marijuana on the body are under study at this time.

Addiction to Marijuana

Is this drug really addicting? Or is the idea of "getting hooked" on marijuana just another of the scare stories that have been deliberately and falsely perpetuated about the drug? The answer is clear and inarguable. As we saw in chapter 3, addiction to a chemical is definable and identifiable. We defined addiction as "the compulsive and out-of-control use of any chemical substance that can produce recognizable and identifiable unpleasant withdrawal symptoms when use of the substance is stopped." There is no question that a great many marijuana users fit this definition of addiction. These are addictive people who use marijuana regularly, steadily, usually daily, often almost continuously — a compulsive, uncontrolled use that has made the drug a major feature of their life's pattern.

This is not to say that everyone who uses marijuana is addicted to it. There are many marijuana users, including some who use it repeatedly or more or less regularly, who are not addicted, never have been, and probably never will be. Most of these people are nonaddictive individuals who are not particularly vulnerable to addiction of any kind. They may be using it because of their association with an addictive person. Generally, nonaddictive persons are not interested in using any addicting drug extensively.

As we saw in chapter 3, addictive persons have an inborn, inherited flaw or defect in the way carbohydrates are metabolized in their bodies. One of the common manifestations of this inborn metabolic error is that these people suffer a more or less continuous physiological hunger that is difficult to quiet or satiate. For many such people, eating sugar can provide a temporary degree of relief from their physiological hunger, and they become addicted to it. But a variety of other chemicals, not necessarily related to sugar at all — including marijuana — can provide brief temporary relief from the internal craving these people have.

In addition, a great many people with the inborn metabolic error also suffer from depression. Sugar and other addicting substances such as marijuana often provide at least short-lived relief from depression as well as from the physiological hunger we have been discussing, some more than others.

Many such persons get stoned on arising in the morning, go to work or school stoned, remain stoned in the evening, and go to bed stoned. Others use the drug only after work or after school, but virtually always use it at these times. Still others don't use the drug at all during the week but get stoned on Friday afternoon and stay stoned until Monday morning. The individual details of addiction may vary, but the pattern of drug use is uncontrolled — a matter not of choice but of compulsion. Obtaining the drug becomes a matter of overriding importance. Because remaining stoned a great portion of the day or week requires time and is disabling, these people tend to drop nondrug social contacts, sporting activities, or scholastic efforts and devote their major time and attention to their addiction. As with every other addiction, this addiction must be taken care of first. Also, as we will see below, when the compulsive, out-of-control marijuana user is deprived of the drug, he or she encounters distinctive withdrawal symptoms unpleasant enough to encourage continued use just to avoid withdrawal, the other key hallmark of addiction.

Although we know that people get addicted because of their addictiveness, they give many reasons for their drug use. One fifteen-year-old explained his heavy and constant marijuana use very simply: "It feels good." Another high school student I treated said he was using marijuana to escape from frustration — the frustration of dull, boring classes, of difficult social adjustments, of worrying about what to do when high school was over, of emerging sexual feelings with no adequate outlets, and of deteriorating relations with his parents. Actually, he was both addictive and depressed, and the marijuana was probably treating his depression rather than frustration. Other users rationalize that marijuana adds an element of sparkle or creativity to their lives that would not be there otherwise, which is another way of saying that it relieves their depression. One of my patients, a writer, imagined that marijuana added greatly to the creativity and imagination of his work. This is debatable, but numerous artists have maintained that drugs open their minds to new pathways. In studies, this is not demonstrable.

It is probably in young people of junior high and high school age that the most unfortunate aspects of marijuana use and addiction are most clearly discernible. Many are in a finely balanced period of transition and social tension, seeking to become strong, independent individuals while still forced to depend upon their parents for support and remain subject to their discipline and demands. Marijuana seems to alleviate the conflicts and depression so common at this age. It tends to cause adolescents to lose their motivation and drive for accomplishment. It prevents the student from learning, since memory is impaired, and the mind jumps around with free association and distractions. They don't learn anything, and they don't care that they don't learn anything. With steady marijuana use at this time, the dropout syndrome becomes abundantly evident among these young people at home and at school. They end up without any goals at all, beyond today.

For addicted marijuana users, marijuana becomes the primary focus. They want to keep on using it more and more often to the exclusion of anything else. Very few addicted young people are ever found in the upper 10 percent of their classes, or even in the upper 50 percent.

The withdrawal symptoms that occur when marijuana use is suddenly terminated are considerably different in nature from those associated with heroin or other addicting drugs, and this can be confusing. Indeed, there are heavy marijuana users who claim that there are no withdrawal symptoms, but this is not true. The symptoms of marijuana withdrawal are simply quieter, more subtle, and different in kind from those related to other drugs. Just as marijuana use seems to affect the head more than the body, the withdrawal symptoms seem more related to the head than to the body. Patients in treatment time and again describe the same pattern of disturbances. When forced to come down from marijuana and abstain, these people tend to become what they call "spacy" — distracted, muddled, confused, and unable to cope well with the ordinary demands of life. Many become depressed, feel shaky inside, and have trouble eating and sleeping; virtually all of them suffer from acute anxiety. They get scared. They become seized with the idea that things are falling apart, that something frightening is going on and they don't know what it is.

Sooner or later a lot of marijuana addicts want to stop using pot for a variety of reasons. The most common is simply that the drug is interfering with their lives. They find it very expensive; it takes up an enormous amount of time; it interferes more and more with other activities, especially productive activities; it creates stresses on the job, at home, in interpersonal relations, and keeps people too much out of touch with reality for too long. Many who choose to terminate their addiction can succeed on their own, but there are some special problems and hazards to be aware of along the way.

Dealing with Marijuana Addiction

Breaking away from marijuana use involves exactly the same basic steps as breaking away from any other addicting substance. First there must be a firm commitment to discontinue use. Once abstinence has begun, there is a period of detoxification, and withdrawal symptoms must be dealt with as they occur. Substitute addictions must be avoided and the body rehabilitated with a rational nutrition and exercise program. Special problems, such as depression, must be anticipated and treated as necessary. Finally, new activities and friends that are unassociated with use of the drug may need to be developed. These basic steps are discussed in detail in chapter 5, but certain points are particularly pertinent to marijuana addiction.

Commitment to Abstain. A solid commitment to abstain from the drug at once, completely and permanently, is every bit as important with marijuana as with any other drug — but in the case of marijuana, the road to abstinence can be booby-trapped in a thousand different ways. For one thing, for most marijuana users, the commitment to abstain can't really be made privately, as it might in the case of a cigarette smoker or an alcoholic. Marijuana is widely perceived as a social drug to be shared and used with others, and very few users, even entrenched addicts, use it alone. They have dozens of friends who will not seriously consider that someone wants to stop using marijuana and stay off it. Those friends will turn up on your doorstep with a brand new supply of very fine stuff to share, or an invitation to gather at somebody else's place for a laid-back evening, and the temptation to just go along with the crowd can be very strong. One must take a look at these friends and activities and decide what is most important. Some people make a commitment to quit despite continued friendship with users, and they fulfil this commitment.

The motivation to abstain from marijuana can be further undermined simply by the lack of alternative interests, goals, and directions that has evolved during a period of heavy marijuana use. Many users, especially young people of junior high or high school age, have spent a period of two or three years during which marijuana has provided the chief pleasure and direction in their lives, helping them to resolve (or, more likely, evade) their problems. For those who have turned away from scholarship, sports, and normal social activities and made marijuana the central pillar of their lives, it can be frightening to try to set that pillar aside and look for ways to reenter the mainstream of life.

All this is not to say that a firm commitment to abstain is impossible, but outside pressures and forces can make it difficult, and a person needs to be prepared in advance to withstand them. More than a mere whim is needed to carry a person through this essential step in treatment. The addict must recognize something important to be gained that is being lost because of marijuana use — something important enough to inspire abandonment of the drug. Each person must lean heavily on the real motivation to be found in his or her own life. For example, it is unlikely to do any good to ground teenagers, attempt to isolate them from their marijuana-associated friends, try to force them to resume studying, or drag them to a doctor. The youngsters must see for themselves the importance of building a real-world future, which marijuana is preventing them from doing. Some users simply become bored with the marijuana scene. Others (although probably relatively few) require some jarring brush with authorities, some alarming experience with the world of drug dealers, or a close encounter with disaster in an automobile to wake them up. Sometimes youth guidance clinics, encounter groups such as Alcoholics Anonymous or Narcotics Anonymous open the door. Each person must seize the motivation closest at hand and use it to the hilt.

Detoxification. Detoxification, as always, begins with abstinence. In the case of marijuana, however, detoxification is unusually prolonged. The cannabinols from marijuana are stored in the fatty tissues of the body and are cleared away very slowly. Half the amount of THC still remains in the body five to seven days after smoking a single joint, and regular and heavy users carry around a prodigious load of the stuff in their bodies that must be eliminated. As described in chapter 5, a detox program using vitamin C powder (sodium ascorbate) in doses of 4,000 mg (one teaspoon) mixed in fruit juice, milk, or water every two to four hours while awake during the day will help accomplish detoxification as speedily as possible; but in marijuana cases the program should be continued for a period of seven to fourteen days as needed.

Withdrawal. As we have seen, withdrawal symptoms associated with marijuana are more a matter of emotional and mental distortion than of body distress, but are nevertheless physiological. For a great many people abstaining from marijuana, withdrawal is perceived as a vague sense of anxiety and disquiet, difficulty orienting to the real world, which can be all the more difficult for the individual whose normal sensorium has been heavily and continually altered by marijuana for a prolonged period of time. Under such circumstances the withdrawal symptoms may be equated in the user's mind with "the normal world," which is perceived as vaguely bad, threatening, distressing, and depressing, whereas the world of marijuana is perceived as mellow, comfortable, and undepressed. Thus the incentive is great to return to the world of marijuana, not so much to escape or avoid any perceived withdrawal symptoms as to simply "feel good again." (Bear in mind that there is nothing inconsistent about a central nervous system depressant drug such as marijuana having the effect of easing or relieving depression; the drug can simply blunt the sharp edges of depression, blot out worries and apprehensions, and make the person feel sort of drowsily "better." We will encounter this same thing later in the case of such depressant drugs as tranquilizers or sleeping pills.)

Fortunately, marijuana withdrawal is not associated with dangerous or threatening physical reactions, nor do the symptoms tend to last more than a week or two — just long enough for detoxification to be completed. Probably the most simple and physiological measures, particularly a regular exercise program and careful attention to nutritional rebuilding, are more helpful in dealing with these symptoms than is any medication.

Some Additional Pointers. As mentioned above, the nutrition and exercise programs outlined in the self-help section of chapter 5 are just as important in treatment of marijuana addiction as in treatment of any other addiction. Even though there may not be any particular overt evidence of malnutrition or physical debility, they will contribute significantly to a speedy recovery.

The appearance of a deep and tenacious depression may require a doctor's attention and medication to help counteract it. For a marijuana user in treatment, however, the problem of depression may be particularly allayed or forestalled by attention to developing new activities and new friends unassociated with drugs. We have seen that sudden abstinence from marijuana almost always means the departure of a number of drug-oriented friends, and the appearance of a lot of unoccupied time on your hands, especially at the beginning of treatment. Joining a drug-free group — something sports-oriented or church-related, or Narcotics Anonymous, to name a few — will help promote new activities and friendships.

Above all, bear in mind that there is nothing at all impossible about dealing with marijuana addiction and winning. The addictive hold of the drug on the body is much less firm than that of, say, nicotine or alcohol. Withdrawal symptoms, although annoying, don't involve marked physical distress or actual danger, and entering into new activities with new friends can provide a highly refreshing and rewarding turning point in your life.

11

The Depressant Drugs: Sleeping Pills and Tranquilizers

JOHN BROWN, as we shall call him, had a very commonplace problem when he went to the doctor: for the past six weeks or so he had been unable to sleep.

It doesn't matter what particular form his sleeplessness took. Perhaps he went to bed exhausted every night but then lay there until one o'clock in the morning, unable to drop off. It may be that he fell asleep immediately upon retiring, but then woke up abruptly at half past two in the morning and couldn't get back to sleep. Or maybe he simply dozed and woke, dozed and woke, all night long, ending up feeling more exhausted in the morning than he had when he went to bed. Many different patterns of sleeplessness plague humanity, but they all have much in common: they are highly distressing, irritating beyond words, and very difficult to live with.

For our purposes, it doesn't matter what was causing John Brown's insomnia. Possibly he was suffering through a period of extreme stress and anxiety, worrying about his job or his finances or his marriage, obsessed with apparently insoluble problems he could not get off his mind. Maybe he was in the early stages of a major depression — one of the most common symptoms of such a depression is insomnia. Perhaps John Brown was drinking too much — alcohol, as a heavily depressant drug, is often associated with sleep disturbances or insomnia. Or possibly his body was biochemically out of balance due to a badly planned diet.

Whatever the pattern of his sleeplessness and whatever the cause, John Brown went to a doctor, who tackled the insomnia problem in the traditional way. After a brief examination, he reached for his pad and wrote a prescription. "Take one of these pills at bedtime," he said. "There's enough to last you for thirty days."

John Brown went home and slept just wonderfully on the doctor's pills for about two weeks, a fact that pleased him greatly. What he didn't realize was that he may well have walked away from the doctor's office with far worse trouble than he had when he went in: a long-term, tenacious relationship with a kind of highly addicting drug that is virtually always supplied by a doctor's prescription.

We have already seen how such addicting drugs as alcohol, caffeine, and marijuana can have both physical effects and psychoactive (mind-influencing) effects on the person using them. The same is true of other drugs as well. As we will see later, for example, the opiate narcotics can blunt the perception of pain (a physical effect) and induce euphoria (a psychoactive effect).

It shouldn't be surprising, then, to find a large group of addicting drugs that act primarily as central nervous system depressants. These drugs tend to depress or blunt the higher nervous activity of the brain — to put a damper, so to speak, on brain activity — and induce a draggy, sleepy, mentally relaxed state in the people who use them. With some of these drugs, central nervous system depression is the major effect they have; sometimes called "sedative-hypnotic" drugs, they have been widely used as sleep-inducers, or sleeping pills. Other drugs in the group, the so-called tranquilizers, are used primarily to calm down tension and anxiety during waking hours, with other forms of central nervous system depression (somnolence or respiratory depression, for example) appearing as side effects. These drugs were designed literally to tranquilize symptoms of nervousness and agitation.

Virtually all of these depressant drugs, in addition to their depression of central nervous system activity, are potentially addicting to addictive individuals. They are commonly known as downers (depressants), and their great popularity is reflected by the active illegal drug market that exists for them. Their addicting capacity has become well known in recent years, but because they are still widely and freely prescribed for everyday patients by multitudes of doctors, they present a particularly insidious threat of addiction to any addictive person.

That threat is real. Like alcohol (itself a depressant drug), caffeine, marijuana, and other addicting substances discussed earlier, the depressant drugs are able to satisfy temporarily and partially the continuing physiological hunger suffered by the addictive person as a result of an inborn error or disturbance in carbohydrate metabolism. Because of their nervous-system-depressing actions, they can help make these individuals feel more "normal" or "relaxed" for a while, however briefly. When sleeplessness is part of the person's physiological distress, these drugs are made to order — and one of the vast attractions of the tranquilizers in particular has always been their apparent ability to ameliorate such recurrent and unexplained symptoms as headaches, backaches, palpitations, and shakiness — the sort of symptoms of addictiveness we discussed in chapter 3.

In addition, the depressant drugs can help, at least temporarily, to relieve the depression that so often seems to be part of the addictive state. Many people are confused by this. Why would a person take a depressant drug to relieve depression? The confusion lies mostly in the terms we're using. Clinical depression — a depressed mental state as a symptom — refers to a depressed *mood,* a feeling of excessive gloominess or grayness of attitude, of inner pain, of uselessness, worthlessness, or helpless worry. These are inner feelings or emotional symptoms. Depressant drugs, on the other hand, have a direct chemical action on the brain cells, slowing down the transmission of electrical information. These drugs may temporarily relieve depressed individuals' gloom and grayness by making them feel more sleepy, relaxed, and less tense, calming their fruitless worrying, and quieting their minds from thinking so hard about how terribly hopeless everything is. In short, for a brief while the depressant drugs can make depressed people feel better and thus ease their depression.

As addiction to the depressant drugs develops, their use tends to be less for the original specific symptoms and becomes more compulsive. Addicts keep taking the sleeping pills not because they can't sleep, but to be sure that they do, and to avoid the sleeplessness they fear will recur if they stop. Tranquilizers are taken to maintain a state of "feeling good," not to treat some specific symptom. Use becomes uncontrolled: fearing that the doctor may not renew the prescription next time, the patient sees a different doctor, maybe two others, and walks away with reserve prescriptions. Final proof of addiction comes when the patient abstains for one reason or another and clearly identifiable withdrawal symptoms appear. In some respects, sleeping pills and tranquilizers have much in common. Both groups are depressant drugs. Tranquilizers are frequently used in lieu of sleeping pills, and at least one (flurazepam, trade name Dalmane) was developed specifically for use as a nighttime sedative and sleeping pill. These two groups of drugs do have significant differences, however, especially in their patterns of addiction and the treatment problems they present, so for clarity we will discuss them as two separate groups.

Sleeping Pills

This group of drugs includes the barbiturate sedatives; chloral hydrate and a number of other volatile and aromatic sleeping drugs in the same general chemical family; and a number of newer synthetic sleeping drugs. They are all potent central nervous system depressants intended primarily for use as bedtime sedative-hypnotics

ADDICTING SLEEPING PILLS

Barbiturates

Chemical name	Common trade names	Common street names
amobarbital	Amytal (Lilly) Tuinal (Lilly) (combined one-half and one-half with secobarbital)	
aprobarbital	Alurate	
butabarbital	Butisol (Wallace)	
butalbital or talbutal	Fiorinal (Sandoz) (in combination with other drugs)	
hexobarbital	Somnalert, Cyclonal	

mephobarbital	Mebaral	
pentobarbital	Nembutal (Abbott)	"yellowbirds" or "yellowjackets"
phenobarbital	Luminal (Winthrop-Breon) SK-Phenobarbital (Smith, Kline and French)	"goofballs" (in common with all barbiturates)
secobarbital	Seconal (Lilly) Tuinal (Lilly) (combined one-half and one-half with amobarbital)	"redbirds" "reds"

Chloral hydrate and similar drugs

chloral hydrate	Noctec (Squibb) Dormal (Ingraham) Somnos (Merck, Sharp and Dohme)
ethchlorvynol	Placidyl (Abbott)

Others

carbromal	Carbrital (Parke-Davis)	
ethinamate	Valmid (Dista)	
flurazepam	Dalmane (Roche)	
glutethimide	Doriden (USV Pharmaceutical)	
methaqualone	Quaalude (Rorer)	"Qs" or "ludes"
methyprylon	Noludar (Roche)	

NONADDICTING OVER-THE-COUNTER SLEEP AIDS

various antihistamines   representative products include Compōz, Nervine, Nytol, Sominex, Unisom or sleeping pills, and except for a few less potent sleep aids sold over the counter, they are legitimately available by prescription only. On pp. 166–167 you will find a listing of many of these drugs by their chemical names, common trade names, and, where appropriate, street names.

The great-grandfather of the barbiturate family, phenobarbital, has been known and used for three quarters of a century. For years before tranquilizers were even heard of, phenobarbital was widely used as a daytime sedative. It is still used today in small daytime doses to block excess electrical activity in the brain in many people who suffer grand mal seizures or epilepsy. It was also commonly used to reduce the overall stress level in people suffering, for example, from severe heart failure. And reduce stress it did; people taking this drug typically were sedated, slowed down mentally, and lethargic. The drug's addicting capability became well known very early, however, and doctors soon became cautious about prescribing phenobarbital except for the specific sort of indications mentioned.

Other barbiturate drugs were developed in hope of finding one that was less addicting — a hope that was never realized. Pentobarbital was and still is widely used, together with other drugs, for inducing surgical anesthesia. Still others, including secobarbital and amobarbital, are longer-acting drugs that were primarily useful as sleeping medicines, inducing (but not forcing) sleep and helping maintain it for periods ranging from three to six hours. For many decades these drugs were given routinely in hospitals to almost all patients as nighttime sedatives, whether or not the patients needed them.

As sleeping medicine, the barbiturates presented a particularly serious problem for many older people: paradoxically, a great many tended to become more agitated or excited than sedated when they took them. For this older group, therefore, a totally different kind of sleeping medicine called chloral hydrate was commonly used. Chloral hydrate is an aromatic, volatile crystalline compound usually dispensed in a gelatin capsule or in syrup form. The drug has a reputation, probably exaggerated, for inducing sleep very rapidly (it is the main ingredient in the Mickey Finn or "knockout drops") and it does indeed work effectively, in moderate doses, for at least a couple of weeks. Another aromatic drug called ethclorvynol (trade name Placidyl) is similar in nature and action to chloral hydrate, even though the chemical formula is quite different.

A variety of other synthetic sleeping medicines have been developed by drug manufacturers in search of that ever-elusive goal, a completely safe and really effective sleeping pill. For example, methaqualone (trade name Quaalude) was introduced in 1965 to induce sleep. It proved to be so popular as an addicting drug, and so dangerous to the user, however, that it is not prescribed anymore through legitimate sources and the manufacturer has discontinued production. Another drug, flurazepam (trade name Dalmane), is actually a benzodiazepine tranquilizer that was developed specifically for use as a nighttime sedative or sleeping pill, rather than as a daytime tranquilizer like most of the rest of that chemical group. Since its introduction in 1970, flurazepam has become one of the most widely prescribed of all sleeping pills, but since its addictive hazards are more closely related to the tranquilizers than to the other sleeping pills, we will include it later in our discussion of tranquilizers.

Finally, various over-the-counter sleep aids have been available from time to time. Some contained such ingredients as bromides or scopolamine (the "twilight sleep" drug), regarded by the Food and Drug Administration as both ineffective and dangerous. Most over-the-counter sleeping medicines available today are based upon antihistamines — and since these are not addicting drugs, we will not be concerned with them here.

Problems and Hazards of Sleeping Pills

All sleeping pills have certain problems and hazards in common.

The Problem of Tolerance. The body develops a powerful tolerance to any sleeping pill very quickly, so that increasingly large doses are required to achieve the same sedative effect. This means that they become relatively ineffective as sleeping pills at ordinary doses after about two weeks. Continued use beyond that time interval, particularly at increased dosage, is suggestive of developing addiction, not normal use.

The Problem of Overdosage. Since the sleeping pills are powerful central nervous system depressants, overdosage with any of them, purposeful or unintentional, can be dangerous. Moderate overdosage can lead to confusion, slurred speech, staggering, and drowsiness. With a large overdose one might see deepening sleep, slow and shallow breathing as the respiratory center is depressed, and then shock and coma. Every hospital is all too familiar with the "overdose case" who must be kept breathing, somehow, for hours or even days until the sleeping pills the patient took are effectively metabolized and excreted from the body. Some such overdoses are outright suicide attempts, all too often successful, but many others are inadvertent. Because of the tolerance that individuals can build up to sleeping pills, with the resulting need for larger doses to achieve the same effect, patients can simply drift into taking hazardously large overdoses, without realizing the danger.

The Hazard of Drug Combinations. Even more dangerous, some people, either by intent or through ignorance, begin mixing these drugs with other depressant drugs, producing sudden profound central nervous system depression. In perhaps the most dangerous situation of all, large doses of barbiturates are taken for sleep after a long evening of heavy drinking. Each drug magnifies the depressant effect of the other, sometimes with the net effect that the user may lie down to sleep and never wake up. The absolutely deadly drug combination of barbiturates and alcohol may well have accounted for the mysterious "pill deaths" of such entertainment world figures as Robert Walker or Marilyn Monroe and contributed to the reputed "overdose" deaths of many heroin users.

Such drug combinations are so threatening because of a property of drugs known as synergism — the tendency of two drugs to work together, each enhancing and multiplying the normal effects of the other. Thus if a person takes two central nervous system depressants simultaneously — a sleeping pill and alcohol, for example, or a sleeping pill and a tranquilizer — the person is likely to end up not with just the normal effects of the drugs taken together, but with perhaps four to eight times the expected effect of the two drugs taken together.

The Problem of Paradoxical or Unexpected Reactions. Some individuals, especially older persons, are extremely sensitive to *any* sleeping medicine, and can tolerate only a fraction of the normal dose.

The Hazard of Addiction. As we discussed earlier in this chapter, all sleeping pills (with the exception of antihistamine-based over-the-counter sleep aids) are actively addicting, and people can become addicted to them, even on relatively low doses. A person who has been taking one or two Seconal capsules as sleeping pills every night for months on end may well be addicted to that low dose without even knowing it. Many patients I have seen in my office, addicted to a prescription sleeping pill, have simply never been told that they should not use the medicine for more than a week or two. They assumed that taking a sleeping pill was intended as a nightly ritual that might go on indefinitely. It is often not until a doctor decides not to renew a prescription, and withdrawal symptoms are encountered, that the patient realizes there is something wrong about the medicine he or she has been taking.

Because of the many problems and hazards associated with sleeping pills, doctors have become far more cautious about prescribing them than they were ten or fifteen years ago. Nevertheless, they are still available in various forms, and addiction still appears. Barbiturates, for example, are still prescribed in combination with other drugs in such preparations as Fiorinal or Esgic, for headaches. In addition, there is widespread illegal street use of all kinds of sleeping pills. They lend themselves to abuse because they are so actively addicting. That is to say, they are among the drugs discussed in chapter 4 that, by their chemical natures and their biochemical effects on the body, are likely to induce addiction in an addictive person. Even before the drug scene of the 1960s, the sleeping pills had become popular street drugs under various nicknames such as "redbirds" (Seconal), "yellowjackets" (Nembutal), or "goofballs," and they remain widely and actively used to this day, often in extremely large doses and frequently in dangerous combination with such other drugs as alcohol, tranquilizers, or cocaine.

Some drugs have become particularly notorious. Methaqualone (Quaalude) became popular with street addicts because of the impressive euphoric high induced by moderately high doses. Even larger overdoses turned out to be bad news indeed, causing acute psychotic reactions and, in some instances, coma accompanied by seizures and death. As the dangers of the drug became known, legitimate prescribing dropped off sharply — but soon counterfeit pills were being manufactured illegally, perfectly matching the original tablets' size, shape, color, and printing. Today methaqualone is no longer available by prescription and has been withdrawn from the legitimate market, but there may still be some underground distribution of the drug from illegal sources.

Dealing with Sleeping Pill Addiction

Sooner or later, even the person who has become addicted to sleeping pills without knowing it comes up with some clues suggesting strongly that something out of the ordinary is going on. Perhaps the most obvious clue will be that the sleeping pills don't seem to work so well anymore. The person again seems to have the same sort of insomnia problem that led to sleeping pills in the first place. Perhaps it was noticed earlier that one pill seemed to be less and less effective, so the person went to two, and is now thinking about three. DANGER! This is very typical of addiction.

A second clue is evidence of dependency on the drug. A person goes on an overnight trip, inadvertently leaving the sleeping pills at home, and there's no sleep at all that night, just nervousness and irritability. Still another telltale clue of addiction appears when a person who has been taking sleeping pills for a prolonged interval stops doing so, either on doctor's orders or on his or her own volition, and walks right into the kind of withdrawal symptoms we will discuss below.

Once the addiction has been identified, the program for treatment detailed in chapter 5 is entirely pertinent: commitment and abstinence, detoxification, dealing with withdrawal, and nutritional and physical rehabilitation through the supportive diet program and regular exercise. A review of those points in the program for treatment is recommended at this time. Many of the steps can be undertaken and applied by the patient himself — but there are several important reasons that a person stopping a long-term sleeping pill addiction should at least begin treatment under the watchful supervision of a doctor.

The main reason for this caution is the matter of withdrawal from these depressant drugs. Termination can produce withdrawal symptoms even when the person is addicted to a very low dose, and some can be serious, even dangerous. It is characteristic of many addicting drugs, especially those with strong psychoactive effects, that the withdrawal symptoms that occur after addictive use often seem directly the opposite of the actions of the drugs, and sleeping pills provide a good example of this. If the normal action of these

TRANQUILIZERS

Benzodiazepine Derivatives

Chemical name	Trade names
alprazolam	Xanax (Upjohn)
chlordiazepoxide	Librium, Libritabs (Roche)
clorazepate dipotassium	Tranxene (Abbott)
diazepam	Valium (Roche)
halazepam	Paxipam (Schering)
lorazepam	Ativan (Wyeth)
oxazepam	Serax (Wyeth)
prazepam	Centrax (Parke-Davis)

Meprobamate

meprobamate	Miltown (Wallace)
	Equanil (Wyeth)
	Deprol (Wallace)
	plus many others

OTHER TRANQUILIZERS

hydroxyzine hydrochloride	Atarax (Roerig)
hydroxyzine pamoate	Vistaril (Pfizer)
chlormezanone	Trancopal (Winthrop-Breon)

drugs is to sedate and suppress the activities of the central nervous system, withdrawal is often accompanied by a high degree of agitation, anxiety, nervousness, and outright fear. Sleeplessness and nightmares are common. Sometimes this agitation is accompanied by sharply increased brain activity, frank hallucinations (seeing things or hearing things that aren't there), and, in extreme cases, grand mal seizures.

The withdrawal pattern of increased nervous activity, without treatment, can go on anywhere from two days to four or five, depending on how long the drug has been used and in what doses. Seizures or convulsions, however, are dangerous and can even lead to fatalities. For this reason I believe that withdrawal from sleeping pills requires the care and supervision of a physician. Not only do the possible hazards of overagitation, hallucinations, and seizures need to be addressed, but in addition many people coming off sleeping pills develop severe depression, with the ever-attendant threat of suicide.

In dealing with these patients, I have found that small doses of chlordiazepozide (trade name Librium) are both safe and effective. Librium, a tranquilizer, helps greatly to prevent or minimize withdrawal symptoms from sleeping pills and other central nervous system depressants. (I prescribe it to help with alcohol withdrawal as well.) Although addicting in itself, Librium does not produce the sense of euphoria commonly associated with other tranquilizers and central nervous system depressant drugs, and therefore usually is not interesting to the addictive person. Used in moderate doses for about a week during sleeping pill withdrawal and then dropped when it is no longer needed, it has proven an effective aid in protecting against the hazards of withdrawal.

Detoxification begins as soon as the drug is withdrawn and should be complete within three`or four days. Here vitamin C powder, 4,000 mg (one teaspoon) every two to four hours while awake will help the body speed up the detoxification process. When I am following a patient closely during this period, I sometimes order additional vitamin C in my office by intravenous drip during the detoxification interval. Such close observation also enables me to be alert for evidence of developing depression and begin treatment, when indicated, with one of the effective antidepressant medicines — an extremely useful group of drugs that, fortunately, is not addicting at all.

Tranquilizers

A continuing search for safe, effective drugs to treat minor anxiety and agitation led to the development of a large group of drugs that have become among the most widely prescribed medicines of all time. The largest family of these drugs, known as benzodiazepine derivatives, includes drugs prescribed under such names as Ativan, Centrax, Librium, Serax, Tranxene, Valium, and Dalmane. In addition there is meprobamate (Miltown, Equanil), which fosters the same central nervous system depression, addiction, and subsequent withdrawal symptoms as the more potent benzodiazepine family and other drug families. (See p. 173 for a selected list of these drugs by group, generic name, and trade name.*)

These drugs are widely used. During one recent period Valium was reported as the most frequently prescribed medicine in the United States today, as meprobamate was thirty years ago, and today Dalmane, although basically a tranquilizer, is widely promoted as a sleeping medication. A newly released benzodiazepine, Xanax, has been presented to physicians as both an antianxiety *and* an antidepressant drug — a sort of "all-purpose medicine."

All of these drugs, however, have similar effects; they are tranquilizers in the truest sense. Although central nervous system depressants, they do not, as a group, induce heavy sedation or sleep. Rather, they quiet and soothe waking nervous system activity, taking the cutting edge off everyday nervous system experience. They do not relieve pain, for example, but they do blunt the nervous system's response to pain sufficiently that it doesn't bother the patient so much, making a much smaller dose of a pain-killing drug effective. The tranquilizers don't relieve tension, but they do relax the jitters that tension brings. They don't relieve the sources of anxiety in any way, but they do smooth over the effects of anxiety, producing a sort of soothing rosy glow. As one doctor once put it, "They make people feel more shiftless — and content to feel that way." Perhaps the bottom line is that these drugs tend to make the patient feel good, even when the patient doesn't really feel good at all. Indeed, there are very few general symptoms of ill ease that these tranquilizers do not help to modify or relieve. Of course, it must be pointed out that they accomplish this by blunting the acuity of everyday nervous system perceptions. This means that the person taking them is not receiving all the sharply focused sensory experi-

---

*These drugs are sometimes referred to as "mild tranquilizers" to distinguish them from a group of more powerful drugs, the "strong tranquilizers," which were developed and are used exclusively for the treatment of major, severe mental illnesses, such as schizophrenia and manic-depressive disease. Since the strong tranquilizers are not addicting drugs, we will not be concerned with them in this book.

ence that the nervous system was built to receive; because of the nervous system depressant effect of the drug itself, the lives of people taking it are somewhat attenuated, all their perceptions somewhat blunted.

There are cases and occasions when these medication effects are highly desirable for a brief period of time — for the person who must deal with acute anxiety, acute grief, or a brief period of excessive and intolerable nervous tension, for example. They can knock the patient down to a desirable low level of nervous system activity for a few days when there is a valid medical reason for doing so — a crisis at work; a death in the family; a brief and unusual period of sleeplessness due to business, financial, or family worries; as a presurgical medication, especially for surgery that is to be done under a local anesthetic, or as a postsurgical medication to help deal with a brief period of postoperative pain. The problem in using these drugs under such circumstances is knowing when to stop, and the fact is that multitudes of patients — and their doctors — don't know when to stop. In most cases, treatment with tranquilizers could and should ideally be limited to two or three days, and then the drug should be terminated. Any continued use for a period of a week to ten days or more can present a real risk of addiction to an addictive person. Yet the fact is that in all too many cases the original short-term prescription good for two weeks is refilled, and refilled, and refilled again.

Patients who first take a drug such as Valium for its "leveling effect" during an acute emotional crisis often continue to take it when the crisis has passed, as insurance or prophylaxis against another crisis. Many continue taking the drug not as a brief acute treatment but as a chronic and continuing crutch; and often the dose is doubled when the original dose no longer seems as effective as it once was. Many people themselves escalate the dosage of a drug like Valium, which their doctor has indicated is "not habit-forming" and "really quite innocuous," until they are taking whopping doses — 50 or 60 mg a day, which is enough to make most individuals continually groggy from dawn until dark. Others maintain the original prescribed dosage, but simply never discontinue the medicine. Thus, hard as it may be to believe of a medication nominally only available by doctor's prescription, there are thousands of individuals who have been taking 20 or 30 mg or more of Valium, or comparable doses of other tranquilizers, daily for years — some for as long as twenty years!

It is mainly these people, who move from an initial brief course of medication for treatment of an acute condition into a regular, steady maintenance dose that goes on for weeks or months, who face the major problem of addiction to tranquilizers. Most are highly addictive individuals of the sort we discussed in chapter 4 — individuals who are far more vulnerable than most people to addiction to any addicting substance. Most have no idea in the world that they are addicted to anything; they make the reasonable but erroneous assumption that because a doctor prescribed the medicine and authorizes the refills, they can't be addicted to it. The doctor may have told them that it can't hurt them, and they think they are taking a mild, innocuous medication to quiet their nerves, treat their anxiety, or make them feel better. In fact, they are taking the medication to stave off the distressing and frightening withdrawal symptoms that occur when they discontinue taking it.

Grace L., a forty-two-year-old woman who ultimately came to me for treatment of Valium addiction after a long safari from doctor to doctor, had a typical history of how this comes about. Ten months earlier, when her husband died, Grace's world was shattered. She could not cope with the sudden and unexpected loss, the grief, the impending funeral, and the insistent demands to get her husband's confusing financial affairs in order all at once. Her doctor, quite reasonably, prescribed four 5 mg Valium tablets a day to help her through the crisis. The crisis seemed to continue, and she refilled her prescription and continued taking the Valium regularly throughout the following eight months. At that point her doctor decided that she should discontinue the medicine. It seemed reasonable to her, since she found the medicine a costly burden and seemed to be mostly over her nervousness by then. After discontinuing the Valium she did fine for about five days, and then, quite suddenly, was overtaken with an attack of extreme nervousness, agitation, anxiety, acute insomnia, and a terrifying sort of free-floating fear of everyone and everything around her — symptoms unlike anything she could ever remember.

Grace put up with these symptoms, completely beside herself, for over two days before she decided to take just one of the few Valium she had left from her last prescription to help her "quiet down." A single 5 mg tablet was all it took, and it worked miracles. All of her symptoms disappeared as abruptly as they had started, and with the help of a second and third tablet, she got through the next twenty-four hours feeling reasonably like herself again. Then the symptoms recurred. When her doctor refused to refill her prescription again and she had only two or three tablets left, she went to another doctor, who listened briefly to her description of her symptoms and promptly wrote out a prescription — for a month's supply of Valium. That doctor did ask her perfunctorily if she had ever taken Valium before, and she told him, "Once or twice in the past." She went home virtually assured of another eight or ten months of renewals.

Although it was ultimately Grace's own idea to consult with a doctor specializing in treating drug dependence, she did not imagine that her problem was one of addiction to Valium. She had been shaken up by that first experience with withdrawal, however, and after two or three months of trying unsuccessfully to discontinue the drug, tapering down the amount she was taking, and repeatedly running into the same wall of symptoms, she knew that something was wrong. "I seem to have to have those pills or everything goes to pieces," she said to me on her first visit, "and that can't be right."

Benzodiazepine Withdrawal Patterns

Grace L. was right: she really did have to have her tranquilizers, and when she didn't, things really did go to pieces. They are addicting drugs, and addictive individuals do indeed become addicted to them. Withdrawal from the tranquilizers, especially from the benzodiazepine tranquilizers, has certain characteristics unique to this group of drugs, and it is easy to see how the withdrawal can frighten and confuse individuals and their families if they do not understand what is happening.

The first unique feature of benzodiazepine withdrawal is that it is delayed. Most doctors regard the benzodiazepine tranquilizers as short-acting drugs, since they exhibit their effects within a few minutes after they are taken and the effects tend to wear off in five to six hours. (Flurazepam — trade name Dalmane — is a longer-acting benzodiazepine used as a sleeping pill and has an effect lasting eight to ten hours.) The fact that these drugs' clinical effects appear and disappear quickly, however, does not mean that the drugs are eradicated from the body rapidly. As a person uses them over a prolonged period of time, there is a build-up of unmetabolized or partly metabolized drug in the tissues and central nervous system. If an addicted person suddenly withdraws from the medication after weeks or months of use, enough of the drug remains in the body for a period up to seven or eight days, or in some cases as long as twenty-one days, to delay the onset of withdrawal symptoms. During that interval nothing remarkable happens except that the individual gradually begins to reacquire the nervous system acuity that the drug was actively suppressing. The individual may feel an increased sense of well-being, perhaps even euphoria, as sights, sounds, smells, and thinking processes begin to clear from the drug effects. Such people, unless warned, may be devastated by the onset of withdrawal symptoms when they *do* begin, usually suddenly.

What are the withdrawal symptoms? The most notable is the exact opposite of the nervous system depressant effect of the drug — a sense of nervousness, jitteriness, anxiety, and sleeplessness, as if the nervous system is suddenly running in high gear. And this, in fact, is precisely what is happening. The nervous system is running in such high gear that it runs away with itself. In some people the excessive brain activity can lead to convulsions — grand mal seizures — which are highly dangerous and can even be fatal unless their onset is anticipated and they are blocked in some fashion. Other people who do not have seizures feel like they are about to explode on the inside. Still others have actual visual and auditory hallucinations, seeing things that are not there, hearing sounds that don't exist, and so forth. Some people exhibit all sorts of peculiar or disordered thinking, developing false ideas, thinking in circles, and coming up with a long series of wrong answers.

One patient, a woman aged sixty-five, presented a typical picture of benzodiazepine withdrawal. This woman had Parkinson's disease, which was only partly controlled with treatment, so that she had continuous tremor, grimacing, difficulty swallowing, and other Parkinsonian symptoms. A doctor had put her on 40 mg of Valium a day because her shaking and grimacing was making her *companion* nervous. She took the medicine for eight or ten months before her family began to complain that she seemed to be sleeping all the time. When the doctor heard this, he took her off the Valium abruptly.

For the first two or three days thereafter, the woman began to perk up and look around, making conversation and seeming much like her old self again. Then, without any apparent change or warning, she began talking about things that weren't there — the pink flamingos she saw in the living room one evening, for example. Next she became convinced that her family had somehow moved their Seattle home cross-country right next door to her old home on the East Coast, and one evening went so far as to pick up the telephone and call an old friend — in Vermont — to invite her to dinner that night. Evidence of confused thinking and visual hallucinations continued for approximately five days before they finally subsided.

Fortunately, this woman did not exhibit one of the most common and difficult of all benzodiazepine withdrawal symptoms: a free-floating sense of anxiety and fearfulness of something terrible about to happen. Most benzodiazepine addicts do experience this in withdrawal; they don't know what they are afraid of, but they are afraid. I have seen patients walk around the bed and touch the bed but refuse to lie down on it for fear that they would never be able to get up again. These fears can be carried to such activities as sleeping, eating, dressing, or almost anything else. A second common element of benzodiazepine withdrawal is depression — the same symptom that we see in withdrawal from virtually every addictive drug, and one that almost always needs treatment.

One final aspect of benzodiazepine withdrawal is the matter of duration: it tends to hang on. For most patients the withdrawal period tapers off after one or two weeks and is over in one to two months. There are, however, cases in which withdrawal persists. This situation has not been well studied or documented in the scientific literature; one hears about such cases anecdotally or encounters such people occasionally in practice. I treated one young man in my practice who had been off Valium for five years after taking the drug for only two or three months, and I am convinced that he was *still* in withdrawal. He maintained that he had never felt the same since taking the medicine. The free-floating anxiety and fear, the nervousness, and the sleeplessness persisted, and all he needed to do to relieve them all completely within an hour would be to take a single 5 mg Valium tablet.

Treatment of Tranquilizer Addiction

Because of the bizarre and sometimes downright dangerous nature of withdrawal symptoms from all the central nervous system depressants, and because unpredictable things can happen, particularly in withdrawal from the benzodiazepine tranquilizers, *I believe that detoxification and withdrawal from these drugs should be supervised by a physician.*

First, however, the patient has an essential contribution to make: determination to discontinue use of the drug immediately, completely, and permanently, as stated in the self-treatment program outlined in chapter 5. This requires a fixed commitment to go the whole distance from the beginning. Once that is undertaken, it is common sense to guard carefully against involvement in any alternative or substitute addictions, tempting as it might be to use sugar, alcohol, sleeping pills, or other addicting substances as crutches to get over the rough spots. Careful attention to the details of the nutritional program set forth in chapter 5 will help restore the body's nutritional balance, while institution of a daily exercise program will rebuild physical strength and endurance and help combat depression.

Meanwhile, the doctor's role is to be on guard against the hazards of withdrawal and depression that can appear and to deal with those hazards as necessary. I have found a number of things reliably helpful. During the "lag period" before active withdrawal symptoms appear — two to five days — one has an excellent opportunity to speed up detoxification of the drug with the use of large doses of vitamin C (sodium ascorbate) and to start improving nutritional status through diet adjustment, protein supplementation, and vitamin and mineral therapy. With the onset of withdrawal symptoms I start the patient on a brief (three to seven days) course of Librium, which seems as useful in blunting benzodiazepine withdrawal symptoms as it is in quieting the agitation of sleeping pill withdrawal. Indeed, Librium aids withdrawal from any sedative drug, including alcohol. In general one does not like to treat addiction to a psychoactive drug by using another psychoactive drug, but in a case of this sort I believe it is justified, especially when used for just a few days and then terminated. When Librium is used in this way the risk of a substitute addiction is extremely small, and I have never actually encountered Librium addiction in my practice. The drug does have the benzodiazepine quality of blunting and suppressing central nervous system activity, but this is desirable, for example, during Valium withdrawal when the central nervous system is extremely irritable and the patient could potentially have hallucinations or convulsions. When these withdrawal symptoms threaten to be frankly dangerous to the patient or so disorganizing as to disrupt treatment, I have found Librium to be a useful weapon.

Detoxification and protection against severe withdrawal symptoms will help carry the patient through the first critical period of treatment, aided and abetted by the patient's own personal motivation to shake off the drug dependence. But the longer-term threat of depression remains a problem and a hazard for many patients. True enough, some have no problem with this, sailing on through, relieved and exhilarated to be free of dependence on a drug that has been blunting and attenuating their central nervous system activity. For those who do become depressed, probably as a natural expression of the deep-seated depression that is part of their addictiveness as discussed in chapter 3, active treatment of the depression is necessary without delay. At the first sign that a patient in treatment is becoming depressed, I prescribe an effective combination of antidepressant drugs, to be used for months if necessary until the depression is gone and remains gone without help from medication. Librium won't do for this purpose; it has no specific antidepressant action and should not be part of a long-term treatment program. Instead, I choose the tricyclic antidepressants, such as amitriptyline (Elavil) or trazodone (Desyrel). These are specific, potent antidepressant drugs with the special advantage that as a group they are not addicting at all.

The history and behavior in early treatment of some patients makes me so certain that they are going to experience depression that I start antidepressant medication before symptoms appear. The important message is that a deep depression is not a natural way of life. There are safe, effective ways to treat this kind of problem, and in the case of tranquilizer addiction, treatment of underlying depression can go a long way toward eliminating exactly conditions that led to the drug use and the addiction in the first place.

12

The Stimulant Drugs:
Speed, Cocaine,
and Other Uppers

IN CHAPTER 11 we discussed a large group of addicting drugs that act to depress — slow down, sedate, or tranquilize — normal central nervous system activity. Elsewhere we have seen that certain other addicting drugs, notably alcohol and marijuana, also act as central nervous system depressants.

Now we come to a group of addicting drugs that tend to do just the opposite: they speed up physical and nervous system activity, making people abnormally hyperactive, with both body and mind churning along frenetically at excessive speed. Physically, these drugs constrict blood vessels, force the heart to beat more rapidly, and drive the blood pressure up, sometimes to dangerously high levels. Psychoactively, they induce a sense of emotional high or euphoria, increased creativity, increased physical capability, and lack of need for sleep. The speeding up of mental activity, heart rate and physical activity (faster typing, restless pacing, hyped-up athletic performance) has led to the drugs' common designation as "speed" in the jargon of the street user. We already encountered one such stimulant drug, nicotine, earlier in this book. Caffeine is another stimulant drug, although very mild and gentle compared to the extremely powerful and dangerous central nervous system stimulants we will be discussing here.

The potent speed drugs are highly addicting substances to addictive persons, according to the definition discussed in chapter 3. They are subject to repeated, uncontrolled, compulsive use, and the user is faced with distinctive and unpleasant withdrawal symptoms when use is terminated. In addition, these drugs seem to be related more closely than other addicting drugs to the element of depression that is present in so many addictive persons. Indeed, before their dangers were fully understood, many speed drugs were actually prescribed as antidepressant or mood-lifting agents for depressed patients.

How these drugs act to counteract depression is not known, but they do — up to a point. All of them, for example, produce a sense of euphoria, an emotional high, that temporarily blots out gray, depressed feelings. For some addicts this is perceived as a definite "lift" into a seemingly better emotional world; for others, including many who are deeply depressed and don't know it, the drugs merely make them feel "normal" or "functional" — bringing them up out of the gloom to a normal operating level, so to speak. Whatever the case, users of these drugs soon come to depend on this euphoric lift — and to sense the pit of withdrawal that waits for them if the supply of drug is not replenished. Eventually it becomes impossible to determine whether they continue using the drug primarily to achieve the "feeling good" plateau once again or just to forestall withdrawal symptoms. In practical terms, it doesn't matter — the addiction is controlling their lives on either side.

Prescription Speed and Street Speed

Over the years there have literally been dozens of different speedlike drugs and drug combinations in this group of central nervous system stimulants. On pp. 185–186 you will find a representative list of these prescription drugs by generic name and by trade name, together with a sampling of related over-the-counter drugs. Among the most commonly familiar and most widely used are the following.

■ *Amphetamines* — the earliest and most widely known of the hard-core stimulants. They include amphetamine, dextroamphetamine, and metamphetamine.

■ *Methylphenidate* (Ritalin) — a potent central nervous system stimulant that does not contain any amphetamines but has very active amphetaminelike stimulant effects. Methylphenidate (and look-alike stimulant drugs peddled as methylphenidate) has been widely abused as a stimulant street drug.

■ *Other amphetaminelike prescription drugs* — a large group of drugs, all chemically different from the amphetamines but producing moderate to marked amphetaminelike stimulant effects. Most of these drugs are still legally prescribed as aids to weight control, considered useful because they have temporary amphetaminelike appetite-suppressing qualities along with their stimulant effects.

■ *Nonprescription* (*over-the-counter*) *"reducing aids"* — preparations containing phenylpropanolamine (PPA), another chemical with some amphetaminelike stimulant effects. These drugs are legally sold in most areas without prescription.

■ *Any number of preparations* in which amphetamines have been combined with vitamins, barbiturate sedatives, or various tranquilizers. Many of these preparations have been withdrawn by their manufacturers, or effectively banned from use in various states, since the mid-1970s due to widespread abuse.

SPEED AND OTHER UPPERS

Amphetamines

Chemical name	Common trade names
amphetamine	Benzedrine
amphetamine aspartate	Obetrol-10, Obetrol-20 (Rexar)
amphetamine sulfate	(amphetamine salts combined with dextroamphetamine salts)
benzphetamine	Didrex (Upjohn)
dextroamphetamine sulfate	Dexedrine (Smith, Kline and French); dextroamphetamine is combined with other drugs under trade names of Bamadex (Lederle); Biphetamine (Pennwalt); Dexamyl (SKF); Eskatrol (SKF); Obetrol (Rexar)

Amphetaminelike stimulants and appetite suppressants

diethylpropion hydrochloride	Tenuate (Merrell Dow) Tepanil (Riker)
fenfluramine hydrochloride	Pondimin (Robins)
mazindol	Mazanor (Wyeth) Sanorex (Sandoz)
methylphenidate	Ritalin (CIBA)
phendimetrazine tartrate	Bontril (Carnrick) Melfiat (Reid-Provident) Plegine (Ayerst)
phenmetrazine	Preludin (Boehringer)
phentermine hydrochloride	Adipex (Lemmon) Fastin (Beecham) Ionamin (Pennwalt)

Phenylpropanolamine appetite suppressants (O-T-C)

phenylpropanolamine	Appedrine (Thompson Medical); Control (TM); Dexatrim (TM); Help (Verex); Prolamine (TM)

Cocaine

Rigidly controlled under narcotics laws; not available by prescription. Obtained only on the illegal drug market except for small quantities for very limited approved medicinal uses.

■ *Any number of look-alike preparations* intended to mimic the appearance of the amphetamines or other stimulant drugs. These street drugs may contain absolutely anything at all — you never know.

Virtually all of the speed drugs originally were developed and dispensed as anorexic drugs — drugs that tended to depress the appetite and thus were considered useful to dieters. Later some, such as dextroamphetamine and methylphenidate, came to be used for treatment of hyperactivity syndrome in children. All displayed a high order of central nervous system stimulant activity, however, and during the 1960s and 1970s came to be seriously misused as speed or uppers (mood-elevators). Since the mid-1970s, various state regulations and actions taken by medical disciplinary boards and medical society ethics committees have led many doctors to limit sharply the amount of these drugs that they prescribe. Most of the amphetamines available for improper use today, therefore, are street speed, either imported from other countries or manufactured illegally in laboratories scattered around the country. However, both the nonamphetamine prescription drugs and the over-the-counter reducing aids are quite legal and are available today.

Addiction to Speed

The amphetamines and other speedlike drugs probably have been abused for as long as they've been known. As early as the 1930s, amphetamine was widely available as the waxy medicated insert in the common benzedrine inhalers that were intended to unplug stuffy noses due to the vasoconstrictor effect of the amphetamine (the same effect achieved with an ordinary Neo-Synephrine nasal spray today). People at that time found that by removing the benzedrine insert from the inhaler and chewing it like gum, they could produce a distinctive high. Soon thereafter, various other amphetamine preparations began coming into widespread use as appetite suppressants in the treatment of obesity, then available either by prescription or, in many cases, in over-the-counter preparations often combined with vitamins. These drugs did indeed have a strong appetite-suppressant effect, at least for a week or two — but many people continued to use them for their other physiological and psychoactive effects without ever actually losing weight at all.

What were the other effects? As little as 5 mg of dextroamphetamine could bring about the sort of euphoric high and supercharged physical and mental activity we described earlier and maintain these effects for several hours. Fifteen milligrams of dextroamphetamine in a so-called sustained-release dosage form would initiate a similar speed high within a few minutes and then sustain it for as long as ten or twelve or fifteen hours. This was truly the "washday miracle" for multitudes of housewives!

There were, of course, some less-than-desirable side effects to these potent drugs. Some people developed pounding headaches on speed; others perspired heavily and constantly as long as the drug was acting. Since these drugs are powerful diuretics, frequent and copious urination was sometimes a bother, and so many people found the high-rolling acceleration of the drug to be accompanied by such an unpleasant degree of high-keyed nervousness, jitteriness, or edginess that many took to mixing the amphetamines with barbiturates or tranquilizers just to take the edge off the speed alone.

Who used these drugs? In the 1940s and 1950s, understandably, a great many college students, medical students, musicians, actors, and others who worked under high tension used amphetamines specifically for their speed effect, or as a hangover cure. And, although the drugs were not classified as narcotics and were reputed not to be habit-forming, many steady users did indeed become addicted, even at relatively low dosages.* Later, as the drugs' popularity as appetite suppressants grew, they were used by multitudes of people, especially housewives, schoolteachers, professional people (including myself), adolescents, and businesspeople, ostensibly to "help control their weight." Most would have been insulted if confronted with the idea that they really persisted in taking the drugs (often for years) because they had become addicted to them, even though that is exactly what had happened. Actually, a variety of modern studies have demonstrated that the drugs' appetite-suppressing effect is limited to five or six weeks at the most; beyond that there is no valid weight-control effect to be obtained, and the appetite comes roaring back.

Later, of course, the amphetamine drugs came into extremely wide use as street drugs with no legitimate excuse whatever for their use other than to achieve the speed effects. Large numbers of street users became addicted, using the drugs not so much for the euphoric and speed effects as to hold off a thoroughly unpleasant gathering of withdrawal symptoms that came about when the drug was discontinued. Many became tolerant of the drugs — requiring increasingly higher doses to achieve the same "high-rolling" effect — and dosage levels among street users began escalating almost unbelievably high. At the height of the Haight-Ashbury drug scene it was not at all uncommon to find individuals taking as much as 1,000 mg of dextroamphetamine a day, together with staggering

*Even today, drug manfacturers deny that speed is addicting; typically these drugs are described in pharmaceutical literature as merely "habituating" or "subject to abuse."

doses of barbiturates or tranquilizers as well. Such doses may have succeeded in maintaining their highs, of course, but at the same time, withdrawal tended to bring them down lower and lower. A few hours after such a high, the individual would inevitably "crash" unless sufficient drug was available to prevent withdrawal.

The widespread idea that only street drifters ever got into trouble with speed was manifestly untrue — thousands of housewives did too, and sometimes found themselves in contact with some very odd people. Many a housewife who started off with a simple prescription for reducing pills soon escalated her habit to such a level that she was forced to make acquaintance with street contacts to purchase "crisscrosses," "black beauties," or "Christmas trees" at the rate of twenty or so doses a day.

Withdrawal and Toxicity

Addiction to speed is another case in which withdrawal symptoms often seem diametrically opposite to the effects of the drug itself. If amphetamines and other speedlike drugs cause euphoria and an overall speeding up of mind and body functions, the two major characteristics of withdrawal from speed are the abrupt onset of depression and a sudden sluggishness of mental and physical function. The speed user in withdrawal is suddenly possessed of the great-grandfather of all black moods, a gray outlook on everything. This mood typically hangs on, unrelieved, for a couple of days or more; but I have seen patients in whom the depression has persisted for weeks and required vigorous treatment with nonaddicting antidepressant drugs. At the same time, people in withdrawal are irresistibly sleepy and sluggish; often they simply sleep for two or three days and then wake up famished, stuff themselves, and go back to sleep. This torpor and physical sluggishness also extends to mental function. The person may be confused, disoriented, and unable to think straight for several days, and a headache may or may not be added to the list of symptoms.

Withdrawal from speed is not pleasant, and it's not the only piece of bad news, either. With long-term chronic use, the amphetamine-like drugs can have toxic effects that are potentially more disastrous than the withdrawal symptoms. The increased and persistent central nervous system stimulation and the increased expenditure of energy by the brain can, over a prolonged period of time, have a profound effect on the chronic user's thought processes and personality, and eventually many of these people begin manifesting distinctly psychotic and paranoid behavior. The addictive and toxic hazards of these drugs to the chronic user are clearly (and chillingly) expressed by a manufacturer's warning regarding one of the amphetaminelike drugs, originally published in the *Physicians' Desk Reference* and edited here only to make it more comprehensible to laypeople:

Abuse of amphetamines and related drugs may be associated with intense psychological dependence and severe social dysfunction. There are reports of patients who have increased the dosage to many times that recommended. Abrupt termination of these drugs following prolonged high-dosage administration results in extreme fatigue and mental depression; changes are also noted on the electroencephalograms recorded during sleep, indicating changes in the basic pattern of electrical activity of the brain. Manifestations of chronic intoxication with these appetite-suppressing drugs include severe skin rashes, marked insomnia, irritability, hyperactivity, and personality changes. The most severe manifestation of chronic intoxication is psychosis, often clinically indistinguishable from schizophrenia.

It has been my personal observation in treating patients for chronic or long-term use of speed that the evidences of psychosis and paranoia are transient and associated only with continued use of drugs; the symptoms tend to disappear within a few days after the drug is withdrawn. There are reports, however, of patients who have shown long-term residual psychosis and paranoia following prolonged use of large daily doses of these drugs. Interestingly, the paranoia or delusions of persecution that many of these patients experience actually prevent them from seeking out the treatment that would help them get rid of the paranoia — they think their doctor is out to get them. Their delusions can also cause them to throw away their drug from time to time. I had one patient, for example, who was certain that the police were staking him out in preparation for a drug bust; every time he heard a police car siren outside, he would assume that they were coming to get him and would flush all the drug he had on hand down the toilet.

Considering the above hazards involved in continued use of speed, it is perhaps fortuitous that the very act of taking speed for a long time, especially at ever-increasing doses, tends to be self-limiting. The constant fast heart rate, the constant elevation of blood pressure, the constant high-speed mental activity, the irregular meals, and the constant difficulty sleeping all tend to wear people out, and heavy users can reach a point where they are more uncomfortable using the drug than not using it, and begin thinking about going off it. Even low-dosage users (those taking the drug for long periods on a doctor's constantly renewed prescription, for instance) often find that the drug is no longer producing the euphoric high it originally did, but seems instead only to be forestalling withdrawal symptoms. Perhaps some of these latter people begin worrying about stories of trouble that they hear regarding other speed users, or perhaps their doctors become alarmed that their blood pressures are consistently too high. Whatever their motivation, many speed users, just by the nature of the drug and what it does, become distressed enough to want to get off it, a matter we will deal with in some detail toward the end of this chapter.

The Decline of Speed

The central nervous system stimulants, when abused, are bad medicine — they beat you up when you use them and they beat you up when you discontinue them. The street warning that "speed kills" didn't arise by accident. And although these drugs have certain limited legitimate medical uses — for treatment of a very uncommon sleep disorder known as narcolepsy, for example, or, according to some authorities, for treatment of hyperactivity syndrome in children — their widespread use for appetite control and treatment of obesity can hardly be supported. The extreme hazard of abuse far outweighs any possible benefit.

As a result, the amphetamines or Ritalin are no longer as available for addictive use as they once were. In the 1970s, for example, the Food and Drug Administration required new warning labels emphasizing the extreme hazards of abuse. Doctors were discouraged from prescribing the speedlike drugs, and some states virtually prohibited their use. In the end, over 95 percent of all amphetamine prescribing ceased. This made speed extremely difficult to obtain as a street drug; addicts were forced to depend almost entirely on homemade basement laboratories to produce what was needed. The prescription restrictions did not dam up all the non-amphetamine prescription diet pills, however, and they did nothing to restrict availability of low dosages of the stimulant phenylpro-panolamine sold in over-the-counter diet aids. These latter are in-deed still available, and although they are generally scorned by speed addicts as pretty weak sisters, they are regarded as better than nothing. I have seen patients taking as many as twenty or thirty diet pills a day to supply their speed habits.

In spite of this, the widespread use of speed began declining, and continues to decline today — it's just too difficult to get reliable, potent supplies, except those smuggled in from foreign manufactur-ers or made in basement labs. As soon as you get one worm stuffed back into the can, of course, another one pops up to take its place. Thus it was that the fall from favor of amphetamines and other speedlike drugs was accompanied by the rise of another even more dangerous stimulant drug: cocaine.

Cocaine

Cocaine, as an addicting drug, has almost as long and illustrious a history of medical use as the opiate narcotics. The white powdery alkaloid, derived from leaves of the coca plant, came to medical at-tention during the late 1800s for its usefulness as a surface anes-thetic; it is still used for that purpose today in the offices of eye, ear, nose, and throat specialists. Around the turn of the century William Halstead, noted surgeon at Johns Hopkins in Baltimore, did consid-erable self-experimentation with the drug, exploring its possible uses as a local anesthetic and getting himself so thoroughly addicted in the process that it nearly ruined his career. At about the same time in Vienna, Sigmund Freud discovered cocaine and may him-self have been addicted at one time. The addicting qualities of the drug were not recognized at first, but Dr. Arthur Conan Doyle, for example, was aware of the drug's potential as an addicting stimu-lant, and made it quite clear in his writings that cocaine was the source of Sherlock Holmes's addiction, of which Dr. Watson so strongly disapproved. Cocaine also became recognized then for its ability, after prolonged use, to cause mental aberrations and psy-choses or paranoid ideas.

Following this early history of cocaine use and abuse, the drug ultimately — and incorrectly — became classified in the United States as a narcotic under the Federal Narcotics Act and was banned for any medicinal use other than certain limited forms of local anesthesia. At this point conflicting stories began to appear. At first cocaine was touted as a fiercely addicting narcotic, even though it was not an opiate narcotic and never had been. Then the story changed: cocaine was not a narcotic, but was merely called that by the federal government, and could actually be used safely and freely without any worry about addiction. This notion is equally untrue; we now know that addictive people taking cocaine can indeed become thoroughly addicted to it. In fact, some experts today contend that it is the most highly addicting of all substances.

What *is* cocaine, then? In simple terms, it is a very expensive form of speed — an extremely powerful central nervous system stimulant. Because it has become so fashionable and widely used as an illicit drug, its sale and trafficking on the underground market bring about the exchange of many millions of dollars a year in the United States alone. In its purest, most highly refined form, cocaine is a fluffy, white crystalline powder that looks like snow, but this degree of purity is seldom encountered in the United States. Because of its scarcity and the enormous demand for it, virtually every person who handles a given lot of cocaine, from the original producer to the smuggler to the dealer to the pusher to the user, cuts the concentration of the drug and doubles the price. As a result, street-grade cocaine today, cut many times with sugar, vegetable starch, strychnine, aspirin, or myriad other elements, is marketed to the final customer at approximately $100 a gram, $700 to $800 a quarter ounce, or $3,000 an ounce. And because of the way the drug is customarily used, this high cost becomes an important limiting factor in how much of the drug any given individual can consume at any given time.

Modern Use of Cocaine

Cocaine is used two or three different ways. Most commonly, a small amount is cut away from the supply on a slab of glass into a thin line with a razor blade and then sniffed or "snorted" up the nose through a straw that is moved quickly down the line of drug — hence the term "a line of coke." Taken this way the drug can become quite irritating to the nose when used regularly, causing chronic inflammation of the mucous membrane and sometimes leading to perforation of the nasal septum. The powder can also be mixed with a solvent and injected intravenously. A third alternative, known as free-basing, involves extracting and purifying the cocaine with a volatile liquid such as ether, then taking the resulting dried residue and smoking it. This latter method is reputed to produce a very potent, concentrated dosage form — highly fashionable, highly addictive, highly dangerous to produce, and highly expensive.

Whatever its cost, and however it is used, cocaine has become an extremely popular and widely used addicting substance in this country in recent years. It is popular not only on the street, but at many middle- and upper-class dinner parties or evening gatherings as well, and the amount of social disorganization it brings about is staggering. There is no question that many people discover cocaine through casual contact among friends, and then continue using it when they discover how good it makes them feel. Many, I am convinced, are people who suffer from genetic depression with its associated symptoms of agitation, anxiety, fear, or anger, and aren't even aware that they are depressed. Addictive people such as these are likely to experience an unbelievable exhilaration on their first encounter with cocaine — and end up in terrible physical and economic distress because of it.

One of my patients, Sue B., demonstrated a classical pattern in her history of cocaine addiction. Sue was a young gay woman in her mid-twenties who had been trying to live on her own and was not getting along well in her relationships, either with other women or with her immediate family. Acquainted with a variety of different drugs, including amphetamines, tranquilizers, and sedatives, she was casually introduced to cocaine by one of her girlfriends one evening, and almost literally caught fire from it. As she later put it, "I knew I'd found the drug for me on that one single acquaintance; cocaine fit my personal needs the way a key fits a lock." Like many other cocaine addicts I've treated, Sue said that after her first experience snorting cocaine she continued to want more. "First there's a rapid, incredible high," she said, "a crazy rush of sensation throughout the body that brings this feeling of extreme well-being. There's a moment when you feel that the high will get so high you'll literally explode from it; my friend kept her high under control by drinking while she snorted, and afterwards to come down, but I made mine hang on longer by taking some Valium. At the peak of the high you feel incredibly efficient and productive, unbelievably creative, you know you can think things out to profound depths, that if you could only hang onto the high long enough, you could write a beautiful book, paint a masterpiece, or compose incredible music. And then the high starts to fade, and you start coming down, and all you want to do is go back up there again, right then and there."

And that was exactly what Sue did. For $100 a gram she could buy this white, snowlike powder, pour it out on a glass block, use a razor blade to scrape a small amount away from the main pile, and draw it into a line. Many cocaine addicts or aficionados announce their acquaintance with the drug by wearing little solid-gold razor blades, or miniature gold or silver "coke spoons" that will hold about a gram of the crystallized powder, and then use a straw — perhaps an elegant silver straw — to sniff up and inhale all the powder that lies in the little straight line. As Sue got acquainted with more cocaine users, she found that some would use only two or three lines — a portion of a gram — at a time, but Sue could never stop at that. She found that she could easily go through three, four, or more grams of cocaine in one evening.

Shortly after her introduction to cocaine, Sue spent just such an evening and found herself deeply in debt before the night was over. She had spent whatever cash she had available and had to borrow the remainder — not unusual among cocaine users, many of whom resort to stealing from family or friends, writing checks on relatives' bank accounts, or getting money in various other devious ways, like purchasing things on a relative's charge account and then returning the items for cash. In Sue's case, she happened to have been employed in her family's business and began writing checks on the company bank account to obtain funds for cocaine. This went on for quite some time. When the family finally discovered how many checks she was writing, and for what, they brought her to me for treatment. Sue had in mind a short term of treatment, followed by a return to her precocaine life-style, but it didn't work out that way. Her family decided she needed commitment to a long-term treatment facility. And if she left treatment, the family told her, they would prosecute.

As it turned out, the family's judgment was right on target. Sue was overdue for treatment of her cocaine addiction when I first saw her. From her account of her use of the drug, it was abundantly clear to me that she was not only stealing to buy cocaine, but also dealing and pushing as well, cutting the drug she bought to half strength in order to sell half at the highest price she could get. I calculated that her drug usage required the exchange of $3,000 to $4,000 cash per week just to keep herself in relatively the same place — not a healthy situation in terms of life and limb. It was not, however, her economic problems that made treatment so urgently necessary for Sue; it was the steady deterioration of her mental faculties. By the time I first saw her, she had developed a whole structure of paranoid delusions. She was convinced that she was being spied upon, that the police were staking her out and closing in on her, that some of her best friends had become agents against her, and that I was on their side too. This paranoid schizophrenic structure of thought disorder cleared up quickly as soon as she was in detoxification.

The paranoid mentation because of the drug was unpleasant, but the withdrawal was a full-blown crash. Sue was thoroughly depressed, lethargic, hardly able to get out of bed in the morning to drag around. It became clear that by the time Sue had finally come to treatment, she had quit using cocaine for a high because the high didn't occur anymore; she was using it more often and in increasingly larger quantities just to hold the depression at bay. She was one patient who badly needed antidepressant medication in the first few weeks of treatment to enable her to stir around at all and, very possibly, to rescue her from the threat of suicide.

Once she came to treatment and committed herself to it, Sue did not relapse. Despite a very stormy period of two or three weeks, she stuck with the program of treatment outlined below, used the time to try to reorganize some of the imperatives of her life, began to develop some solid human relationships with family and friends, and ultimately made a new life for herself.

It was not so easy for Frank K., a man of thirty-five who came to my office seeking help to get away from cocaine. Frank had both alcohol and cocaine habits to deal with, which made his problem more complex and more difficult to handle. Frank was also far more deeply enmeshed in the dealing and pushing end of the cocaine habit, constantly owing increasing amounts of money that he could not pay back to some extremely unpleasant and unsympathetic people. I am convinced that Frank would have died — been murdered — if he had not extricated himself from his circle of drug-connected people. This didn't seem to worry him, but something more important to him finally brought him to treatment. He had a job as a hotel chain executive, which he loved, but his work was deteriorating fast, and his superiors had finally confronted him: either the cocaine went, or Frank went. He refused inpatient commitment to a treatment center, but agreed to come to my office on an outpatient ' asis.

Frank relapsed three times before he finally got enough of a grip on himself to make a solid and lasting commitment to stop. The cocaine was too tempting, his drug-connected associates too close. Too much was expected of him by these people — until he finally realized that nothing they "expected of him" was ever in any way to *his* benefit. Relapse is a hazard in treating any addiction, and a major symptom of all forms of addiction. It tests the mettle of the physician, the family, the employer, and everyone else involved. Relapse cannot be accepted as lasting and meaningful; it simply means that you back off and start over, try a little harder, and build more safeguards into your program. Frank did back off and start over three separate times, but at this writing he has been "clean" of cocaine for over six months and may well stay clean for good.

Not everyone who encounters cocaine becomes addicted. Many nonaddictive people can use cocaine casually on a one-time basis, usually in a social setting, and either get no kick out of it at all or find their experience to be actively unpleasant. This is not usually true of an addictive individual. Although a few don't get hooked on cocaine after using it a few times — because they don't like it, they have some other drug of choice that cocaine doesn't replace, or there are strong social reasons for them not to use it — addictive people run an extremely high risk of becoming thoroughly addicted if they do try it.

Treating Addiction to Speed or Cocaine

Like any of the addictions we have already discussed, addiction to speed or cocaine can be treated effectively. Treatment of addiction to any of the central nervous system stimulants is essentially the same, and we could probably find no better example of the way the doctor's role in treatment and the patient's own self-help program discussed in chapter 5 can dovetail to achieve the best possible results.

The Doctor's Role. In many cases of speed or cocaine addiction, the doctor's role in treatment is essential to guard against the hazards of withdrawal and detoxification. The most imminent, and common, danger is that the withdrawal depression so common when a patient terminates these drugs can be deep and enveloping enough that the patient begins to consider suicide. I put such a patient on one of the potent tricyclic antidepressant drugs without a moment's hesitation whenever I get a signal that suicide is a possibility. These drugs require long-term use and are sometimes associated with a variety of undesirable side effects — dryness of the mouth, urinary hesitancy, and gastrointestinal disturbances, among others — but they are not addicting, and usually are effective in controlling depression at a time when it *must* be controlled.

Fortunately, most patients do not go into such profound depression, but with any of the stimulant drugs there will always be a basic period of withdrawal lasting around four to five days. During this time I tackle the problem of detoxification as vigorously as I can. The patient is started on a high-dosage schedule of vitamin C (sodium ascorbate) by intravenous drip in my office, with additional doses of 4,000 mg (one teaspoon) of the powder every two to four hours while awake at home. In addition, I prescribe as much as 3 g a day of niacinamide, one of the B vitamins that acts as an effective antidepressant, together with large doses of the amino acid tryptophan, another natural antidepressant.

Aside from withdrawal hazards, many patients during this critical period become brittle emotionally — moody, changeable, or unpredictable. Thus another part of the doctor's role is to keep close contact with such changes of mood and motivation in order to help keep the treatment program on a smooth, even keel. I try to touch base with a patient daily during the first critical days — or even more often if necessary — through daily office visits or by telephone. The patient's failure to comply with what is really a simple, straightforward treatment program is often a clue that depression is getting out of hand; another sign is evidence that the patient is getting discouraged. If things are going well, patients don't feel discouraged, because they can see their improvement and begin feeling better from the first day on. When deep depression is developing, they tend to feel discouraged that treatment isn't getting rid of it. At such times treatment has to be individualized. In some cases more vigorous antidepressant treatment is required.

The Patient's Role. Perhaps more than any other, the speed or cocaine addict needs a high degree of convinced, solid self-motivation in order to launch treatment successfully. Part of this motivation can come from learning about addictiveness, what addiction is, and what these stimulant drugs do to the body and mind. Part can also come from recognizing the physical deterioration and mental aberrations that begin to show up with continued use. Careful attention to the patient's self-help program discussed in chapter 5 is essential here.

As a first step in that program, the patient's firm commitment to discontinue the drug immediately, completely, and permanently is, of course, critical — but this can present some special problems. Like marijuana, speed and cocaine often are perceived as social rather than solitary drugs; the drug experience is often pursued and shared with others, even when the cost isn't. Addicts who determine to stop using and break away from this social fold of drug users will have lots of friends who would be delighted to see them fail, and who in fact encourage them to fail. In addition, in the case of cocaine, there will be at least one supplier who will have a solid cash stake in seeing to it that the addict fails to quit. In the face of such negative and defeating influences, the patient's best course may be to make as much change in life-style as possible simultaneously with abstaining — new friends, new activities, new recreations, perhaps even a new location if this seems necessary to cut off the old patterns.

The avoidance of alternative or substitute addictions makes obvious sense, but attention to nutritional restoration and physical rehabilitation through regular exercise is also extremely important. Speed or cocaine addiction typically is characterized by inattention to nutritional well-being or general physical conditioning. The appetite-suppression effects of speed can lead to grossly disturbed eating habits, with little or nothing eaten for days or even weeks at a time, while cocaine use becomes such a fierce preoccupation that both nutrition and exercise are forgotten. Speed or cocaine addicts, therefore, are likely to be physically ill when they come into treatment, and physically weak as well. Careful adherence to the patient's self-help nutrition and exercise programs set forth in detail in chapter 5 will help establish and maintain a common-sense restoration routine.

13

The Opiates

IN EARLIER chapters we discussed addictions to a wide variety of addicting substances, such as sugar, alcohol, caffeine, and tranquilizers. Still, for many readers, when the word "addiction" is mentioned, the first thing to come to mind will remain addiction to the "hard drugs" — the opiate narcotics.

This is not surprising, considering the enormous amount we have read and heard about the hard narcotic drugs over the years. Novels, articles, and news accounts are enough to make one think that narcotics addiction is the only addiction that really matters in today's world. We know that isn't true, of course. Narcotics addiction is not by any means the most prevalent or destructive addiction we have to deal with in this country, and a great many beliefs that people regard as facts about narcotics addiction aren't true at all. Consider the following widely held ideas, all generally regarded as true, and all of them incorrect.

- A single dose of a narcotic such as heroin is sufficient to hook an individual into addiction — the larger the dose, the more unshakable the addiction.
- Everyone who uses a hard narcotic such as heroin at all regularly inevitably becomes addicted.
- Once addicted, addicts must continually use increasingly large doses of the narcotic to feed their habit.

■ Once an addict, always an addict: it is a hopeless task to try to treat heroin addiction successfully, or to enable addicts to break their addiction.

■ Heroin addicts must have one or more "fixes" every day in order to keep going.

■ When heroin addicts can't obtain their drug, the inevitable result is the onset of agonizing and intolerable withdrawal symptoms.

■ Narcotics withdrawal is so terrible that no one can reasonably be expected to tolerate it.

■ There is a great difference between real physiological addiction and so-called psychological addiction, and this difference distinguishes hard narcotics addiction from any other kind.

Everyone has heard these "facts" about narcotics addiction expressed in one form or another. Yet in the course of treating hundreds of narcotics addicts over the years, I have come to realize that not a single one of these mythical beliefs is always true in any absolute sense. Several of them, as we will see, are almost never true. The one thing that *is* universally true is the incredible amount of variation in the patterns of hard drug addiction, which I have observed from one addict to the next.

Where did so-called hard narcotics come from, and what are their general properties?

Virtually all of the true narcotic drugs are basically analgesic, or painkilling, drugs derived in one way or another from the sap and seedpods of opium poppies (see list on pp. 204–205). The painkilling and euphoric properties of these substances have been well recognized for many centuries. The original opium, largely associated with China of the last century, was a gummy, black, resinous substance made by crushing the seedpods and drying the residue. This substance was smoked in pipes or dissolved in an alcohol solution known as laudanum, which was drunk or eaten. Today, camphorated tincture of opium, or paregoric, is still used as an antidote for diarrhea because of the opiate side effect of slowing down intestinal motility. Another side effect of virtually all the opiates is a marked depression of the respiratory centers. Because of this, the opiate drugs are used with extreme caution in patients with pulmonary emphysema or chronic obstructive lung disease.

When the alkaloids of raw opium are refined and crystallized, two major narcotic derivatives are obtained: morphine and codeine. Morphine is the oldest and one of the most potent of the natural refined narcotics still in use today. It is a powerful painkiller and, when injected hypodermically or intravenously, is capable of controlling severe degrees of pain with comparatively small doses of medication. In addition, because of its calming and euphoric effects, it can be immensely valuable in treating the crises of congestive heart failure. Its side effects include nausea and constipation, and it is highly addicting. Codeine shares the same side effects, but it is a far less potent painkiller than morphine. Nevertheless codeine has widespread legitimate medical use for controlling lesser degrees of pain and as a highly effective cough suppressant in cough syrups. Finally, raw opium alkaloids and alkaloid hydrochlorides are still found in such refined opium products as Pantopon.

Over the years the highly addicting qualities of morphine and the other opium derivatives have led to a search for natural or synthetic narcotics that would be less addicting. Around the turn of the century one such refinement product of morphine was developed, known as diacetyl morphine or diamorphine — now commonly known as heroin. Although at least as effective as morphine as a painkiller, heroin soon proved even more quickly and vigorously addictive. Although it is still used for pain therapy in England and other countries, it has been declared "without known medical value" in the United States. A whole series of other synthetic and semisynthetic narcotics developed more recently have fared better, with acknowledged medical uses. These are legitimately manufactured and prescribed. Among the best known are meperidine hydrochloride (trade name Demerol), methadone hydrochloride (trade name Dolophine), hydromorphone hydrochloride (trade name Dilaudid), and levorphanol tartrate (trade name Levo-Dromoran). Various other narcotic preparations derived from morphine or codeine are known under such trade names as Percodan, Numorphan, Fentanyl, and so forth.

All of these drugs closely resembled morphine or codeine in their painkilling potency, but all, unfortunately, proved to be highly addictive as well (no nonaddicting drug with the analgesic potency of morphine has been discovered to this day). Most are legitimately

THE MAJOR OPIATES

Prescription drugs

Generic name	Trade names
alphaprodine hydrochloride*	Nisentil (Roche)
codeine, codeine sulfate, codeine phosphate	Many products under many brand names containing codeine alone or in combination with aspirin, acetominophen, phenacetin, or other nonnarcotic analgesics.
dihydrocodeine	Synalgos (Ives)
fentanyl*	Sublimaze (Janssen) Innovar (Janssen)
heroin** (diacetyl morphine or diamorphine)	
hydrocodone bitartrate*	Damacet, Damason (Mason) Duradyne (O'Neal)
hydromorphone hydrochloride	Dilaudid (Knoll)
levorphanol tartrate*	Levo-Dromoran (Roche)
meperidine hydrochloride*	Demerol (Winthrop-Breon)
methadone hydrochloride*	Dolophine (Lilly)
morphine sulfate	Many products under many manufacturers' labels for oral and/or injectable use.
nalbuphine hydrochloride*	Nubain (DuPont)
⎰oxycodone hydrochloride*⎱ ⎰oxycodone terephthalate* ⎱ combined with aspirin	Percodan (DuPont)
oxymorphone hydrochloride*	Numorphan (DuPont)
propoxyphene hydrochloride*	Darvon (Lilly) — plain and many combinations
pentazocine hydrochloride* (a nonnarcotic drug with opiatelike actions and addictive capabilities)	Talwin (Winthrop-Breon)

Over-the-counter preparations

Note: Many opiates are contained in preparations sold over the counter either because the dosage is very low or because the opiate is considered of very low addicting capability. These products are mainly cough-suppressant medications or antidiarrheal medications. They may not be available in all states, nor on open shelves; often they must be requested of the pharmacist. Following is a representative sampling.

antidiarrheals

codeine	Kaodene with Codeine (Pfeiffer)
diphenoxylate hydrochloride	Lomotil (Searle) Loflo (Spencer Meade) Colonaid (Wallace)
opium, powdered	Diabismul (O'Neal) Parepectolin (Rorer)
opium, tincture	Parelixir (Purdue Frederick)
paregoric (camphorated tincture of opium)	Corrective Mixture with Paregoric (Beecham)

cough suppressants

codeine phosphate or dextromethorphan	Combined in many products, mostly cough syrups, tablets, or capsules, from many manufacturers.

* Denotes synthetic or semisynthetic opiatelike narcotic analgesics.
** Heroin is not currently available by prescription or any other legitimate way in the United States. It is legitimately dispensed by physicians for pain control in England and by prescription in certain other countries.

available only on a doctor's prescription, but not all are controlled by prescription. A wide variety of cough syrups, for example, containing codeine or codeinelike drugs, can be purchased over the counter. And many prescription narcotics turn up on the street market for sale and distribution among addicts as a result of supplies stolen from hospital stocks or pharmacies, or else illicitly manufactured. All the heroin that appears on the street market in this country is, of course, illegal, and since heroin is one of the most widely used of all narcotics among street addicts in the United States, we will pause here to examine it more closely.

Heroin ("Horse," "Junk," "Smack," "Shit," "H," "Big D")

Highly refined pure heroin is a white, bitter-flavored, odorless crystalline powder that is readily soluble in water. Most users, however, practically never see the drug in this degree of purity because, by the time it filters down to street users, it has been cut or mixed any number of times with any number of materials, such as milk sugar, vegetable starch, or strychnine. Thus, on the street, it may be anything from an off-white powder to dark brown. Like morphine, heroin provides only about half its potential painkilling or addiction-satisfying effect if it is taken orally, so the most common way that addicts use it is to dissolve it in water, suck it up into an eyedropper with a hypodermic needle on the end, and then inject it intravenously.

What kind of effect does heroin (or any other hard narcotic) have on a person who takes a dose? For the nonaddict who is receiving the medication to counteract pain, there is dramatic pain relief within a few minutes of receiving an injection. For many there are a number of side effects as well, including light-headedness, dizziness, a feeling of faintness, nausea, and sometimes vomiting. Even addicts may suffer some of these unpleasant side effects; one nurse I was treating who had been shooting up Demerol told me that she became nauseated and threw up every time she took the drug, a "disadvantage" that never seemed to interfere with her use of the stuff. The majority of addicts report, however, that the most common and striking effect following an intravenous dose of narcotics, especially at first, is a characteristic rush of euphoria, a soaring high, worry-free — a sudden sense of well-being and exhilaration and a feeling of "being on top of things."

These sensations appear to be felt and interpreted quite differently depending upon whether the individual is addictive or nonaddictive. The narcotic high often is not recorded by patients receiving narcotics in the hospital for the relief of pain, probably because many are nonaddictive people. Generally, such people find the sensations they experience to be not necessarily pleasant or desirable at all, and certainly not "natural." Indeed, it has long been a belief (valid, to my mind) in medicine that most patients who are first introduced to narcotics in a hospital for treatment of pain relief, perhaps even for a prolonged period, and are then withdrawn from narcotics because the pain is no longer present, suffer few or no withdrawal symptoms whatever and walk away from the hospital free of any craving. These, I believe, are nonaddictive people.

On the other hand, the addictive person who first encounters this kind of euphoric high, in a hospital or anywhere else, may light up like a Christmas tree. Some patients describe it as the most fabulous sensation they have ever encountered. This phenomenon may be closely linked to the narcotic's capacity suddenly to relieve a long-term depression that the patient may never even have realized was present — narcotics clearly do act as potent temporary antidepressants. One addict, a highly addictive person, told me that he found his first narcotics experience (in a hospital) to be so intensely pleasurable that he had never felt so good in his life. It impressed him so much that the moment he got out of the hospital he went to the library and read everything he could find on narcotics before embarking on a long period of addiction. The addictive person sometimes develops withdrawal symptoms in the hospital when a narcotic is discontinued. All too characteristically, doctors and nurses tend to treat such a patient as "an offender" when this occurs — as though the patient is being devious and is not to be trusted.

The narcotic high, when it is experienced, typically lasts anywhere from a few minutes to half an hour or more and then subsides into a general feeling of ease or relief, often ending in drowsiness or, in some people, in agitation. Sexual stimulation does not seem to be a part of this phenomenon; most heroin addicts do not appear to be interested in sexual activity, whether or not they are high on their drug of choice.

Thus for the first user the euphoric heroin high, however short-lived it may be, seems a generally pleasant, rather sleepy experience, and as it fades there may seem to be no particular discomforts or drawbacks involved. There are even a few people who use heroin socially, taking it only on very discrete, specific party occasions and never otherwise. They may be nonaddictive people who never become addicted at all — or more likely, addictive people who have a lot of self-discipline and actively intend not to become addicted. Most established addicts that I have treated, however, have reported repeated use two or three times a day for as long as a week before evidence of addiction occurred. A significant period of repeated exposure seems to be necessary; I think the popular notion that a person can be hooked with a single large dose of heroin is not true. An inexperienced person might well be made very ill by a large dose, or conceivably even killed by an overdose, but not addicted to the drug. However, novices to narcotics might well find the high from an initial dose to be so great that they are drawn to using it over and over again — and become addicted.

For the most part, sad to say, the pleasurable aspect of heroin use does not last very long. Tolerance to the drug develops very quickly, so that more and more narcotic is needed to produce a significant high. At the same time, the cost of the drug is so great that the amount most addicts can manage to purchase is sharply limited. Thus most heroin addicts quickly end up taking just barely enough drug just often enough to stay out of dreaded withdrawal, but not enough to produce a pleasurable high.

Patterns of Withdrawal

What exactly do we mean when we speak of "withdrawal symptoms"? "Withdrawal" or "withdrawal symptoms" can be broadly defined as any combination of unpleasant physical symptoms and/or psychological or emotional stresses that characteristically appear after a period of abstinence from a given drug or chemical substance. We have already seen that there is no single pattern of withdrawal symptoms that applies to all addicting drugs. Each addicting substance has its own characteristic withdrawal pattern, and among addicts to each substance there will be substantial individual variation in the withdrawal symptoms that are suffered. For one heroin addict I treated recently, withdrawal consisted primarily of being very sleepy — he literally slept his way through it — whereas another patient developed such severe abdominal pain that had I not known she was addicted, she would surely have been rushed to surgery.

In fact, about the only thing that can be said about all withdrawal patterns is that they tend to make the individual uncomfortable in one way or another, and scared to death! The discomfort can range from a minor degree of tension and ill ease on the one hand to a sequence of thoroughly unpleasant physical symptoms on the other. Much fuss has been made about the difference between so-called physical withdrawal and psychological withdrawal. I have found this to be a useless distinction, simply because withdrawal patterns to any addictive substance can embrace the whole spectrum of physical and psychological distresses. Certainly the emotional tone of the abstaining addict depends largely upon how much or how little physical distress the individual is feeling during abstinence from the drug. On the other hand, the individual's emotional reaction to withdrawal can often be influenced by his or her attitude toward the addiction and the degree of determination to terminate the addiction. In general, I have found that the higher and more genuine a given addict's individual desire and motivation to get off a drug or addicting substance, the less withdrawal distress, physical or psychological, that person will suffer. People who are pressured or bullied into abstinence against their will, with little or no motivation of their own, will be the ones who suffer more severe withdrawal.

It must be pointed out, however, that withdrawal from heroin or other hard narcotics usually is not a pleasant experience. In fact, it can be unpleasant indeed. In most cases the withdrawal symptoms occur in two recognizable steps or stages: early or first-stage withdrawal, and late or second-stage withdrawal. Early withdrawal can be subtle; it may not involve any specific or overt symptoms at all. Occurring in some addicts just a few hours after the last dose, early withdrawal may manifest itself as nothing more than the addict wanting to have another dose. This can occur long before anyone could recognize it as a stage of withdrawal. It is not that the addict is feeling bad, particularly; it is simply that the addict knows that if another dose of the drug were taken right then, he or she would be feeling good — better, that is, than at the moment.

The addict is feeling, at this point, a vague, indefinable sense of craving — with withdrawal just around the bend! This phenomenon of uneasiness experienced in early withdrawal is particularly subtle because its timing may be completely different for different users. Some people use narcotics only once a day, for example, or just on certain nights. I have treated a number of nurses who never use drugs except when they're at work. If they're on vacation they don't use, on weekends they never use, some of them never take the drug home with them — they shoot up only on the job. And these people begin to develop symptoms of early withdrawal only when it gets close to the time for their next dose, according to their individual pattern of use. In many ways such people resemble binge drinkers, who go on a binge but then don't have withdrawal until maybe a week later. They may drink on Friday and Saturday nights and get drunk both nights, for example, and then be perfectly fine all week — go to work, function well, no drinking at night when they go home — until the next weekend. *Then* withdrawal appears in the form of craving, and they head for their favorite bar.

This sort of individual withdrawal pattern would seem to make more sense if withdrawal were purely psychological rather than physiological. This, however, is not the case. The individual's mental set and individual physiological pattern of drug use combine in such a way that withdrawal symptoms occur only according to the patterns of drug use that are established.

The onset of uneasiness in early withdrawal is generally the point at which heroin addicts begin to think about and plan for their next drug dose; when they don't treat the earliest signs of withdrawal with a drug dose, the first real physiological symptoms of early withdrawal gradually begin to appear. The blood pressure goes up. The addict begins to sweat. The nose runs, the eyes water. He or she begins to complain of abdominal cramps, and can't sleep. You may see goosebumps appearing on the skin, and the addict will tell you that he or she feels terrible. Underlying all of these physical symptoms is a pervading sense of fear and anxiety, which continues to grow the longer that abstinence is maintained.

The combination of physical and psychological stresses makes withdrawal terribly scary, and narcotic addicts will do anything not to experience it. At this point in withdrawal, doctors' wives write prescriptions on their husbands' prescription forms; addicted doctors themselves call in prescriptions and do anything necessary to obtain their drug dosage; addicts steal money from their mothers' purses, lie diligently to their best friends, and become involved in all manner of violent street crime because they are desperate to stay out of withdrawal.

With further abstinence the physiological symptoms become accentuated. Although vomiting is itself not a physical symptom of the withdrawal, abdominal cramping is very much so, together with increased intestinal activity, increased bowel tone, with diarrhea following the cramps. Both blood pressure and pulse rate are elevated in this second stage of withdrawal, and there is marked dilation of the pupils. There is also a remarkable thermal reaction — the addict gets goosebumps and complains of feeling bitterly cold but is sweating profusely at the same time. Addicts arriving for treatment during second-stage withdrawal feel so cold that they often come in wrapped up in many layers of clothing. They're scared, they're cold, they're perspiring, and they're doubled up because their bellies hurt. Their pupils are huge with very little iris showing; lacrimation and dripping of the nose may be dramatic in some cases, absent in others.

Rarely do all of these symptoms show up all at once all of the time; some symptoms come and some go. The addict with goosebumps may sometimes have them and sometimes not. Almost always, however, if you touch an addict in advanced withdrawal, the person will jump. It's as if the nervous system is stretched like a tight rubber band, and any loud sound like slamming a door or any sudden action such as touching will make the addict jump. It's not that the addict is jerky or twitchy, like a person about to have a convulsion; it's more as though the nerves are laid out raw on the outside of the body.

The unpleasant nature of second-grade withdrawal helps to explain some of the curiosities one observes about heroin addicts and their addictive behavior. For example, if you happen to be looking around an addict's living quarters, you may not find any standard syringes, even though they are readily available at any drugstore. You may find other paraphernalia that addicts use for shooting up, however. A "kit" characteristically contains a spoon, some cotton, an eyedropper outfitted with some kind of hypodermic needle, and a pacifier. Addicts will melt the drug in water in the spoon held over a flame or a stove burner, cook it up good, and then use the eyedropper with the needle and pacifier for sucking it up and injecting it. They don't like to use syringes, if they can help it, because a standard syringe wastes about one tenth of a cc of the preparation that stays in the syringe. Because of the impurities that may be present, they use little wads of cotton to strain the stuff through before injecting it. Then when they run out of heroin, they get out all their old cottons, rinse them out with water, and shoot that — it's called "shooting cotton." It is like using coffee grounds a second or third time, and is a last resort to stay out of withdrawal.

For all their concern about staying out of withdrawal, however, heroin addicts do not characteristically keep any extra supply of the drug around in reserve unless they deal. Whereas the alcoholic may keep supplies of booze stashed away here and there and prescription-drug addicts may keep small supplies of their drug hidden in the dresser drawer or in the trunk of the car as a reserve against withdrawal, the heroin addict typically uses up every last bit of the drug, and worries about getting a new supply later.

What do these people do when they can't score a new supply? First of all, they are not likely to go into withdrawal until the time that their body's pattern of use demands it. The weekend user may go all week without any drug and not begin withdrawal until the following weekend. Even then there are ways to postpone withdrawal — like eating sugar, for example. I got one of my first clues that addictiveness is an inherited carbohydrate defect when I saw how much sugar heroin addicts eat. They eat sugar all the time — but when approaching withdrawal, they simply gorge on it, eating heaps of candy bars, drinking can after can of sugar-sweetened soda. It helps them handle withdrawal. In addition, they can substitute any other narcotic drug in place of heroin and do just as well. If the heroin addict can get some Dilaudid, for example, that's fine. (In fact, that's better than heroin because it's more reliable.) They can even postpone withdrawal with a supply of cough syrup containing codeine or dihydrocodeinone. Heroin addicts soon lose the ability to feel pleasure from their drug, however. They live an existence almost always on the thin edge of withdrawal and are constantly driven to find some way to support a very expensive habit that offers them little but postponement of withdrawal symptoms.

Withdrawal Variations

What we have identified as "typical" or "characteristic" of heroin addiction applies to the great majority of heroin addicts — but not necessarily to all of them. Some addicts to heroin or other narcotics suffer comparatively little from withdrawal, or even go off a narcotic habit cold turkey without any significant amount of discomfort.

Much seems to depend upon individual circumstances, and individual motivation. One of my early narcotic addict patients was a nurse named Mary Ann, who developed her habit while working on the acute postsurgical floor, one of the areas in a hospital where narcotics are widely and frequently used. Three times she was caught in the act of shooting herself up on the job, and each time she was transferred off the surgical floor and told that she had to get herself straight. Each time she did exactly that — simply by not using any narcotics. Each time the nursing board subsequently returned her to work on the surgical floor, contending that she couldn't possibly be an addict because she showed no evidence of withdrawal. In fact, she *was* an addict and she *did* have withdrawal symptoms; hers just weren't all that severe, and she refused to let any sign show when her job depended upon it.

I saw a similar case in Dr. John T., one of the multitudes of doctors who get started shooting up narcotics just for a lift at the end of a hard day, to enable them to work longer hours more efficiently. One day the Drug Enforcement Agency men came into his office, produced a record of the drugs he had been obtaining far beyond the amounts necessary to his practice, and told him they were revoking his narcotics privileges. Caught flat-footed with direct evidence of his use, and threatened with professional exposure as an addict and possible loss of his license, the doctor went cold turkey off high daily doses of Demerol without showing any significant evidence of withdrawal. He had some withdrawal symptoms, all right, but simply went along with them and kept working because he felt he had to.

In yet another case, I knew a patient supposedly on methadone maintenance therapy in a program where the amount of methadone she was given each day had slowly been reduced to none. She hadn't been receiving any at all for a month. She was still taking the colored fruit juice that she thought contained methadone, however. This woman suffered no withdrawal symptoms until the day the people running the program informed her that she hadn't actually received any methadone for weeks. As soon as she learned this, she immediately developed acute second-grade withdrawal symptoms.

I think it is occasional observations of this sort, and the many apparent contradictions in the nature and expression of withdrawal symptoms, that account for the great argument about whether withdrawal is physical or psychological. I still maintain that the distinction doesn't make any difference. You can get physiologic withdrawal symptoms with your head at certain times and at other times you can *prevent* physiologic withdrawal symptoms with your head. The psychology affects physiology and vice versa, and we just don't understand how. Any given human being is a completely integrated package of emotion, intellect, physiology, and spirit, and you can't separate those parts into nice neat piles. In the matter of withdrawal, what is emotional and what is physiologic is constantly overlapping, and just as you can get an ulcer as a result of emotional stress, you can get rid of physiologic pain with the right kind of thinking. These close interconnections are merely underlined, in the case of addiction and addictive people, by the discoveries that are currently being made in the area of natural endorphins.

Beta-Endorphins and Endorphinless People

There has never been any real argument that the strong physically addicting qualities of virtually all of the opiate narcotics have some kind of physiological basis — they result from some discrete biochemical mechanism in the body. Until recently, however, nobody had the slightest clue to what that physiological basis might be. Obviously, a drug like heroin hooked onto something in the human body and produced biochemical changes, and then caused a lot of physiological distress when it was withdrawn. But hooked onto what? Caused what kind of changes? And why the withdrawal distress? Nobody knew.

Then in the early 1970s, S. H. Snyder and C. B. Pent, both of Johns Hopkins University School of Medicine, and other researchers, discovered that people have certain natural biochemical receptors in the brain and central nervous system that seem able to take up or "bind" opiate narcotics. At first glance this discovery didn't make sense; why on earth would our bodies have evolved specific receptor sites to match up with opiate narcotics unless opiate narcotic chemicals were already present — or expected to be present — in the body? The question was answered in 1975 when J. Hughes and H. W. Kosterlitz of the University of Aberdeen discovered that the body actually did produce its own opiatelike chemicals capable of binding to those opiate receptor sites. The predominant chemicals in this group came to be known as beta-endorphins.

The beta-endorphins, first isolated from the pituitary gland, are produced by the body in response to such things as pain and stress and, indeed, help relieve pain much as if they were opiate narcotics. In fact, these natural substances are so closely akin to narcotic drugs that when narcotic antagonists (drugs that counteract the effects of narcotics) are given to a person, not only does the endorphin-quieted pain recur, but the individual begins feeling withdrawal symptoms.

These discoveries have led to a great deal of speculation and experimentation with regard to the possible behavior of natural endorphins in the body as compared with the opiate narcotics. Might it be possible to stimulate or manipulate natural beta-endorphins as a means of pain control? For centuries Chinese and other Oriental physicians have used acupuncture needles as a means of reducing pain or even inducing anesthesia. Western physicians had always dismissed this as "magic medicine" until a few of them began considering that these needles, which were used to barely tickle nerve endings in the skin, might actually be stimulating the body's production of natural beta-endorphins, which in turn serve to counteract pain or induce anesthesia. And what about the possible use of synthetic or laboratory-derived beta-endorphins for pain control? Would these substances prove superior to morphine or Demerol? What about addictiveness? Are natural beta-endorphins addicting? If they were supplied from the outside for pain control, would patients suffer withdrawal symptoms when the supply was terminated?

The questions still are not answered definitively, but some patterns are becoming clear. We know that the body's natural production of beta-endorphins can indeed be stimulated by a number of conditions, including pain, stress, acupuncture needles, and even prolonged vigorous exercise such as long-distance jogging. We know that these chemicals do fill up endorphin receptors, and when there is a superabundance of the endorphins, additional receptors seem to be created. We know that the beta-endorphins behave with uncanny similarity to morphine, Demerol, and other opiate narcotics; people do suffer withdrawal symptoms when beta-endorphin production is, for some reason, terminated; the jogger does indeed experience a high at the peak of jogging and definitely "comes down" slowly after the jogging ends. More than anything, beta-endorphins seem to have something to do with the individual's overall emotional tone; they seem to contribute to "feeling good," and there is some evidence that certain people who chronically and continually "feel bad" may be people who simply have a poor natural supply of beta-endorphins. Some have no identifiable endorphins at all, and they are miserable most of the time.

Certainly there is similarity enough between natural endorphins and narcotic drugs that we can expect narcotics to interact with endorphins one way or another when they are taken into the body. So far, however, we don't know what actual interactions occur. It seems possible — but has not been proven — that narcotics placed in the body might tend to upset the balance of natural endorphin, or depress the amount being produced, so that when the narcotic is withdrawn a number of receptors are left empty, leading to withdrawal symptoms. Researchers also have discovered receptors other than the opiate receptors that seem to respond to drugs such as Valium. Clearly, there is no reason that the body should possess receptors for a specific synthetic drug introduced in 1963 — but if the body has natural products that are chemically similar in nature to diazepam, this could not only account for receptors that appear "made" for Valium, but also could account for the fact that Valium seems to help relieve the withdrawal symptoms of narcotics so well.

There is no question that scientists in a dozen different fields will continue to study beta-endorphins most intensively in the laboratory. The possibilities are exciting, and so far the surface of knowledge of these substances has hardly been scratched. Already endorphins have been synthesized, and soon clinical doses of endorphins will be available to scientists for investigational use with patients. It is also possible at this time to run blood endorphin levels on patients, and thus to identify and observe a small, fascinating, and exceedingly peculiar special subpopulation: a group of individuals who appear to be virtually bereft of any natural endorphins.

So far I have identified five or six such people in my practice, and the possible relationship between their endorphinless state and their addictiveness and addictions is intriguing. I've observed that these people seem to feel absolutely miserable all the time. Their muscles ache, they have frequent headaches, they feel depressed and anxious — indeed, they never seem to feel good in the same way that normal people do. On the surface they may manage to function reasonably well in their everyday life, but they never seem to enjoy life to any degree and they appear to be poor at interpersonal relationships, always maintaining a well-marked emotional distance from other people. For two of those patients in my practice, life looks absolutely impossible to them, so painful and hard that there is no joy in it. The only things that give them relief are narcotics and Valium, and they become addicted readily.

A third patient, a doctor, also falls into this bizarre category of individuals. The only way that Harold can keep himself feeling halfway decent is by exercising energetically for two hours or more every day. He either runs or plays racquetball or tennis, and that seems, temporarily, to get enough natural endorphins produced in his system to keep him feeling half alive. He does not ordinarily drink, but reports a curious thing: on those rare occasions when he does drink, a single drink has a remarkable effect, producing in him a feeling of well-being that he rarely experiences otherwise. I strongly suspect that he would be a user of narcotics, if he ever discovered them. Cocaine would probably produce the same effect in him.

Quite recently Harold was at a medical conference and thus unable to keep up on his regular daily exercise. During this brief time you could see him running down like an old-fashioned phonograph. Finally he couldn't stand it anymore and left the conference abruptly, without farewells. As he climbed into his cab, he looked and acted as if he were totally drained — as though he couldn't go another inch forward. I would guess that he has such experiences quite often; he is fortunate that he has been able to build a lot of exercise into his life.

What is happening in these people? Although a great deal of work is currently being done to clarify what is going on, so far we don't really have answers — just speculations. It seems plausible that there might be a certain small number of people who — for reasons as yet unknown — produce far fewer natural endorphins than normal people, or produce them with greater difficulty, or require greater stimuli to produce them, just as there are certain people who — for reasons still unclear — produce less natural insulin than normal. As we have already pointed out, there are definitely people who develop withdrawal symptoms just a few hours after their last dose of a hard narcotic, whereas others can go for a week without withdrawal, and still others can withdraw cold turkey without any serious withdrawal symptoms at all if their motivation is high enough. Such differences could be based largely on individual differences in production of natural endorphins. People with a high supply of natural endorphins may use them to "fill in" for hard narcotics, so to speak, when the supply is suddenly cut off. Or, equally plausibly, natural endorphin production might become attuned to the pattern of narcotics use of a given addict; if that addict used narcotics only once a week, for example, or only three nights a week, that might be the pattern that his or her body's natural endorphins have adjusted to. None of these speculations is clearly valid, at this point, but the connection between endorphins and narcotics addiction patterns seems far too close to evade us for long, and soon we will begin to develop useful answers.

Patterns of Narcotic Use

When nonaddictive people come into my office, they usually stick out like a sore thumb because they don't display the addictive pattern. I recall one patient, an osteopathic physician, who came to me and said, "My doctor wanted me to come and see you because he thinks I'm addicted to Demerol."

"Well, are you?" I said.

"I don't know; I certainly don't feel any need for it, and I never had withdrawal symptoms."

It turned out that this doctor had been on Demerol for over six months while being treated for a painful hip fracture. The doctor who referred him assumed that he was addicted because he'd been using Demerol regularly for six months. But there was no family history of addiction, no history of addiction to other drugs such as tobacco or sugar, and no evidence of depression or that he was either addictive or addicted. So I said, "There's no evidence of any kind that you're an addictive person, and you're not addicted," and sent him home. Typically, such people are nondefensive at the question of whether they are addicted or not. They say, "If I have an addiction to these pain pills that I've had to take, I certainly want to find out because I wouldn't want to be addicted." They tell you exactly how much they're using, and they're eager to have treatment if they need it. This approach is not typical of addictive people, who may have all kinds of defenses, denials, and rationalizations for their drug use, trying to convince me and themselves that they're not addicted.

Many people have the idea that hard narcotics addicts invariably increase the amount of drug they use, so that the frequency of their habit becomes ever-greater. Actually, a couple of outside factors exercise very rigid control over this kind of escalation. One such factor is plain economics. Narcotics addiction is very expensive, and most addicts have certain realistic limits on how much drug they can afford to buy. Usually only dealers can afford to use large or increasing amounts.

A few addicts have a family source of money, but in most such cases the family uses the funds to maintain control of the addict — the money is by no means freely available. By far the majority of heroin addicts must either hold down some kind of job to help pay for the addiction, or do something illegal to get the money. Essentially, then, it is much more accurate to say that heroin addicts use as much drug as they can afford to buy or otherwise obtain, and this sets a limit on how much they can escalate their usage. Dealers often have the biggest habit because they have the most dope!

The other limit is simply the amount of time that has to be spent acquiring funds, making contacts with dealers, and so forth, so that the time the addict has left for *using* the drug tends to be limited. An addict may, for example, spend literally all day long going from doctor's office to doctor's office, either following up on doctors who have already supplied narcotics prescriptions or seeing new doctors in attempts to con them into supplying new prescriptions, and this can be hard, daylong work. Stealing enough money to cover a day's habit can involve even more time — a point most people would never even think of, but many addicts must. Thus a number of factors, in combination, pressure addicts into using as little narcotic as they can get along on, rather than escalating their dose, as many people imagine they do.

What most people do not imagine, however, is the knife-edge of sheer violence upon which the street addict lives. This is especially true of those addicts who are trying to support their own drug habits in part by cutting or diluting the supply of drug they obtain and then selling part of it, so that they become dealers themselves, in effect. This activity exposes them to all kinds of potential violence. Many of these people carry guns — they never go anywhere without them. They never know when somebody is going to shoot them, or burn their house down, or assault them on the street. The amount and sort of random violence they encounter can be phenomenal — enough, one might think, to force them out of addiction altogether.

That actually happens, at least temporarily, more often than most people believe. Contrary to the popular picture, most hard narcotics addicts do not remain constantly and continuously addicted from the time they are hooked until some nebulous end point is reached. Most of them, in fact, are on and off their drug at irregular intervals, and actually spend a significant amount of time *not* using. This may occur because of unevenness in the supply of drug, poor quality of heroin, or temporary embarrassment over lack of funds (narcotics are not sold on credit); because of some intercurrent illness that makes it impossible to obtain money or drug; because of a period of incarceration in jail, where narcotics are at least somewhat more difficult to come by than on the street, though not much; because of entry into a voluntary or involuntary treatment program; or for other personal and individual reasons.

What do addicts do during such a period? If they aren't taking their addicting narcotic of choice, they usually are seeking a substitute of some kind. They may be getting by on Valium or the codeine in cough syrups, for example, or drinking alcohol, or eating lots of sugar; overall, they may spend considerable time off the drug of choice altogether. They may be off for a day or two or even a week — probably not more than a month, although it's possible. The phenomenon is so common that addicts have a word for the times during which they were using: "runs." They will say, "This run is two months old," meaning, "I've been using for two months."

Finally, one of the most widely reported "hazards" of narcotics addiction isn't actually a hazard at all, at least not in the way people think. This is the matter of overdosing on narcotics. My experience has convinced me that heroin addicts do not overdose themselves — indeed, they probably *cannot* overdose themselves — on the narcotic alone. I have seen cases in which huge amounts of narcotic were injected, even over a prolonged period of time, without death occurring. Some of my patients have deliberately tried to commit suicide by overdosing, without success. In one striking case, a nurse took the entire stock of narcotics from the surgical floor of the hospital where she worked and went to a motel with the intent to end it all. There she began shooting up until she passed out. She did this repeatedly every time she regained consciousness. After twenty-four hours she couldn't continue, because the drugs were gone — but she was still very much alive.

Of course, people do die in relation to narcotics use, but they may not have been addicted. In virtually every case you hear about — people like Jimi Hendrix or Janis Joplin, for example — the fatal event occurs as a reaction to a variety of other drugs that can be particularly deadly. Heroin taken on top of a heavy dose of alcohol, for example, can be highly dangerous. Valium and alcohol are well recognized as a deadly enough combination just by themselves; add heroin and you could have a killer mixture. It's also true that addicts may not know — often *cannot* know — exactly what is in the supply of drug they buy. There is "good stuff," and there is "bad stuff" — heavily contaminated stuff; some of the contaminants in combination with other drugs that may have been taken can be more than the body can tolerate. And finally, according to such authorities as Washington State's King County Medical Examiner, many deaths ascribed to overdose may actually be due to acute respiratory depression, Sudden Death Syndrome similar to crib death, aspiration of food or vomitus leading to choking or aspiration pneumonia, or other causes only peripherally related to narcotics use.

Treating Narcotics Addiction — The Traditional Method

If most narcotics addicts are not actually using their drug of choice all the time, and if most of them do not overdose themselves, then it follows that most of them from time to time have periods of abstinence from their drug, whatever the reason. Some actually seek or receive treatment during these periods.

Addicts seek treatment for a number of reasons. Some of them simply get tired of the rat race of constantly trying to gather the funds necessary to maintain their habits. It's not exactly an easy life to lead. Others — doctors, nurses, housewives, or otherwise reasonably solid citizens — suddenly find themselves under terrific professional, social, or family pressure to stop and seek treatment. Still others "enter treatment" involuntarily by virtue of being arrested and put in jail where they are forced to go cold turkey. In such a case, "treatment" may amount to enforced abstinence and nothing more.

For those who so choose, there are various publicly supported and private programs for the treatment of addiction, including live-in therapeutic communities and outpatient programs. Most of the latter depend heavily upon one of two programs: either methadone detoxification, or methadone maintenance. These plans employ a synthetic narcotic known as methadone (trade name Dolophine), which was developed during World War II under the illusion that it was a weaker or less addicting narcotic than morphine or heroin. The drug was intended to help relieve the withdrawal symptoms of heroin and other narcotics. In actual use, however, methadone is every bit as addicting as other narcotics, and has a much longer period of action, so it prevents withdrawal for up to two days after a single oral dose. Withdrawal from methadone lasts for weeks or months, untreated.

In either the methadone detoxification program (intended to detoxify or "de-poison" the heroin addict through gradual withdrawal) or the methadone maintenance program (intended to maintain the addict on methadone indefinitely so he or she won't need heroin), the methadone is given in oral dosage form, mixed up with fruit juice or some such beverage, usually on a daily basis. This is done on the assumption that methadone addiction is in some way better or more desirable than heroin addiction. In the methadone detoxification program, the amount of methadone given each day is reduced or tapered off, with the idea of ending up with no narcotic at all. This actually works in some cases, when the addict's motivation to break free is high enough and the withdrawal is sufficiently tolerable for the addict to make it through the tapering process. It works in only about 2 percent of all cases, however — which means it fails about 98 percent of the time. Unfortunately for this program, the tapering process goes on for about three weeks before the zero-narcotics point is reached. By that time, all too often the addict has long since dropped out of the program and gone back to the original drug, or has become addicted to methadone, so that he or she leaves the program with a larger habit than before!

Methadone maintenance and methadone detoxification both have other serious flaws. One of the most important, and most obvious, is that unless the addict really *wants* to break free of narcotics addiction, the methadone programs provide all kinds of incentive and opportunity to play games. Both programs customarily require the addict to demonstrate clearly that he or she is already in severe or second-grade withdrawal before any methadone is given. The intent is to make sure that a true addiction is present so that the methadone doesn't kill the addict on the third day. (The blood level increases for about three days, then levels off.) A nonaddicted person could die from the usual dose of methadone.

Although methadone was standard treatment for heroin addiction, it seemed to me so replete with problems, and the idea of treating one narcotics addiction by inducing another seemed so ridiculous, that I didn't even apply for permission to administer methadone when I went into private practice. Using my own approach to treatment, I obtained just as good or better results without using methadone, so I could see no reason for adding an addicting drug to the one that was already entrenched.

Treating Narcotics Addiction —
An Alternative That Works

So how does one approach treating this particularly difficult kind of addiction? The basic rules outlined in chapter 5 for the doctor's contribution and the patient's self-help role in treating any kind of addiction apply to narcotics addiction as well, with the help of a number of special weapons from the treatment armamentarium.

The first prerequisite for successful treatment — perhaps the single element that we really must have in order to win — is the proper motivation. This is the patient's initial and most essential contribution; nobody else can provide it. The patient must want to be "clean" of addicting drugs if treatment is to be successful. Neither I nor anyone else can work toward successful treatment until the addict reaches a point where he or she really *does* want to give it up.

Thus when I begin managing a patient's treatment I try in every way I can to establish the individual's basic motivation as strongly as possible. Sometimes it is there and waiting — the patient really is fed up, and wants help. Sometimes the motivation is supplied by pressure from the outside. Whatever will help the patient develop motivation, I am for it, but the bottom line is that the motivation ultimately must be the patient's own. At the same time I find out about other factors that can be crucial to successful treatment: Is the patient involved in other drug, alcohol, or sugar-food addiction? Does the patient's DST suggest the possibility of endogenous depression? Is there any evidence of active depression present then and there?

The next two steps in treatment, simultaneously, are withdrawal and detoxification. As with other addictions, withdrawal must be both immediate and complete — no tapering, no "one last fling." The patient who isn't ready for this isn't ready for treatment, and thus is not treatable. It doesn't mean that I throw the patient out of my office; it simply means that more time and effort — perhaps a lot more time and effort — must be spent preparing the person for treatment. I have known patients to come back seven or eight times, thinking they were ready to go when they really weren't ready to make that final, firm personal commitment.

Once the commitment is made and acted upon — that is, the drug is stopped — detoxification can help clear residual drug out of the body and minimize withdrawal. I administer large doses of vitamin C in the form of sodium ascorbate, 8 g daily, by intravenous infusion in my office during the first week following cessation of the drug. In addition, I give vitamin C powder, 4 to 8 g by mouth, every two to four hours for two to five days. I do not know precisely how vitamin C works, but its detoxification properties are well known and I have observed that these patients do better than similar patients did before I used this approach. It may be that ascorbate's antioxidant effect helps. It acts like magic, in any case, relieving withdrawal almost instantly.

Along with the ascorbate, I count heavily on the detoxifying and supportive effect of a carefully structured nutritional program and exercise program to accompany cessation of the drug. In many cases heroin addicts are in terrible physical and nutritional condition when they come to treatment. Some are so physically debilitated that they can barely walk around the block. Both the nutritional rehabilitation program and the exercise regimen I recommend are discussed in detail in the patient's self-help program in chapter 5, including elimination of sugar-foods, frequent small feedings of protein supplement and unrefined carbohydrates, and vitamin and mineral supplements as well. The exercise program is started simultaneously, as soon as the patient is able. The doctor can outline these programs and be on the alert for any physical limitations that require special attention, but the patient must implement the programs faithfully as part of his or her contribution to the treatment.

Withdrawal, to whatever extent it is going to emerge, will make its appearance on the first, second, or third day in most patients and be over by the fifth day if they don't use in the interim. In helping patients deal with the severe withdrawal symptoms of narcotics addiction, I use any aspect of treatment available, including drug therapy — except, of course, I do *not* use addicting drugs. Control of withdrawal symptoms and manipulation of the individual patient's response to withdrawal becomes something of an art in this kind of treatment program because there can be so much individual variation both in symptoms that develop and in response to therapeutic measures.

A drug that can be helpful in combating narcotics withdrawal is clonidine hydrochloride (trade name Catapres), which came on the market in the mid-1970s as a new antihypertension medicine. Quite by coincidence, it was discovered that clonidine also worked remarkably well in relieving narcotics withdrawal symptoms — possibly through the same pharmacological activity that lowers blood pressure. Excellent studies have been done at Yale University demonstrating the efficacy of this drug in treating narcotic withdrawal.

Fortunately, narcotics withdrawal symptoms, at their worst, only last a matter of a few days, but other deleterious things can last much longer. One major problem that can appear to hinder the treatment of any addiction is that many patients become deeply depressed during the course of treatment. Once again, drug treatment can greatly relieve a patient's depression and at the same time help save the patient from possible treatment failure. There are a number of medications, most notably the so-called tricyclic antidepressants, which are useful in treating endogenous depression when it arises; since one patient may respond better to one such drug and another patient to another, finding the right drug in each individual case may require therapeutic trials of one or two or several. The whole course of treatment literally depends in many cases upon medication at the first sign of depression.

Does the program I have described actually work in treating a long-term, entrenched heroin addict? That, of course, is the acid test, and the answer is that it does indeed work — if the doctor and the patient each fulfills his or her part in the treatment program to the fullest extent possible, and if the patient really wants to become drug-free. Here is a record from my files of how one narcotics addict's treatment progressed.

When I first saw Harry N., age twenty-seven, he had been addicted to heroin off and on for more than six years. For the past six months he had been on a government-supported methadone maintenance program — 50 mg of methadone every day. Because of a rules violation (his urine tests showed he had been back on heroin in addition to his methadone), Harry was told that he would be given twenty-one-day methadone detoxification and then kicked out of the program. On the tenth day of detoxification he called our office and asked for help. He had heard that we could help people get off methadone, and that they were able to stay free of drugs thereafter. He dreaded the prolonged period of withdrawal symptoms he faced after the methadone was completely terminated, and was afraid he'd resort to going back to heroin.

First Day

On a Monday morning Harry arrived at my office on time, accompanied by his wife, who had driven the car because Harry didn't feel well enough to drive. Because of the methadone detoxification schedule, Harry was already in quite severe second-stage withdrawal discomfort. He said that his bones and muscles ached constantly, and he felt absolutely terrible, with abdominal cramps, diarrhea, and intermittent hot and cold flashes. He said he had not slept at all for three nights. He was clearly depressed and appeared very apprehensive.

In addition to his narcotics addiction, I ascertained that Harry's diet was loaded with sugar-foods; he took no vitamins or minerals; he smoked two packs of cigarettes a day and drank six to eight cups of coffee daily. He did not drink alcohol because he didn't care for its effects. This history was taken in my office with Harry and his wife both present; spouses are included whenever possible, since their support is an enormous contribution to successful treatment. Harry's wife did not use drugs and wanted to help him in any way she could.

In reviewing his history with him, I kept looking for clues suggesting that Harry was truly motivated to become drug-free. Finally convinced that he was sincerely prepared to make the necessary serious commitment, I outlined the treatment program I had in mind for him to follow. I explained how this treatment could help keep him reasonably comfortable during the next few days, but that he would have to work at staying away from his former drug associates, and that attendance at Narcotics Anonymous and Naranon would be important for both him and his wife.

For the first few days, starting that day, I explained it would be necessary for him to come to my office daily for injections of vitamin C and other vitamins and minerals. Daily counseling with one of my office staff would also be vital. At first, each day, he would receive a very large dose of vitamin C intravenously in the form of sodium ascorbate to help control withdrawal and keep symptoms at a minimum. In addition, I outlined a schedule of other vitamins, amino acids, and protein supplements that he was to take on a regular schedule at home between office visits. I ordered two prescriptions — clonidine and Darvon N 100 — to help counteract the withdrawal symptoms he was already suffering, and in addition prescribed one of the potent antidepressant drugs because of the marked degree of depression I observed to be present.

By the time Harry had received the office medications, had his initial counseling session, and was ready to leave, a great deal of the apprehension he had demonstrated on arrival had vanished — an important first step in the right direction.

Second Day

Although his energy level was very low, and once again his wife had driven him to the office, Harry's mental attitude seemed much improved on the second day. For one thing, he had slept well for the first time in almost two weeks. He was taking his supplements and medications as directed and found the withdrawal symptoms, although unpleasant, much more tolerable than he had expected. A second injection of sodium ascorbate was given intravenously, and Harry had a second counseling session. I reviewed with him exactly how his day had gone and how he felt. His wife had been very supportive and had helped him take his supplements on schedule. He was eating very little, but the protein supplement was helping keep his nutrition up.

As he prepared to leave I praised him heartily (and sincerely) for the progress he had made already and urged him to remain confident that things would continue to improve. I reminded him that he must not use any drugs except those I had ordered. I also urged him to make his first contact with Narcotics Anonymous without delay, even though he insisted that they wouldn't be able to help him. I offered as much support and encouragement as possible, knowing that the next twenty-four hours would be critical to his continued recovery.

About eight o'clock that evening I heard from my answering service that Harry had called me on an "urgent matter," and I returned his call promptly. I was afraid that a disaster had occurred and that Harry would be high on heroin, but he wasn't. All he really wanted was to touch base, perhaps just to reassure himself that help was there if he needed it. He was discouraged and depressed, afraid the program wasn't going to work. We talked for about fifteen minutes, during which time I encouraged him to restate to me (and for himself) all the positive reasons why he wanted to stay drug-free. I pointed out that as long as he stuck to the program, it couldn't help but work, and urged him to recognize that the hardest part was already behind. The conversation ended on a more positive note than it had begun, and I remained hopeful.

Third Day

This morning Harry was smiling and remarking on how good he felt. He said he had decided to discontinue the last week of the methadone detox program because there was "no point to it," and for the first time he voluntarily reiterated his commitment to becoming drug-free and his conviction that he was going to make it. He said he felt well enough to take a ten-minute walk that morning, and intended to increase the time the next day. After his office medication I drew some lab studies to monitor his medications and his physical condition.

Fourth Day

Harry continued doing well, with a marked decline in his withdrawal symptoms. His energy level still was not great, but at least was improving. Since he had developed diarrhea from the vitamin C (a common side effect of high dosages), the amount was cut in half. He was tolerating the clonidine well, with no evidence of symptoms due to low blood pressure.

Fifth Day

Harry seemed particularly apprehensive on day five — something we often see in a recovering patient with the approach of a weekend — but otherwise his progress continued satisfactorily. His appetite was finally beginning to return, and he was taking two ten-minute walks a day. Perhaps more important, from my viewpoint, he had attended his first Narcotics Anonymous meeting the previous evening. When I spoke privately to his wife, she was both delighted and slightly bewildered at what was happening — his personality seemed to be opening up day by day, she said, and he was becoming a different and more stable person than the sick, addicted Harry she had married. I pointed out how much help the Naranon organization could be to her in adjusting her own feelings to the "different Harry" she would be continuing to see. As for Harry, his apprehension seemed markedly relieved when I assured him that he could reach me by telephone over the weekend if the need arose. If necessary, I could meet him at the office to give him an injection, but I thought he could do without it.

Sixth and Seventh Days

No weekend calls. Harry later reported that he had felt stable and reasonably comfortable all weekend.

Eighth Day

Although some residual withdrawal symptoms remained, Harry appeared cheerful, comfortable, and confident on Monday morning. I reduced his clonidine dosage but maintained the antidepressant because he still had episodes of depression. During this second week I planned to see him three times and have him continue his program of supplements at home. Meanwhile, Harry felt well enough to make plans to return to work. He continued to go to Narcotics Anonymous meetings three times a week, and his wife attended Naranon for family members of addicts. For the first time, I began to feel confident that Harry was indeed going to get out of the woods.

* * *

Harry N.'s recovery from this point on was remarkably uneventful. The same, of course, cannot be said for all addicts in treatment. Indeed, in treating most narcotics addicts, the most dangerous threat of all is the threat of readdiction — plain old backsliding — and once the initial intensive week of withdrawal is over, this becomes the major enemy to fight. Every possible external support must be called upon to supplement and bolster the patient's own internal motivation and commitment. The doctor and the doctor's office staff are most deeply involved on the initial day and days, touching base with the patient in person or by telephone two or three times a day, if needed, to maintain support and encouragement. Daily or every-other-day office visits, adjustments of medications, and review of the nutritional support program are carried out as needed as the patient moves through the most trying period. At the same time, external support is sought from such organizations as Narcotics Anonymous, with the patient attending regular and frequent meetings. The patient can obtain powerful support by going to gatherings of once-narcotics-addicts who are all off the narcotics and have been for weeks and months. These contacts can help maintain abstinence long after the acute phase of treatment is over and provide a bulwark against the kind of complacency and overconfidence that can all too easily lead to relapses. Close family members should also be involved so that they can provide ample support from another direction.

Relapses do occur, of course, sometimes repeatedly. Indeed, in regard to any addiction, one could say that relapses are more the rule than the exception, and once again it is critical that everyone — patient, doctor, office staff, family — keep their eyes firmly on the long-term goal and not on the sometimes circuitous path necessary to achieve it. The patient who has been off drugs for two months and has started to rebuild his body and his life and then relapses is, at least, two months and some achievements ahead of the person who has not started at all.

Clearly, then, treatment of hard narcotics addiction is a long-term and multifaceted campaign, probably more dependent upon the doctor's guidance and intervention than many other addiction treatment problems. In fact, there is no distinct end point to be reached. Recovering narcotics addicts, like recovering alcoholics, must make peace with the fact that they are, and always will be, *recovering,* not recovered or cured.

14

To the Physician

ADDICTION IS a disease of denial and relapse and is frequently hidden behind physical and emotional complaints. We are handicapped in treating addictions by the lack of training in this area in medical school. We are further handicapped by lack of training in nutrition. Consequently, we are not alert to early signs and signals of addictions in our patients, nor are we alert to significant vitamin and mineral deficiencies and the value of treating them.

Often we recognize addiction only when it is glaring and advanced or when the patient comes to us asking for help with addiction. It is vital that the physician diagnose alcoholism and/or drug addiction before the patient progresses so far that the physical signs are visible to all.

Identifying Addictions

The disease of addiction is no respecter of individuals and is found in all groups of people, no matter how educated, how wealthy, or how influential they may be.

It is important to consider it in every patient. Basic questions about alcohol and drug use are vital in each patient's history.

Minimal Alcoholism History

As part of the routine history and physical, these questions can elicit important information that screens for alcoholism hallmarks: tolerance change, loss of control, and secondary physical and psychological symptoms.

Tolerance Change
1. How much do you usually drink a day?
2. How much can you drink in a twenty-four-hour period?
3. Does it take more or less alcohol now to achieve the same effect?

Loss of Control
4. Has anyone suggested that you drink too much?
5. Do you drink more than you intend?
6. Have you ever tried to control your drinking or promised to go "on the wagon"?
7. Do you use any drugs to cut down on your drinking?

Secondary Complications
8. Has drinking ever caused a problem in your life (family, work, courts, finances)? How often?
9. Have you ever had health problems from drinking?
10. Have you ever had loss of memory from or after drinking?

Watch for the patient's attitude as a subjective indicator of alcoholism: defensiveness, rationalization, denial, projection of blame, and so forth. How the questions are answered is important.

Drug history, both prescription and recreational, should be covered with every patient regardless of how unlikely you think it is that he or she is a candidate for drug use. Dietary history, as well as use of cigarettes, caffeine, and sugar, may be helpful as well.

Addiction occurs only in persons who have genetic "addictiveness." Addictiveness is a physiologic condition that includes a dysmetabolism of sugar and some degree of genetic depression with adrenal dysfunction. The adrenal glands seem clearly involved in this inherited defect. The addicted person often is unaware of the addiction and may deny it adamantly. Addicting substances may be used alternately and interchangeably to maintain a certain lifestyle, for example, sugar by day, alcohol by night, or sugar and pot by day, and cocaine by night.

Sometimes family members will come to you for help when their loved one is clearly addicted but refuses to accept it or get help. A formal intervention may be the answer, and an expert to lead it can be found through local treatment centers. He or she will meet with the family, rehearse the loving confrontation, and then present it to the patient, urging immediate treatment that has already been arranged.

Treatment

Once an addiction is identified, the most suitable treatment for that patient should be chosen. If a patient can afford inpatient treatment at a residential treatment center for alcohol and drugs, that often is the best choice. If the patient lacks motivation or needs the strong educational process that comes with residential treatment, this may be the only effective way to go.

Some patients want to try an outpatient approach of intensive care. This may be chosen with the understanding that if it fails, inpatient treatment will be next. Many cities now have multiple intensive outpatient programs that can be combined nicely with medical treatment from a physician. All addictions are treatable, and no patient should be considered hopeless, regardless of the number of previous treatments or relapses.

Do not tell the patient to "cut down" on drinking or drug or sugar excesses and go on to the next subject. This is impossible for an addicted person to accomplish. Successful treatment requires total abstinence of all addicting substances, not just the patient's drug of choice. Attempts to taper or cut down are rarely successful or helpful. The patient needs to quit entirely and completely.

There are numerous nonaddictive and safe drugs that can ease the detoxification period and eliminate the dangerous aspects of withdrawal. Sedative-hypnotic withdrawal can be life-threatening if seizures occur when the brain becomes unsedated. This group includes alcohol. The drug of choice for alcohol withdrawal (approximately three to seven days) is Librium, 25 mg, one or two up to four times a day. Occasionally, more will be required by a given patient, or occasionally a patient will do well on 10 mg, one or two, four times a day. This drug is very safe and has a high lethal threshold. A moderate overdose may cause some sedation but not respiratory depression. Although it can be addictive, it is seldom anyone's drug of choice because it induces no high or euphoria as most of the benzodiazepines do. However, it is deleterious and harmful to maintain an alcoholic on chlordiazepoxide for any length of time, and it may cause relapse. It is also my drug of choice in withdrawing patients from tranquilizers such as Valium, Azene, Tranxene, or meprobamate. This kind of withdrawal may last much longer, even months. I switch the patient at once to chlordiazepoxide, find the comfortable substitution dose, and gradually taper it to zero as the patient tolerates it. They need much reassurance, because usually they have tried getting off by themselves and were terrified by the withdrawal symptoms they experienced. On this plan they will be comfortable throughout.

Withdrawal from the other groups of drugs generally is not life-threatening, with the possible exception of cocaine withdrawal depression. Clonidine is helpful in treating narcotics withdrawal. Start with .1 mg three times a day. Watch for orthostatic hypotension as a side effect, since the blood pressure may be lowered in the process. On the second day, many patients will tolerate .2 mg three times a day. Some show considerable sedation, which may be an advantage, since many narcotics addicts cannot sleep in withdrawal. The original work on this came out of Yale Medical School.

Darvon-N 100, one or two, four times a day may be helpful for a few days during detoxification from narcotics; however, it should be discontinued as early as possible since it is an addictive substance. Withdrawal from Darvon addiction results in symptoms similar to those of narcotics withdrawal. Using it for narcotics withdrawal is a common trap that is easy to fall into, because it is so effective. I have stopped using it, because too many patients became dependent on it.

Tricyclic antidepressants are sometimes necessary to treat depression, which, if left untreated, may lead the patient to relapse. Depression, in my opinion, is the most common cause of relapse or treatment failure. It is often long-standing genetic depression rather than just the depression of relapse. There is no way to know which drug is the best for a given patient without trying them. One antidepressant may cause excessive side effects, whereas another is dramatic in its benefits. Sometimes two drugs in low dosage work best. It is ideal to start out with a low dosage and gradually build the dosage up as tolerated, for example, Elavil 10 to 25 mg q hs, increasing as tolerated to 75 to 150 at bedtime, or Asendin 50 mg, ½ tablet at bedtime, increasing in increments to 100 mg as tolerated. Recently, I have had excellent success with Desyrel (trazodone), which has few side effects, low overdose toxicity, and highly effective antidepressant benefits.

Vitamin C is the single most valuable substance I use in detoxification. If I could only use one thing, I would choose vitamin C even over the drugs mentioned above. Sodium ascorbate, intravenously, offers dramatic relief of withdrawal symptoms from any addicting substance. The exact ingredients and proportions I use are as follows:

vitamin C	8,000 mg
calcium gluconate	1,000 mg
magnesium sulfate	500 mg

This may be given once or more daily during the detoxification period as needed. Dramatic improvement often is noted shortly after the injection.

Sodium ascorbate by mouth, given ēvery two to four hours while the patient is awake, is extremely valuable in detoxification. I use the crystals, containing 4,000 mg per teaspoon, giving one teaspoon every two to four hours during the detoxification period. If diarrhea develops (which is desirable for a short time), one may cut back the dose but maintain the frequency of dosages. The diarrhea is short-lived and probably therapeutic in ridding the body of the toxic products of the addiction. It is important for each patient to find his or her body's best dosage of vitamin C.

Free-form amino acid complex given orally three times a day seems to stabilize the metabolism and give the patient additional energy and a feeling of well-being. Much has been written on this recently in medical journals. Vitamin B_6, 100 mg, is given with each dose.

A potent multivitamin and mineral carries many benefits, since it is safe to say that all addictive patients are malnourished and have significant vitamin and mineral deficiencies. I use a specially designed product called NutraBalance (see the resource list in chapter 5, p. 48).

The high-protein supplement drink described in the treatment chapter is often the only source of nutrition the patient can tolerate during detoxification. It can be used alone or with additional food.

Exercise as soon as tolerated is vital. It stimulates endorphins and helps the patient to feel much better.

Counseling is very important. I and my staff provide it in my office, or you can refer the patient to a good outside counselor with knowledge of addictions.

Alcoholics Anonymous and Narcotics Anonymous can provide a strong support system to maintain the patient's direction and motivation. It offers an alternative to using drugs and alcohol and fills in much of the spare time that is created by abstinence. Meetings are available almost everywhere and can be located by calling Alcoholics Anonymous in the phone book or contacting the local police or a church.

Always inquire of the patient at each visit as to his or her progress in recovering from the addiction. Recovering people love to talk about the joys of recovery. If the patient has relapsed, it is important to uncover that fact and start again. It is vital to assure addicts that addiction is a disease and not a moral or character disorder, and that they are not bad people because they have the disease or because they relapsed. They need love and understanding, not scoldings and dire predictions. The fact that their addiction is harming their health is not enough to get them to abstain.

If you cannot show loving patience with this disease, let someone else treat it. Then take some continuing education workshops on addiction.

Dealing with addicted patients can be a most rewarding endeavor. It has been for me.

Afterword

You have taken a brave new look at addiction. Perhaps it is because you love someone who is addicted, or maybe the addiction is closer to you — your own. I hope that in either case you have gained some valuable ammunition to combat this powerful, baffling, cunning disease. Do not be discouraged; it takes patience and time to recover from addiction.

You have learned how genetics set the stage for addiction and then how our bodies' physiology plays a major role. Sugar contributes heavily to the early development of addiction, as does genetic depression. The unusual response of the addictive body to addictive chemicals is the third ingredient in my working model for addiction.

Recovery lies in moving the body biochemically back into natural balance. The state of balance will contribute greatly to the well-being expressed simply in the words "Now I feel really good."

This occurs when the use of sugar, alcohol, caffeine, and other addicting drugs is stopped and the body is encouraged to function in as pure an environment as possible. Balance expands when a complex carbohydrate diet is chosen with as many fresh foods as possible, along with dairy products and fish and poultry. Exercise and support groups help round out one's new recovery program.

The rewards of recovery increase indefinitely: the longer one is "clean" and sober, the greater the returns. Suddenly your world lights up and new joys are experienced. You learn that your destination is less important than the quality of the journey and the goals you set along the way.

Good traveling, my friend. I wish you well. May your growth and creativity never cease, and may love fill your universe.

Janice Keller Phelps, M.D.

Index

Abstinence, 1, 6, 37, 43–45, 65, 108
  from alcohol, 109
  from all addicting substances, 233
  from caffeine, 128–130
  from heroin, 210
  from marijuana, 161
  from nicotine, 139, 140–142
  from sleeping pills, 172
  from tranquilizers, 181
Accidents, and alcohol, 110
Activities, new, as therapy in addiction, 63
Acupuncture, as beta-endorphin stimulant, 215
Addicting substances
  effect on central nervous system, 39
  strength of, 34–35
  types of, 40
Addiction
  acceptance of, xi
  to alcohol, 86–124
  basics of, x
  to caffeine, 125–135
  cause of, 5
  control of life by, 4
  and "cures," 41
  definitions of, 7–8, 31–32, 79
  and denial, xi, 40, 89, 90, 95, 100, 107–108, 110, 231

  to depressant drugs, 163–182
  and depression, 24–25
  as a disease, 5, 7–8
  and habit, differences between, 38–39
  and heredity, 28–29, 33
    See also Genetics and addiction
  identifying, 231–233
  and life-style, 6–7
  to marijuana, 146–162
  to nicotine, 137–145
  and nonaddictive persons, 7
  to opiates, 201–230
  physiological basis of, 23–24
  as a psychological problem, 5
  reasons for, 22
  similarity between various types, 5
  to sleeping pills, 170–173
  to speed, 187–189
  to stimulant drugs, 183–200
  substitute, avoidance of, 45
  to sugar, 26–27, 73–85
  to tranquilizers, 174–182
  unknowns about, xi
  and withdrawal, 29–30
    See also withdrawal
  working model of, 21–32
Addictiveness
  degrees of, 34
  identifying, 9, 19